AZAADI, FREEDOM AND CHANGE IN KASHMIR

Laura Schuurmans is an independent writer specializing in the Kashmir conflict. For more than a decade she has been actively working on international security issues in the wider Asian region and she has published a number of articles, research papers and book chapters. Her prime focus has always been the Kashmir conflict. From 2011-2013 she followed a postgraduate programme at the prestigious School of International Studies at Peking University, China. Based in Jakarta where she has lived for more than two decades, she has actively witnessed the development of political Islam in one of the world's most populated Muslim nations which has provided her with a more in-depth understanding of the interplay between issues of international security and religion.

Azaadi, Freedom and Change in Kashmir

LAURA SCHUURMANS

Arena Books

© Laura Schuurmans 2023

The right of Laura Schuurmans to be identified as the author of this work has been asserted in accordance with the Copyright, Design and Patents Act 1988.

All rights reserved. Except for the quotation of short passages for the purposes of criticism and review, no part of this publication may be reproduced, stored in a retrieval system, or transmitted, in any form or by any means, electronic, mechanical, photocopying, or recording or otherwise, without prior permission of the publisher.

First published by Arena Books in 2023
www.arenabooks.co.uk

Laura Schuurmans
Azaadi, **Freedom & Change in Kashmir**

ISBN 978-1-914390-10-4 Paperback
ISBN 978-1-914390-14-2 eBook

A Catalogue record for this book is available from the British Library.

Thema: GTU; 1FKA-IN-AJ; JPS; 1FKA; 1FKP; JPWL; JPVH; JPVR1; JWLP; JPSL.

BIC categories: GTJ; JPS; JPSL; JPSN1; JPV; JPVH; JPVR; JPW; JPWQ; JPWL; JPWS; 1FKA; 1FKAH; 1FKP; 1HFMS; 1FMNT; HBJF; HBTR; HBTQ; HBTV; HBTZ; LB; LBH; GT; GTB.

Distributed in America by *Ingram International, One Ingram Blvd., P.O. Box 3006, La Vergne, TN 37086-1985, USA.*

Cover design by Jason Anscomb. With thanks to NASA Worldview for use of the satellite imagery for cover image.

"She was the last warrior left on the battlefield"

To my mother (1949-2017),
who bravely fought one of the toughest battles against cancer

Acknowledgements

This book would not have been completed without the encouragement, patience, and commitment of the former Commander of the Sri Lankan Navy, and the current Ambassador to Indonesia, Admiral Prof. Jayanath Colombage. I am grateful for his expertise on the Indian Ocean Region and on China, and for his support during the final stages before publication – support that was so graciously given despite his round-the-clock duties as an academician and later also as Sri Lankan Foreign Secretary. Admiral Jayanath patiently guided me through the modification of this manuscript without compromising on the academic analysis and overall contents.

Moreover, the book would not have become what it is today, without the support of many more people. André de Bussy, the French diplomat first based in Jakarta and then in Islamabad, connected me to today's President of Timor-Leste and Nobel Peace Laureate José Ramos-Horta. Willem Geerlings, the Political Counsellor at the South African Embassy in Jakarta, introduced me to Ivor Jenkins, Director of the Pretoria-based In Transformation Initiative (ITI) who arranged all my meetings in South Africa. The latter also introduced me to former President and Nobel Peace Laureate F.W. de Klerk. The In Transformation Initiative is an organization with decades of experience in peace building in South Africa and other conflict-ridden regions throughout the world. The Norwegian Ambassador to Indonesia, Vegard Kaale, connected me to former Prime Minister K.M. Bondevik.

I am grateful for all the time the former Vice President of the Republic of Indonesia, Mr. Try Sutrisno, took during my interview, and for providing me with such an insight into the Indonesian perspective of the reconciliation with East Timor. I had been keen to interview him after seeing him on an Indonesian TV program, Super Mentor, in discussion with other leaders from both Indonesia and Timor-Leste who had all been actively involved in the conflict; they had come together amicably to commemorate the 1999 referendum resulting in East Timor's independence.

I would also like to thank Mr. de Klerk for answering my questions in writing. I was sad to learn of his passing away in November 2021. It was heart-warming to listen to Mr. Bondevik during my phone interview who told me about all his experiences in both India and Pakistan and his aspiration to get involved in the peace process in Kashmir. I am grateful for the warm hospitality of both José Ramos-Horta and his brother Arsenio during my visits to Timor-Leste where I connected with dozens of East-

Timorese and learned about their personal experiences during the conflict with Indonesia. And I would like to thank both of these brothers for taking the time to show me around Timor-Leste. I hope that the contribution of all these leaders will generate more interest in Kashmir and open doors for the aggrieved parties to sit around the negotiating table and start a long-lasting peace dialogue.

I am thankful to Prof. Gui Yongtao of Peking University in Beijing, where I was a post-graduate student, who always critically combed through each and every page of my research projects. I probably spent the best years of my life studying long hours in the library of the School of International Studies. I am also grateful to Ye Hailin of the Beijing-based Chinese Academy of Social Sciences, one of China's leading think tanks, for all his patience and moral support during completion of the manuscript. Ye Hailin is one of the few Chinese experts on South Asia, and I am grateful for his expertise, experience, and insistence on maintaining a balanced viewpoint throughout the manuscript.

I am also grateful to the Pakistani authorities for facilitating my visits to Pakistan and the wider Kashmir region. I consider myself fortunate to have been granted the opportunity to travel to some of the world's most beautiful, unique and remote regions in Pakistan. These are regions that are homes to so many different tribes, ethnic minorities, and kind-hearted people with their own distinct cultures – and a face of Pakistan mostly unknown to the outside world. The Pakistani establishment always extended a hand of friendship and warmly welcomed me despite our diverging viewpoints on the question of Kashmir. I have been asked whether or not I believe that Pakistan is sincere in its efforts to resolve the tensions in Kashmir. Yet, why not ask the same question of the international community? Regional geopolitical dynamics have created complexities which have hampered efforts on all fronts to find political solution. Moreover, while the international community at large advocates human rights, it seems that these rights are overlooked with regard to Kashmir.

The authorities in Pakistan also arranged my interview with their former president, Pervez Musharraf, in Dubai, who despite his involvement in the 1999 Kargil War, initiated a peace process with India over Kashmir after he became the country's President in 2001. I was impressed with the humble straight-forwardness and kind disposition of a leader who had been a prominent figure on the international political stage following the September 11 attacks on the United States. I also met with Major General Zafar who planned and executed Pakistan's operation in North-Waziristan in 2015 – an assignment reserved only for the bravest and most capable of officers in one of the world's most dangerous and complex battlefields. We met when he was based in Jakarta as Defence Attaché and he always encouraged me in my work on Kashmir.

This book, moreover, would never have been possible without the encouragement of Major General Jamshed Ayaz Khan (Retd.) whom I met for the first time in March 2007 when he was President of the Islamabad-based Institute of Regional Studies. I had asked the then Ambassador of Pakistan in Jakarta, Major General Ali Baz (Retd.) to arrange a trip to the Pashtun tribal regions and the legendary Khyber Pass, as my father had extensively travelled through the West and South Asian region in 1968.

When I was young, I would listen to my father's intriguing stories – especially when his Japanese friend, Kenji Numata (with whom he had travelled), visited us in both the Netherlands and in Indonesia during his business trips. My father once told me that in the middle of the night, people were shooting at each other right below the window of his hostel in Peshawar, and when he asked about the gunshots at the reception desk the following morning, the clerk behind the counter was evidently not impressed – he stoically answered "but they did not shoot at you," and continued with his office duties. My father always said that the Pashtuns are a kind-hearted, straight forward and brave people. His advice before one of my trips to Pakistan was that I would have to be brave if I wanted to be respected.

While I was initially interested to learn more about the frontier tribal region bordering Afghanistan, General Jamshed introduced me to Kashmir where I quickly learned about the injustices happening to the people there while the international community looked away. General Jamshed and Pervez Musharraf were childhood friends who would both like to have seen a peaceful resolution in Kashmir and for it to have achieved friendly and stable relations with its neighbours. But sadly, both of these eminent men did not live long enough to see the final publication of this book; General Jamshed passed away in August 2021, and Pervez Musharraf passed away in February 2023. I am grateful for the personal effort that Jamshed took to keep me motivated. And during my hectic trips to Pakistan with tight schedules, he always managed to find some spare time for us to drink tea at his home in Islamabad.

The people of Kashmir are all close to my heart and without their moral support, I would not have completed this project. I am thankful especially to those Kashmiri friends who gave of their precious time to help me with the manuscript. There are too many friends to mention, some of whom I have not even met in person, others whose names I cannot mention, and one who left this world too soon. Shujaat Bukhari, Editor in Chief of *Rising Kashmir* was a loyal friend to so many of us but his voice for peace in

Kashmir turned into eternal silence when unknown gunmen assassinated him in Srinagar in June 2018. He was one of the first friends who had called after he heard my mother had passed away in 2017. And the solidarity among Kashmiri women, and their silent support, should also not be underestimated. I hope that this book will give the people of Kashmir a voice on the international stage and generate more understanding of the question of Kashmir.

My mother was a staunch supporter all the way through and it was her wish to be with us to see the final publication of the manuscript. I am thankful to my father, and my sister and her family, for all their support especially at difficult times. Thank you, Kala, whilst far away, for always being such a loyal friend. The list would not be complete without Suryo Sulisto, who always had faith in me and who encouraged me to publish the book. I am thankful also to Arena Books, for believing in the potential of this manuscript and having it published in its original form.

CONTENTS

Acknowledgements viii
Azaadi defined xvi
Acronyms xvii
Map of the Disputed Region of Jammu and Kashmir xviii
Map of South Asia and the Wider Region xix
Foreword by the Former Vice President of the Republic of Indonesia,
Try Sutrisno xxi
Foreword by the President of Timor-Leste and Nobel Peace Laureate,
José Ramos-Horta xxiii

CHAPTER 1: INTRODUCTION TO KASHMIR 1
Introduction to Kashmir 1
Kashmir's Wall 5
The Urgent Need for Peace 6
The Inclusion of Kashmiris 11
Kashmir and the Instrument of Accession 15
The Jammu and Kashmir Region 16
Gilgit-Baltistan 17
Azad Jammu and Kashmir 19
The Chinese part of Kashmir: Aksai Chin 20
The Indian part of Kashmir 21
The Predicament of Kashmir 24
Why this Book on Kashmir? 26

CHAPTER 2: INDIA & KASHMIR: THE ARMED STRUGGLE 29
The Youth Take up Arms in Jammu and Kashmir 29
Talking with Farooq 34
Jammu and Kashmir Liberation Front (JKLF) 35
Mirwaiz Farooq's Assassination 37
Militancy in Kashmir 38
The Israeli Hostage in Kashmir 41
The Armed Struggle Continues: 1990-1995 43
1995: Brutal Modus Operandi 44
Developments in the Kashmir Valley in the Later 2010s 45

CHAPTER 3: PAKISTAN & KASHMIR 47
The Strategic Importance of Gilgit Baltistan 47
China and the China-Pakistan Economic Corridor 49

Aksai Chin, Kargil and Siachen 50
Regional Political Dynamics.. 52
A Brief History 55
The Gilgit-Baltistan Region 58
Azad Jammu and Kashmir 60
The Political System in Azad Jammu and Kashmir and its link with
Gilgit Baltistan 61
The Azad Jammu and Kashmir Region 64

CHAPTER 4: CHINA'S GEOSTRATEGIC CONTEXT 67

Introduction.. 67
Sino-India Relations 69
US-India Relations... 72
The Sino-Pakistan "All Weather Friendship" 73
The Uighur Communities and China 74
The Belt and Road Initiative (BRI) and the China-Pakistan Economic
Corridor (CPEC).. 75
China and Kashmir 78

CHAPTER 5: SILENCE IS A CRIME IN TIMES OF CONFLICT 91

The Human Cost of Conflict in Kashmir 91
Khurram's Narrative of the Attack in 2004 95
Human Rights Abuses in Kashmir... 98
The Kashmir Disappearances... 100
Violence Against Women in Kashmir 102
A Summary of Events.. 104
Pakistan's Role in Kashmir.. 105

CHAPTER 6: THE INDIA-PAKISTAN DISCORD 109

Kashmir and the Shifting Balance of Power in Asia 109
The Simla Agreement vs. the UN Security Council Resolutions........ 115
Terrorism vs. *Mujahedeen* or Freedom Fighters 119
South Asia's Nuclearization... 121
Musharraf's Out-of-theBox Solution 124
Regional Conflicts and Dynamics.. 127
Bilateral Disputes over Water Resources and Boundaries 129

CHAPTER 7: TRANSITIONAL JUSTICE: TWO CASE STUDIES 131

Independence for Timor-Leste 131
South Africa 1948-1990 133
Transitional Justice in Timor-Leste and South Africa 136
Timor-Leste: Leaving the Past Behind 138
Turning point in Timor-Leste-Indonesia Relations 142
The "Hearts and Minds" Strategy 142
Santa Cruz Massacre 144
The Gusmão-Sutrisno Nexus 146
Lasting Regional Peace 147
Parallels with Kashmir 148
Breaking the Deadlock in South Africa 152
CODESA 1991-1994 155
National Peace Accord 156
Truth and Reconciliation Commission 157
South African Parallels with Kashmir 158

CHAPTER 8: PATHS TO RECONCILIATION 163

India and Pakistan 163
The Inclusion of Kashmiris 165
Violence and Terrorism in Kashmir 165
Gilgit-Baltistan and Azad Jammu and Kashmir 167
The China Factor 168
Human Rights Abuses in Kashmir 169
India-Pakistan Relations and Kashmir 171
The Case Studies of Transitional Justice in South Africa and Timor-Leste 172
The Independence *(azaadi)* Factor 175

APPENDIX 177

THE NIAGARA DECLARATION 177

NOTES 181

AFTERWORD 203

Azaadi defined

Azaadi means freedom. However, in the Kashmiri context, it does not only mean freedom in the sense of independence or self-determination; it can also mean freedom from military occupation, freedom from human rights abuses, and freedom from any subjugation by India or Pakistan. Improved living conditions and greater freedoms for individuals and communities, is *azaadi*. Peace in Kashmir, in whatever political from that eventually takes, is *azaadi*.

Acronyms

AFSPA	Armed Forces Special Powers Act (Indian Kashmir)
ANC	African National Congress (South Africa Timorese the
APHC	All Parties Hurriyat Conference
APODETI	Associação Popular Democratica Timorense (Timorese Popular Democratic Association)
ASEAN	Association of South East Asian Nations
BCM	Black Conscious Movement (South Africa)
BRI	Belt and Road Initiative (same as OBOR)
BRICS	Brazil, Russia, India, China, South Africa
BSF	Border Security Forces (Indian Kashmir)
CODESA	Convention for a Democratic South Africa
CPEC	China-Pakistan Economic Corridor
CTBT	Comprehensive Test Ban Treaty
DAA	Disturbed Areas Act
FATF	Financial Action Task Force
FCR	Frontier Crimes Regulations (Gilgit Baltistan)
FRETILIN	Frente Revolucionária de Timor-Leste Independente (Revolutionary Front of Independent East Timor)
IPTK	International People's Tribunal on Human Rights and Justice in Kashmir (Indian Kashmir)
ISI	Inter-Services-Intelligence (Pakistan's intelligence agency)
IS	Islamic State
JKLF	Jammu and Kashmir Liberation Front
KANA	Ministry of Kashmir and Northern Areas Affairs
KKH	Karakoram Highway
KOTA	Klibur Oan Timor Asuwain (The Association of Timorese Heroes)
KOPASSUS	Komando Pasukan Khusus (Special Forces Command of the Indonesian Armed Forces)
LoC	Line of Control
MK	Umkhonto we Sizwe (military wing of the ANC, South Africa)
MQM	Muttahida Qaumi Movement (political party in Pakistan)
NPT	Non-Proliferation Treaty
NSG	Nuclear Suppliers Group
PSA	Public Safety Act
RAW	Research and Analysis Wing (India's external intelligence agency)
SACP	South African Communist Party
TRC	Truth and Reconciliation Commission
UAPA	Unlawful Activities Prevention Act
UDT	Uniao Democratica Timorense (Union for a Democratic Timor)
UNMOGIP	United Nations Military Observers Group for India and Pakistan
XUAR	Xinjiang Uighur Autonomous Region

Map of the Disputed Region of Jammu and Kashmir

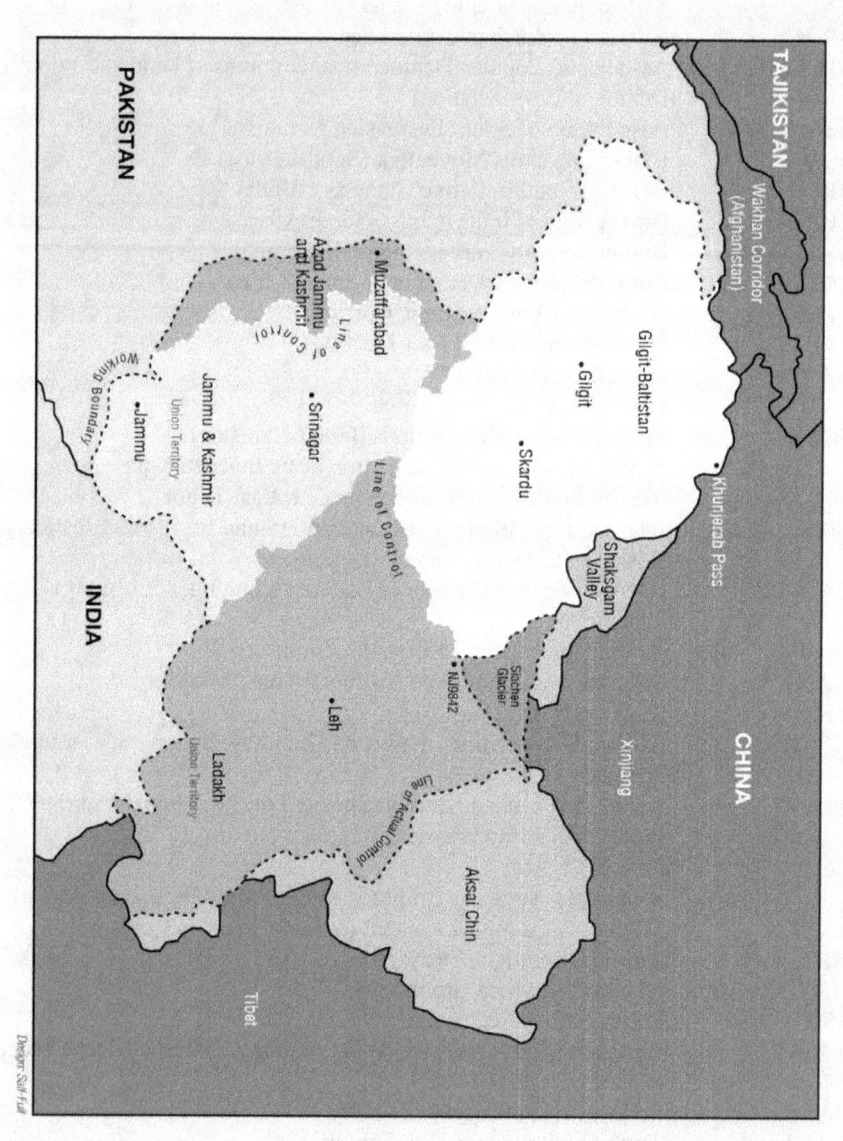

Map of South Asia and the Wider Region

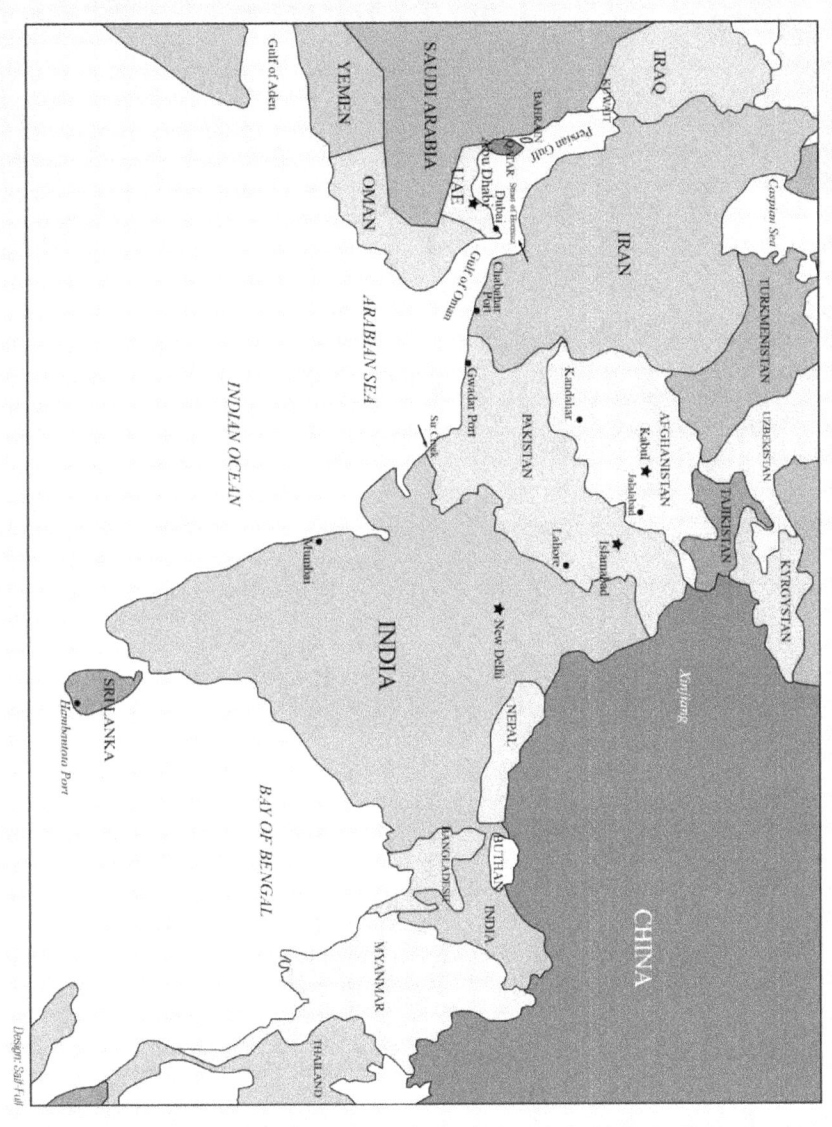

Foreword by the Former Vice President of the Republic of Indonesia, Try Sutrisno

In the twenty-first century, the world has become increasingly prone to regional conflicts and limited wars which have endangered international peace and security. The conflict between India, Pakistan – and also China – over the disputed region of Jammu and Kashmir, moreover, is not only a conflict that includes three nuclear powers, it is also one of the longest unresolved conflicts that the world has witnessed since the Second World War. A sustained dialogue among the aggrieved parties has always been absent, and has resulted in the loss of tens of thousands of innocent lives.

This book, *Azaadi, Freedom and Change in Kashmir*, elaborates on the urgent need to build peace in the disputed region of Jammu and Kashmir. It aims to break the deadlock in Kashmir and establish a fruitful dialogue among the aggrieved parties – including the people of Kashmir, who have for too long been the victims of this conflict. Based on my experiences, I agree with the author's viewpoint that a sustained dialogue that includes the people of Kashmir must constitute the first step towards creating stability in the region.

The author, moreover, has emphasized that a sustained dialogue in the disputed region of Jammu and Kashmir would not only have a positive impact on the people of Kashmir; it would also reduce the wider regional tensions that pose such a grave threat to peace and security in South Asia and to the world at large. In chapter 7, the case studies of Indonesia and Timor-Leste, and of South Africa – where opposing parties have succeeded in reconciling after decades of oppression and conflict – provide unique examples which have the potential to act as inspiration to other nations, leaders and citizens, and from which we can all learn valuable lessons.

In this book, the author has been simultaneously critical and compassionate in her analysis; Schuurmans has written the book independently, with impartiality and integrity, taking into account the grievances of all the different parties. I personally fully support her approach and analysis, and her efforts in bringing about change in Kashmir.

When I served my country as a military officer in the Armed Forces and later as Indonesia's Vice President, I was actively involved in the question of East Timor for more than two decades. During this time, I came face to face with armed conflict and witnessed first-hand the loss of lives of both military and civilians on both sides of the conflict zone.

Although national interests always played a predominant role in Indonesia's dealings with East Timor, a humane approach with the adversary is an essential requirement in starting a sustainable dialogue. In addition, *all* the aggrieved parties will need to make considerable concessions in order to be able to sit around the negotiating table in a peaceful and just manner.

The road to dialogue and peace-building has never been an easy one, and plenty of hurdles will be met along the way. Patience, political will, and most importantly, sincerity and flexibility, are a prerequisite. Today, I take pride in the fact that Indonesia's relations with Timor-Leste are based on mutual trust and respect; and the fact that our friendship has continued to strengthen is something that we are proud of as a nation.

Foreword by the President of Timor-Leste and Nobel Peace Laureate, José Ramos-Horta

In today's increasingly troubled world where the major power players are competing for regional and global supremacy, dialogue has become an ever more vital instrument in bringing back stability. This also counts for the disputed region of Kashmir where three nuclear powers have been in armed conflict with each other over territorial grounds for decades. This conflict, over which India and Pakistan have never been able to maintain a sustained dialogue, has cost the lives of tens of thousands of innocent civilians in Kashmir.

This book, *Azaadi, Freedom and Change in Kashmir*, is a comprehensive analysis of the conflict. While Pakistan aims to internationalize Kashmir and seeks a multilateral approach and mediation through the United Nations, India vehemently opposes these steps and insists on a bilateral approach between the two nuclear powers. The people of Kashmir have never been a formal part of the discourse and they have remained voiceless.

In this book, the author has not only included an objective analysis of the on-the-ground realities on both the Indian and the Pakistani sides of the Line of Control, she has also included the China factor. In recent decades, China's rapid rise to global power has been aided by its Belt and Road Initiative – a revival of the ancient Silk Road that, in part, runs through the Kashmir region. The author has provided an in-depth analysis of Kashmir within the geostrategic context of China's foreign policy and has thereby contributed to raising awareness of the oft-overlooked fact that China also controls part of this disputed region.

While this book has focused on all the different aspects of the conflict – often with reference to historical events – Schuurmans' prime emphasis is on the humanitarian suffering that the people continue to endure; the author has conducted dozens of interviews with Kashmiris who have become victims of the conflict, from both the Indian and the Pakistani sides of the Line of Control, and she has incorporated their viewpoints.

Azaadi, Freedom and Change also elaborates on the armed uprising in the Kashmir Valley that took place in the 1990s. It explains the role of Pakistan and its support for the armed militants who fractured Kashmiri society along Hindu and Muslim lines, and divided communities who had been living peacefully side-by-side in the Valley for centuries. And in the spirit of impartiality, the author also details the gross human rights abuses that have been committed by India, and the risks that Kashmiris have faced, as a result, while working for peace in the region.

I have witnessed the brutalities of armed conflict, and I commend the author for her inclusion of case studies that might provide solutions to the political deadlock over Kashmir. These case studies – namely our reconciliation with Indonesia, and the fall of apartheid of South Africa – show that through commitment and selfless effort, it is possible for leadership to overcome difference and to bring an end to chronic human hardship and suffering. In presenting these examples, the author ultimately aims to find ways in which the aggrieved parties might begin long-lasting dialogue in the disputed region of Kashmir, and provide a roadmap to peace in the wider region.

I highly recommend this book which provides a fresh look at this decades-long conflict that has been too-long neglected, and in which innocent civilians are still paying the price.

CHAPTER 1

INTRODUCTION TO KASHMIR

"The weak can never forgive. Forgiveness is the attribute of the strong."
Mahatma Gandhi (1869-1948)

"Our object should be peace within, and peace without. We want to live peacefully and maintain cordial relations with our immediate neighbours and with the world at large."
Quaid-i-Azam Muhammad Ali Jinnah (1876-1948)

Introduction to Kashmir

On 14 June, 2018 Shujaat Bukhari, chief editor of *Rising Kashmir*, one of Kashmir's leading English-language newspapers, left his office in Srinagar, summer capital of Kashmir. As he left to go home and join his wife and two teenage children for *Iftar* (the breaking of the fast during the holy month of Ramadan) he was assassinated together with two of his bodyguards.[1] This was not the first time that Shujaat had faced threats; he had earlier survived several assassination attempts, once simply because the trigger of the gun got blocked as the assassin pointed it at him.

As in other conflict regions, reporting in Kashmir has always come with dangers, and tragically, the assassination of Shujaat is just one example of the elimination of a Kashmiri intellectual. Farooq Siddiqi, alias Farooq Papa, a Kashmiri living in Canada who was actively involved in the armed uprising of the 1990s, had been talking to Shujaat on the phone just a few hours prior to his assassination. He told me, "so many intellectuals have been killed in Kashmir over the past few decades. Where is our voice of the people of Kashmir if our intellectuals who are advocating for peace in the region are being killed?"[2] The Indian authorities held the Pakistani-sponsored terrorist group Lashkar-e-Taiba accountable for Shujaat Bukhari's killing, yet Lashkar-e-Taiba have vehemently denied any involvement. State and non-state actors alike, on both sides of the Line of

Control or LoC (the de-facto border that splits Kashmir between India and Pakistan) declared him a martyr in the name of *azaadi* (freedom) in Kashmir.

Shujaat was killed on the same day that the Office of the United Nations High Commissioner for Human Rights (OHCHR) published its first ever human rights report *On the Situation of Human Rights in Kashmir*. Shujaat and I met for the last time in Jakarta in November 2016. He, and the writer and intellectual Ershad Mahmud, had been attending a week-long meeting and working session in Karawang with Kashmiris from both sides of the Line of Control, organized by the UK-based organisation, Conciliation Resources.

I joined them one evening in Karawang for dinner where we discussed the latest developments in Kashmir and the possible ways in which the situation might move forward. After the working session ended, we met for a second time in Jakarta. We talked about Khurram Parvez, a common friend and Kashmiri human rights defender who had been arrested and imprisoned under the Public Safety Act – one of Kashmir's draconian laws that allow the detention of anyone in Kashmir without a trial for up to two years. Ershad suggested starting a campaign to release him from jail, but Shujaat warned "there is always a risk in Kashmir. If you do too much or try to achieve something in Kashmir that people, organizations, or countries disagree with, you always run the risk of being imprisoned, or even assassinated."[3] I had never anticipated that just over one-and-a-half years after our last meeting in Jakarta, Shujaat himself would become a target.

But hope nevertheless came with the release of the OHCHR report in June 2018, and a second report in 2019, when the voices of the people of Kashmir finally began to be heard on the international stage. India rejected the findings; it alleged that the report was based on fabricated material and they condemned the United Nations for using language such as "armed groups" for groups that India – and the rest of the world – considered terrorists. India also took pains to remind the international community that the entire State of Jammu and Kashmir was an integral part of India.[4]

Furthermore, a few months after the first report, India pointed the finger at the Pakistani-sponsored terrorist group Jaish-e-Mohammed when in February 2019, a suicide attack in Pulwama, in the Kashmir Valley, killed forty men from the Central Reserve Police Force. Pakistan denied any involvement. India nevertheless decided to retaliate, and on 26 February 2019 the Indian Air Force claimed that it had crossed the border into Pakistan and had attacked a Jaish-e-Mohammed training camp, killing a large number of terrorists. In turn, Pakistan denied the existence of any such camp and, as a tit-for-tat, conducted an airstrike into Indian Kashmir, shooting down an Indian MiG-21 and capturing its pilot. As a result, the two nuclear-armed nations came to the brink of war. Based on credible intelligence, Pakistan claims that India had planned two missile attacks in Pakistan which they succeeded to thwart.[5] Pakistan closed its airspace to avoid the conflict from spiraling out of control. They also handed back the Indian Air Force pilot on 1 March of that year as a gesture of goodwill and peace.

In the following months, the tension between the two nations calmed down somewhat until 5 August 2019 when the Indian government revoked Articles 370 and 35A of the Indian Constitution. These two articles had been incorporated in the Indian Constitution in 1950 and 1954 and had granted special status and relative autonomy to Jammu and Kashmir within the Indian Union. Pakistan vehemently denounced the revocation of the articles and India's subsequently increased control of the region. Pakistan viewed it as a breach of the disputed territory under United Nations Security Council Resolutions – especially after India re-drew the maps to incorporate Azad Jammu and Kashmir and Gilgit-Baltistan, located in the Pakistani part of Kashmir, into the Indian part of Kashmir. In a counter move, Pakistan also redrew the maps and included Indian Kashmir, Siachen, Sir Creek and (surprisingly) also Junagadh as parts of its territory.

A few days prior to India's revocation of Kashmir's special status, tens of thousands of additional security forces were brought into Jammu and Kashmir and Ladakh located in the Indian part of Kashmir. A curfew was imposed and anyone who planned a demonstration against the move was to be arrested under the Public Safety Act. No-one was spared – prominent Kashmiri women who came out to protest on the streets of Srinagar were also put behind bars. People were not granted the right to free speech. And on the day of the revocation, an estimated 450 Kashmiri businessmen, journalists, lawyers and political activists were put on a temporary no-fly list.[6] Gowhar Geelani, a Kashmiri journalist who had just released his first book *Rage and Reason in Kashmir* was stuck for hours at Delhi airport, only to receive the news that Indian intelligence had stopped him from leaving for Germany.[7] In the weeks and months that followed, there were reports of innocent youth being taken away from their parents which further spread fear and distrust. Some of the children arrested were as young as ten years old.

Although initially, these events received the attention of the international media, this attention soon faded away. India does not want to highlight the suffering of the Kashmiri people and argues that as an internal matter, it should be free to resolve it without outside interference. Meanwhile, the people of Kashmir are frustrated that nobody hears their voices. Their frustration is also directed against Pakistan with many Kashmiris feeling that they only matter to the Pakistani government when it suits the Pakistani political agenda, and they are angry that Pakistan has not done more to bring Kashmir to the attention of the international community. On the Indian side of Kashmir, the oppression has continued and human rights are being violated on a daily basis; it seems that appeasing India as part of the geopolitical game has been more important to the international community than speaking out against the violations.

In the autumn of 2019, to show their solidarity with the people in the Indian part of Kashmir, the Kashmiris on the Pakistani side (known as Azad Jammu and Kashmir) organized demonstrations. Some Kashmiris were injured when they demonstrated too close to the de-facto border. Sardar Anwar, a Kashmiri whom I once met in Doha, was one of the injured. The then Pakistani Prime Minister, Imran Khan, made repeated emotional appeals to the people not to cross into the Indian part of Kashmir as this would be considered an act of aggression from the Pakistani side for which he would get the blame. Intermittent cross-border shelling between the Indian and Pakistani border forces continued after these events – with both sides blaming the other.[8] And so the Kashmir conflict reached yet another deadlock with no clear sign of any possible peace dialogue in sight.

While the international community at large considers the Kashmir dispute a bilateral issue that should be resolved through dialogue between India and Pakistan, the European Union believes that the people of Kashmir should be included in the political process and have a say in their own future.[9] Sweden also issued a statement, two days prior to a Royal visit to India, expressing its concern about the ongoing humanitarian situation there and urging the Indian government to lift the restrictions.[10]

Over the years, the de-facto border has remained heavily militarized. Innocent civilians living alongside the border have become victims of cross-border fire, targeted killings, and anti-personnel landmines. The 2003 Ceasefire Understanding between the two countries has been repeatedly violated; and these violations increased in 2014 following Narendra Modi's election as India's fourteenth Prime Minister. In 2015, Indian soldiers shot dead two Pakistani military officers when they crossed the border along the Working Boundary, into the Indian side for a regular flag meeting. The two officers were holding a white flag (the Working Boundary is the name given to a relatively short section of border that runs between the Punjab Province in Pakistan to its west, and Jammu in the Indian part of Kashmir to its east). Likewise, in 2017, Pakistan killed two Indian soldiers along the Line of Control and embarked on the barbaric act of mutilating their bodies. During my visit to Sialkot, I talked to villagers who had been living on the border for generations and had been having to protect their cattle from cross-border shelling at night by giving the animals shelter inside their own tiny homes. Some respite from the violence came in February 2021, when talks restarted and the two nations agreed again to adhere to a ceasefire along the Line of Control.

Antagonism between India and Pakistan began when millions of people witnessed the brutalities that took place during the partition of British India and the Princely States in August 1947 – when the borders between Pakistan and India were created. The enmity was consolidated following Kashmir's accession to India in October of the same year. Antagonism does not always easily fade away in the minds of people; it too often leads to ongoing hatred, mutual suspicion, and ultimately revenge. As long as people continue to fall prey to brutality, bloodshed will linger and the vicious cycles of violence will continue to be carried down from one generation to the next.

Kashmir's Wall

The Berlin Wall was constructed on the recommendation of the Soviet Union during the Cold War. The 38th parallel divides North and South Korea. And Israel's Wall in the West Bank separates the people of Palestine. The Line of Control is yet another "wall" dividing people in the disputed State of Jammu and Kashmir. Closed borders, military checkpoints, and landmine fields along this de-facto border, have divided Kashmir and separated it from India and Pakistan. During one of my visits to Chakothi, a border town on the Pakistani side of the Line of Control (in Azad Jammu and Kashmir), I talked to a Kashmiri whose sister had lost a limb after stepping on a mine. To prevent militants from crossing into the Indian part of Kashmir, India has fenced-off vast areas of land along the Line of Control and minded the area with thousands of anti-personnel landmines.

Originally known as the Ceasefire Line (1949-1972), the Line of Control divided tens of thousands of families in the aftermath of the first Indo-Pakistan War in 1947. Yet more families were divided with the armed uprising in the Kashmir Valley in the 1990s. For example, during the height of the armed insurgency in the early 1990s, Allaudin Butt, a retired primary school teacher, fled his home village of Keran in Kupwara, located in the Indian part of Kashmir, and crossed the then volatile Line of Control into the Pakistani part of Kashmir because Indian authorities had accused him of supporting the militancy during the uprising – allegations that he denies.

As a result, in the decades since that time, he has been living in a camp in Muzaffarabad designated for displaced Kashmiris who fled Indian Kashmir during the conflict. Some of the camp's residents were actively involved in, or supporters of, the armed uprising against Indian occupation, but others, including many women, were quiet bystanders who were left with no choice but to flee. Many of the women I spoke to live with the unhealed scars of conflict – leading to trans-generational trauma and the distress of war being transferred down to the next generation. I listened to the story of one woman who had fled all alone at night; she had spent four days and three nights in the forest crossing landmine fields into the Pakistani part of Kashmir to be reunited with her husband who had fled earlier to escape persecution by Indian security forces.

While having a chat with Allaudin and some of his relatives, over a cup of Kashmiri tea and fresh oranges in Muzaffarabad, Allaudin started talking – while trying to hide his emotions, he said, "do you know that when I travel to the Line of Control, I can see my elder brother on the other side of the Jhelum River? I can even wave at him, and he waves back, but we cannot talk, we cannot meet either. All I am longing for is to go home."[11] As he speaks, Allaudin sits on the floor of his nephew's home. He stares at the sliced oranges in front of him and then gazes into space before quietly breaking down into tears. It is moving to see these tears rolling down the cheeks of an elderly man. After some minutes of silence, he wipes his tears, apologizes, and when I ask him what he would like to see happening in Kashmir, he answers "I always get sad when I think of my brother and of those troubled years of armed conflict. I am sorry that I cried but I hope that India and Pakistan will engage in a dialogue so that I can be reunited with my brother again."[12]

The Urgent Need for Peace

In the past few decades, terrorism has replaced conventional warfare. Some of the first seeds of this terrorism, or "unconventional warfare," were planted in the years after 1979 when the Soviets invaded Afghanistan and when the *mujahedeen* defeated the Red Army in 1989. At that time, the United States and Pakistan were staunch allies, and it was in the interest of Pakistan to join the United States during the Cold War as the Soviets were advancing into the region, attempting to get access to the warm waters of the Indian Ocean through Pakistan.[13] In the following decades, the terrorist threat steadily spread throughout the world, reaching cities such as London,

Paris, and Boston, and attacking places as far apart as Indonesia, Egypt, and Tunisia.

Innocent Muslims and non-Muslims from all walks of life have become victims of what seems like widening division and a never-ending conflict that threatens diverse, democratic and secular societies. International politics in today's world, especially after September 11 2001, has been dominated by ethnic and religious conflict, and by people identifying with religion to a greater degree than any enlightenment thinker could have imagined.[14] There does not appear to be a quick and easy solution to bridging the growing gap between the West and the Muslim World. This gap, moreover, is unlikely to narrow as long as Muslims back in their homelands feel as though they are occupied or subjugated by non-Muslims.

The sound of jackboots marching through cities, towns, and villages has reminded the majority Muslim population in the Kashmir Valley of India's "occupation" and top-down control. This subjugation has led to a strong sense of alienation, injustice, and resentment, and a lack of democratic values, ongoing human rights violations, and draconian laws, have harmed innocent civilians. This gives the victims of oppression a reason to pick up arms, and in turn, creates the excuse for state and non-state actors alike to stage brutal attacks. It is an undeniable fact that terrorism in Pakistan will never be rooted out as long as the Kashmir conflict remains unresolved. In the early 1990s, Pakistan created the militant organisation, Hizbul-Mujahideen, who favour full integration with Pakistan, to counter the efforts of the Jammu and Kashmir Liberation Front (JKLF) who have fought for the creation of a fully independent state in Jammu and Kashmir.

In 2017, the United States declared Syed Salahuddin, the commander of the Hizbul-Mujahideen, a global terrorist. Another militant organisation, Lashkar-e-Taiba, was also formed in Pakistan and is notorious for staging brutal attacks against the Indian state and also the Hindu minority in the Valley. In 2008, Lashkar-e-Taiba was allegedly held accountable for the Mumbai attacks. Although the security situation in Kashmir stabilized somewhat following Pakistan's crackdown on militancy after the September 11 attacks in the United States, the militants did not denounce violence and lay down their weapons for good. The killing of Burhan Wani in July 2016 resulted in mass protests, violence, and an entire shutdown of the Kashmir Valley. Human rights have continued to be violated. Terrorist-sponsored activities in Kashmir and against India, remain a serious hurdle in starting peace talks.

To get a deeper insight into the political dynamics of Kashmir I engaged with the former Norwegian Prime Minister, K.M. Bondevik, in 2019. Bondevik has an interest in finding a peaceful resolution in Kashmir and has visited the region on several occasions. I asked his viewpoint on the ongoing terrorist threat in South Asia:

> India has continued to state that Pakistan-sponsored terrorism is the main hurdle to resolving Kashmir. Pakistan, on the other hand, has continued to claim that it condemns all forms of terrorism and it has even offered to discuss terrorism as the first point of the agenda of bilateral talks. India, however, has said that it first wants to see concrete results of Pakistan's crackdown on terrorism and will only then start the debate.[15]

The lack of dialogue has resulted in a continuously deteriorating security situation in the Kashmir Valley. Against this backdrop, I also reached out to Kashmiri human rights lawyer Parvez Imroz who was awarded the Ludovic Trarieux International Human Rights Prize in 2006, and also the prestigious Thorolf Rafto Memorial Prize, in 2017, for his efforts to bring about justice in Kashmir. I asked him what actions he thought both India and Pakistan should be taking to stop the human rights abuses in Kashmir, and whether there is any action that the people of Kashmir could be undertaking to ease the tensions in the Valley? He responded by saying:

> There is no action plan in the foreseeable future and the Government of India is intransigent. There is complete deadlock between the two countries and Kashmir is off the table. On the contrary, belligerency from both sides is evident from the repeated violations of the Line of Control. Kashmiris are besieged and they have no action plan so far, that too when the Indian state has initiated Operation "All Out" i.e., to use more repressive measures against the activists including human rights activists and also against the people who are confronting the occupation through non-violent means, which is more difficult for the state to deal with than the militancy which is easy for them to deal.[16]

Apart from today's ongoing terrorist threat and the human rights abuses in Kashmir, the conflict between Muslims and other groups in Kashmir has much deeper historical roots which both India and Pakistan inherited from the erstwhile colonial power. Long before the partition of the British Raj in 1947 and Kashmir's subsequent "accession" to India, Muslims never wanted to succumb to Hindu rule in Kashmir. In 1846, the Hindu Maharaja Gulab Singh (1792-1857) purchased Kashmir from the British through the Treaty of Amritsar. In 2014, Sameer Bhat, then a Kashmiri PhD candidate of the Department of History at Aligarh Muslim University in India, asked

Introduction to Kashmir

me to review one of his draft papers before publication in which he quoted the Kashmiri Muslim poet Muhammad Iqbal (1877-1938) who wrote:

> Their fields, their crops, their streams,
> Even the peasants in the vale,
> They sold, they sold all, Alas!
> How cheap was the sale?[17]

Seven decades later, the people of Kashmir are still being subjugated and moreover, are living under the shadow of guns. Today, an estimated 350,000-700,000 security forces are keeping a population of seven million Muslims under control. But the people have no intention of giving up their struggle for *azaadi*.

After the partition of British India and the Princely States in 1947, India and Pakistan fought three wars – in 1947, 1965, and 1971; all three conflicts were the result of disputes over the Kashmir region, and the last one ended with the secession of East Pakistan, today's Bangladesh. In 1998, both India and Pakistan declared their nuclear arsenal to the world, and in 1999 and 2003 they fought limited wars over the Kargil and Siachen regions.

On the one hand, Pakistan's ongoing support of terrorist activities against India has been a grave threat to South Asian peace and security; as the world's largest democracy, the constant terrorist threat in India not only undermines its own national integrity, but also its democratic and secular principles and those of the wider region. On the other hand, Pakistan has claimed it has sufficient proof that India has been attempting to destabilize Pakistan by supporting violent political movements in Karachi and also in Balochistan, where pro-secessionist movements have been active. Pakistan has also repeatedly accused India of staging attacks against Pakistan from Afghan soil. And Pakistani officials have continued to point out, in vain, the refusal of the international community to condemn any sort of Indian-sponsored terrorism against them.

With the growing threat of the Islamic State (IS), the need for an effective strategy to bring stability back to Muslim regions has become even more vital. The Indian military has claimed that the IS threat cannot be ruled out in Kashmir.[18] However, Kashmiris at large have stated that IS will never succeed developing roots in the Kashmir Valley – and some have claimed that the threat of Islamic State has been exaggerated by India as an excuse to sustain the large military presence and subjugation of the people there. The hoisting of IS flags in Kashmir has often been seen primarily as an act of anger against Indian occupation rather than a genuine desire to create an Islamic state. Nevertheless, even if only a handful of young boys were to join IS forces out of sheer frustration of India's occupation in the Kashmir Valley, what might happen?

It is a known fact that only a handful of angry men are needed to plan an attack and moreover, many attacks are carried out by just one lone wolf – the Pulwama attack of 14 February 2019, in Kashmir, being one mere example. Pakistan, moreover, has a solid history of turning a blind eye to antagonistic elements against India, and the volatile Line of Control has continued to be a flashpoint where, indisputably, militants from Pakistan have crossed into the Kashmir Valley.

On the political level, improved Indo-Pakistani relations would reduce this militant threat. On the grassroots level, in recent years, some innocent Kashmiri youths have abandoned school and have picked up Kalashnikovs in their struggle for *azaadi*. This has not been an effective solution to the conflict and will only aggravate the already dire security situation. Faced with these realities, it becomes clear that an effective peace dialogue between India and Pakistan would not only make a fundamental contribution to a more stable security environment in South Asia as a whole, but it would also provide a vital space in which the voices of the people of Kashmir could at last be heard.

The Kashmiri human rights defender, Khurram Parvez, once told me when we met over a coffee in Jakarta that "India has to treat us as equal. We are now having guns pointed at our heads, military boots are marching around the city, and innocent children are being killed. We need to sit around the table and talk."[19] The former Norwegian Prime Minister, K.M. Bondevik, later reiterated this point when he argued that, "Kashmir is not only a bilateral dispute between India and Pakistan but also one which includes the people of Kashmir from all the different regions who cannot be excluded from any long-lasting peace dialogue." And he went further, saying, "Kashmir is not only a conflict about territory but one that involves ethnicity, religion, natural resources and also the economy. Lasting peace in Kashmir would boost tourism in Kashmir which has great potential.[20]

The absence of the opportunity, over the past decades, for the people of Kashmir to address their grievances in talks has resulted in an increasing number of Kashmiris (on both sides of the Line of Control) siding with the idea of the creation of an independent nation. The ideal scenario sought by those who argue for Kashmir's independence, is the erasure of the Line of Control and the reunification of the pre-1948 Princely State of Kashmir as a sovereign entity.[21] Professor Sumantra Bose of the London School of Economics considers this a fantasy in practical terms since India and Pakistan are tacitly united in their absolute opposition to the emergence of a sovereign authority in all or any part of Kashmir's territory. But even if the scenario were to be permitted by the two countries, it would be extremely problematic.[22] When I spoke with the former President of Pakistan, Pervez Musharraf, he also reiterated that "both India and Pakistan are strategically opposed to an independent Kashmir." However, he added that "we can fall short of that by giving the people of Kashmir the maximum level of self-governance."[23]

On the political, diplomatic, and military level, both India and Pakistan have only engaged with the Kashmiri people when it has served either of their national interests. In a more cultural capacity however, with Kashmir and Pakistan sharing a proportionally similar number of Muslims in relation to other religions, the people of Pakistan have generally shown support for the people of Kashmir and been committed to Kashmir's *azaadi* struggle. Pakistan, moreover, has been the *only* country in the world that has provided moral, political and diplomatic support to the people of Kashmir both domestically and also on the international front. This is despite the fact that Pakistan had considerable constraints dealing with Kashmir following the loss of East Pakistan in the 1971 Indo-Pakistani war; to calm down a nation that had been militarily, politically, and diplomatically defeated, the then President of Pakistan, Zulfikar Ali Bhutto, had to secure the release of 93,000 Pakistani prisoners of war, and was left with no choice but to surrender to Indira Gandhi's demands and settle for what was considered a meagre accord. It is not without reason that Kashmir was not put on Pakistan's political agenda in the decades following the 1972 Simla Agreement.

The Inclusion of Kashmiris

It has been widely argued that the people of Kashmir should be granted a voice and be included in formal talks with India and Pakistan. However, as mentioned earlier, many Kashmiri intellectuals have been killed over the decades and many more have been imprisoned and tortured. Kashmiris in the Kashmir Valley especially, know that their lives are at risk if they say or do something that does not suit their country's political agenda. It is therefore incumbent that the Kashmiri Diaspora, from both sides of the Line of Control, play a role in representing the voices of the various individuals and groups in Kashmir and in advocating for a peaceful resolution to the conflict. To date, there is no single unanimous voice that represents the people of Kashmir as a united front – however, there have been efforts made towards this goal.

Farooq Siddiqi alias Farooq Papa was one of the faction leaders of the Jammu and Kashmir Liberation Front during the armed struggle in the 1990s. He was forced to go in exile to escape assassination in 1994 and he subsequently settled in Canada. Farooq is a widely experienced veteran of the struggle who started out as a young student in the 1970s by organising peaceful demonstrations. He was often arrested by the Indian security forces, and in 1989, he eventually joined the armed struggle together with Yasin Malik. Until this day, he cannot return to Kashmir. Based on his decades-long experiences of the struggle in Kashmir and his subsequent campaigning as a member of the diaspora, Farooq believes in the creation of a platform where all Kashmiris from different regions, ethnicities and religions come together. He believes that this is a necessary first step forward and that it will pave the way for an all-inclusive peace dialogue. He argues that as long as the people of Kashmir are not included in any peace talks with India and Pakistan, a peaceful resolution of the conflict will remain elusive. In 2012, he laid down a technical framework which he called the *Niagara Declaration* (not to be confused with another declaration of the same name created in 2020). The declaration states:

> The two countries have not been able to maintain steady progress in establishing peace in South Asia; both have intermittently engaged themselves in bilateral talks without any substantial outcome that could have benefited the Kashmiri people in particular and the people of South Asia in general. The rigid stand that both countries have taken with respect to a resolution of Kashmir is manifest in deadlock and will continue to be so. In such a state of antagonism, the Kashmiri people, irrespective of their religious group, linguistic background, political ideology and social background, have suffered in the absence of hopes for peace.[24]

The *Niagara Declaration* is not intended to challenge the stated stands of India and Pakistan, but to find the way forward for the people of Kashmir to be a part of the progress that South Asia will witness in the twenty-first century, given the condition of peaceful co-existence. It will be left for India and Pakistan to resolve the Kashmir conflict, if and when they become mature enough to realize that the Kashmir conflict should be resolved in the name of humanity, as the threat of nuclear war is always an ominous danger in the absence of peace. Until that time India and Pakistan, together with the international community, must help in removing the impediments that the Kashmiri people are confronted with.[25]

The chairman of the Jammu and Kashmir Liberation Front, Yasin Malik, is another of the four *azaadi* leaders who have received widespread support from Kashmiris. He endorsed the *Niagara Declaration* and in 2015 issued the following statement in an effort to unite the people of Kashmir and promote peace:

> The people of Kashmir have been voiceless for the past seventy years. I appeal to the people of Kashmir to join hands, and speak with one united voice. The *Niagara Declaration* will be a first step forward towards peace in South Asia.[26]

At the time of writing, Indian security forces had incarcerated Malik in the notorious Tihar Jail in India's capital New Delhi, and in May 2022 he was sentenced to life in jail. International condemnation has remained absent.

Hypothetically, pressure from the international community on both Pakistan and India to move towards peace talks would be an effective tool. Successive United Nations Secretary Generals have offered mediation in Kashmir, provided that both India and Pakistan would agree, but this agreement, at least to date, has seemed unattainable.

The longer that Kashmiris are ignored, the stronger the desire for independence will become, and the risk of yet another armed uprising against Indian occupation in the Kashmir Valley will increase. Because the Kashmir conflict has been ignored for so long outside of South Asia, the vast majority of people in the world have no knowledge of the existence of an unresolved territorial conflict between India and Pakistan. The international media, politicians and academia have shown limited or no interest in Kashmir. India has become known only as the world's largest democracy, for its rapidly growing economy, and for its Bollywood movies and secular values.

Although Pakistan was an ally of the United States during the Cold War while India sided with the then Soviet Union, the tide has turned. Lucrative nuclear deals, business and trade contracts worth billions of US dollars, and US efforts to contain a rapidly growing China have become priorities in the relationship between the western powers and India. As a result, the world at large has turned a blind eye to Kashmir's oppression – especially the oppression of the Kashmir Valley.

In 1948, The United Nations Security Council Resolutions on Kashmir pledged to hold a plebiscite for the people of Kashmir on the future of the Princely State. After seventy years, it appears these resolutions have become obsolete. It is said that Nehru abandoned his earlier commitment to a plebiscite already in 1956 when Kashmir's status as semi-autonomous state within India was formalised.[27] In an interview with *Rising Kashmir*, former chief of Indian intelligence, Amarjit Singh Dulat, who dedicated most of his career to Kashmir, reiterated, "it [the plebiscite] will not happen here [in Kashmir]. Let us be realistic."[28] And in 2004, President Pervez Musharraf became the first leader in Pakistan's history to communicate the withdrawal of his support of the 1948 UN Security Council Resolutions and to publicly acknowledge that he thought it pointless to flog the dead horse of the plebiscite. He argued that an alternative path to settling Kashmir should be found, and his solution was what became known as the "Four-point Formula."[29] In 2015, Dulat wrote:

> Musharraf's four-point proposal is the closest that we (India and Pakistan) have come to some kind of forward movement.[30] All four points were not acceptable to either side but we were quite close. Coming in and going, opening of borders, making borders irrelevant, that is the general idea. There was a forward movement.[31]

In 2018, I had the honour of meeting former Pakistan President Pervez Musharraf at his residence in Dubai. I asked him how he had reached the decision to divert from Pakistan's traditional stance of supporting the idea of the UN Security Council Resolutions on Kashmir. He replied:

> India has violated the UN Resolutions to prevent the people from their right to self-determination. Having a military background, every soldier gets involved in war games and military exercises on Kashmir. The Line of Control cross border shelling, Siachen, or Kargil are just a few examples. It makes our hearts bleed to learn about what has been happening to the Kashmiris on the Indian side. When I was President, I asked various people in the Kashmiri leadership how to resolve Kashmir, but nobody had any answer. Then the four-point solution came to my mind.[32]

I then asked Mr. Musharraf how he thought the move toward building peace in Kashmir should proceed and he answered as follows:

> What both the Indian and Pakistani leaderships require to move towards a resolution on Kashmir are: the sincerity of both countries; flexibility; and the willingness to agree to a half-way solution. We need to be committed with our heads and hearts to a peaceful resolution for which

a lot of flexibility is required to meet half way. Leaders are often scared to compromise, because they do not want to deal with opposition and extremist forces in the country that will go into the streets to protest. As leaders, however, we have to deal with this. This is what leadership is about.[33]

Describing the challenges for peace in Kashmir, former Norwegian Prime Minister K.M. Bondevik also emphasised the necessity of a willingness to compromise, and a readiness to dialogue, between the leaders moving forward:

> The main hurdle to resolving Kashmir is the lack of confidence between India and Pakistan. The two countries need to start building confidence and trust in each other. This is the only way forward. In February 2019 for instance, the Prime Minister of Pakistan, Imran Khan, made one concrete step forward by releasing the Indian pilot which they had captured and which reached worldwide headline news. Earlier, he had already opened the Kartarpur crossing for religious worship where Indian Sikhs can cross the border into Pakistan without even holding a visa. Much more, however, needs to be done. Both nations need to reach out to one another by creating a platform where they can meet each other.[34]

Kashmir and the Instrument of Accession

For the past seventy years, there has been much debate around the Instrument of Accession – the document that was created to legalize Kashmir's accession to India. On 14 and 15 August 1947, both Pakistan and India became two independent nations. Based on the two-nation theory, the 584 Princely States which were part of the British Raj had the choice to join either India, Pakistan, or in some cases to become an independent nation. These Princely States were scattered throughout the South Asian continent. Both Nehru and Gandhi had been very anxious that the Maharaja of Kashmir should make no declaration of independence.[35] It was widely anticipated that Kashmir would join Pakistan based on demographic grounds, geographic location, and the overall aspirations of the majority of the population. However, the Hindu Maharaja Hari Singh was unable to take any decision – and as the decision kept on lingering, the tension between the two countries surged and the first war between India and Pakistan over the accession of the Princely State broke out in October 1947.

India accused Pakistan of sending Pashtun tribal warriors (from the North-West Frontier with Afghanistan) into Kashmir. Pakistan on the other hand, accused India of landing its armed forces in the Princely State on 27 October 1947. It is said that the Maharaja of Kashmir signed the Instrument of Accession with India on 26 October 1947 – the day before the arrival of Indian troops in Jammu and Kashmir.

However, Alastair Lamb, one of Britain's most prominent historians on Kashmir, has, among others, disputed the validity of this document. He highlights the controversy around the details of the events that took place around 26 October 1947 and questions whether the Instrument of Accession was ever signed at all.[36] On the other hand, British historian and author on Kashmir, Victoria Schofield, argues that there is no such dispute. In *Kashmir in Conflict*, Schofield writes, "unhappy as (Maharaja) Hari Singh sometimes became with the states' accession to India, he never suggested that he had not signed an Instrument of Accession before Indian troops landed nor that he had never signed one."[37]

During the conduct of my research over the past decade, I found that many Kashmiris and Pakistanis express doubts about the validity of the Instrument of Accession, and the majority believe that it was never signed at all.[38]

The Jammu and Kashmir Region

The Princely State of Jammu and Kashmir lies between the vast mountain ranges of the Himalayas, the Karakoram and the Pir Panjal, and was once a popular tourist destination known for its serene beauty. The Mughal Emperor Jahangir rightfully called Kashmir a Paradise on Earth. Today, the name Kashmir is applied not only to the Princely State of Jammu and Kashmir, but denotes the wider surrounding area that is divided into various regions. While the vast majority of people in Kashmir as a whole are Muslim, it is also home to a number of other religious minorities.

Kashmir as a whole has a total estimated population of roughly thirteen million people. The Kashmir Valley is home to a population of four million people of which ninety-five per cent are Muslim and four per cent Hindu. Jammu is home to three million people of which sixty-six per cent are Hindu, thirty per cent Muslim and the remaining four per cent are of other faiths such as Sikhism and Christianity. The population in Ladakh is comprised of fifty per cent Buddhist, forty-six per cent Muslim, and three per cent other religions. Azad Jammu and Kashmir has a total population of four million people who are primarily Muslim. And lastly, Gilgit-

Baltistan is home to approximately two million people of which ninety-nine per cent are Muslim. There is no reliable data available on *Aksai Chin* and the *Shaksgam* Valley which are the parts of Kashmir that are under China's control.[39]

Gilgit-Baltistan

Gilgit-Baltistan came under Pakistan's administration through the Karachi Agreement of 1949 following an earlier act of "self-liberation" in 1947. Traditionally they are two separate regions. Gilgit is the capital, and Skardu (in Baltistan) is the region's largest city. The region is known for its splendid beauty with the high snow-capped mountains of the Karakoram, the Hindu Kush, and the Himalayas, all converging in Bunji located near Gilgit. In summer time, long stretches of lush green valleys covered in colourful flowers lie between the mountain hills and plains. The narrow and dangerous trade paths that wind deep through the mountains are today's traces of the ancient Silk Road which has been restored along the Karakoram Highway. The rock carvings and Buddhist faces that are carved out of mountain walls have continued to attract archaeologists from around the world. Today, some remnants of Kashmir's rich Buddhist history can still be found in the British Museum in London. Turquoise coloured lakes, and streams of fresh water flowing downwards from the mountain summits add to Gilgit's natural splendour. Rich in natural resources of minerals, vital water flows, and also precious stones, Gilgit-Baltistan is Pakistan's national pride.

The region is home to a predominantly Shia population of which many have enjoyed close ties to either Chinese or Tibetan Buddhist culture. The region has its own distinct language, culture and cuisine, and the people of Gilgit-Baltistan are proud of their Chinese and Tibetan heritage. In the area of the Hunza Valley in northern Gilgit-Baltistan, the followers of the Aga Khan, the Ismailis, have a strong presence. In this valley, the vast majority of women have been educated – with a literacy rate of around eighty per cent. The people of this region share no allegiance, be it on cultural, religious, or ethnic grounds, with the Kashmiris from the Vale of Kashmir more commonly known as the Kashmir Valley. While it is estimated that the majority of the population in Gilgit-Baltistan favour full integration with Pakistan, there is also a minority who favour the creation of an independent state. The founding father of the Jammu and Kashmir Liberation Front, the late Amanullah Khan, was from Astore in the Gilgit region, and he favoured the reunification of Greater Kashmir.

Gilgit-Baltistan is strategically placed, being close to Afghanistan in the west, Central Asia in the northwest, China to the north, and India's Kashmir to the east. Gilgit-Baltistan is also home to five of the world's highest mountain peaks making it of vital importance with regard to water flows into Pakistan.[40]. And so, although Gilgit-Baltistan is a disputed region of Jammu and Kashmir, under no conditions would Pakistan want to secede this region and lose access to its rich water resources.

The region is largely tribal, and large parts of it remain impoverished. Although literacy levels are relatively high in school-age children in places such as the Hunza Valley, only a handful of people have access to higher education.[41] There is one university, the Karakoram International University, that was established only in 2002 on the orders of the then President of Pakistan, Pervez Musharraf.[42] When I visited the university during my stay in Gilgit, its leadership was proud that Mr. Musharraf had gifted the university to the region; only a minority can afford to send their children to universities in Pakistan.

In 2015, Gilgit-Baltistan came briefly into the political agenda when Pakistan proposed converting the region into Pakistan's fifth province. Kashmiri political leaders on both the Pakistani and Indian sides strongly condemned this proposal which they believed would harm Pakistan's chance of arriving at a peaceful resolution in Kashmir. However, in 2020 the idea came to prominence again, and this time the Pakistani Prime Minister Imran Khan granted Gilgit-Baltistan provisional provincial status.[43] On 9 March 2021, the Gilgit-Baltistan legislative assembly unanimously adopted a resolution to make the region an interim province of the country.[44]

Although Gilgit-Baltistan officially acceded to Pakistan with an Executive Order, the region does not, essentially, enjoy any constitutional framework, and falls directly under Islamabad's control. It is believed that the Pakistani military exercise strong regional control and that political freedom has been restrained. During my field research in the region, one Balti intellectual said, "if we cannot get the status of a province of Pakistan, then Pakistan could alternatively grant us the same status as our "friends" in Azad Jammu and Kashmir."[45] He also continued whispering in my ear "please suggest to both India and Pakistan to re-open the ancient Kargil-Skardu trade road, so there will be more people-to-people contact between the two disputed regions of Kashmir."[46]

Azad Jammu and Kashmir

Unlike Gilgit-Baltistan, Azad Jammu and Kashmir has its own interim constitution that was enacted in 1974. Azad Jammu and Kashmir was said to have been "liberated" following the first Indo-Pakistan War in 1947, yet, the Kashmiri political activists who favour the creation of an independent Kashmir have no voice. The Kashmiri activist Sardar Anwar has been arrested and imprisoned four times for his views on the creation of an independent nation. Article 7.2 of the Azad Jammu and Kashmir interim constitution states that no person or political party in Azad Jammu and Kashmir shall be permitted to propagate against, or take part in activities prejudicial or detrimental to the ideology of the state's accession to Pakistan.[47]

In 2010, the UK-based policy institute, Chatham House, published a paper titled *Kashmir: Paths to Peace* in which it stated that an estimated fifty per cent of the Azad Jammu and Kashmir population favours full integration with Pakistan.[48] "If the federal government in Islamabad claims that Kashmiris of Azad Jammu and Kashmir favour full integration with Pakistan, why don't they hold a referendum like in Scotland,"[49] said Ahmed (a Kashmiri whose name has been changed) as we talked on the phone. The Pakistani security forces may not be as visible as the Indian security forces in the Kashmir Valley, but they undoubtedly have a presence in Azad Jammu and Kashmir as well. Foreigners who want to visit the region need a special permit which is usually not valid for more than a few days. During my last visit, I had to wait for thirty minutes at a security checkpoint to finally be allowed in. Those who attempt to enter the region without a valid permit find themselves at the mercy of the security forces.

It is widely believed that the Pakistani government separated the regions of Azad Jammu and Kashmir from Gilgit-Baltistan for political purposes. Many political activists in Azad Jammu and Kashmir would like to build closer relations with the people of Gilgit-Baltistan, but the Pakistani authorities have always countered such attempts. Ethnically, the Kashmiris from Azad Jammu and Kashmir are different from those in Gilgit-Baltistan; the people of Gilgit-Baltistan often have blonde hair and blue eyes like many people from Afghanistan and the Pashtun tribal regions. The level of education in Azad Jammu and Kashmir is higher than in Gilgit-Baltistan as a whole (discounting the higher level of education in the Hunza Valley). Azad Jammu and Kashmir is politically more vibrant than its Gilgit-Baltistan neighbour, and the people of Azad Jammu and Kashmir tend to enjoy more prominent positions in Pakistani public and political life. For example, Kashmiris from Poonch, in Jammu, are famous for their military skills and many joined the British Indian Army during colonization. Today, many enjoy high ranks in Pakistan's Armed Forces.

The Chinese part of Kashmir: Aksai Chin

On the international political stage, it is a little-known fact that the People's Republic of China controls two parts of the disputed region of Jammu and Kashmir – Aksai Chin and the Shaksgam Valley. China took the Aksai Chin regions under its control following the 1962 Sino-India border war, and the dispute about the Shaksgam Valley was settled with Pakistan following the Sino-Pakistan Frontier Agreement which was signed by Pakistan's Foreign Minister, Zulfikar Ali Bhutto and the Chinese Foreign Minister Cheng Yi on 2 March 1963. The intention was that this temporary border agreement would be renegotiated once India and Pakistan found a final resolution on Kashmir.[50]

In the subsequent decades, Pakistan has been widely accused of ceding territory to China. Indian writers have insisted that Pakistan has surrendered no less than 2,050 square miles of territory to China to which, they argue, it had no right to in the first place. Moreover, Pakistan has likely gained around twenty square miles in these transactions rather than lost territory overall.[51] Not much is known about these sparsely populated regions, but they are of vital strategic geopolitical interest. Aksai Chin used to be home to the only road into Tibet that was accessible all-year round. Although this is no longer relevant, the region's close proximity to both Pakistan and India contribute to it still being coveted by those nations. The Shaksgam Valley also has some strategic mountain passes. In 1960 and 1980, Zhou Enlai and Deng Xiaoping offered India a swap – Aksai Chin for Arunachal Pradesh. The latter is an India-controlled region which is seen by China as "South Tibet". However, India refused the offer citing security, economic, and political reasons.

A final settlement for Kashmir would fundamentally contribute to peace and stability in Pakistan and the wider region, creating a more stable regional security environment. This would also positively impact the security conditions in the Xinjiang Uighur Autonomous Region – China's far western province and home to the Uighurs, a Muslim ethnic minority group which has a long history of revolting against the Han Chinese. The region, also known as East Turkestan, has long been prone to social and political unrest; the Uighurs have been held accountable for a number of deadly attacks in China and in turn, many have been rounded up and held in "re-education" camps by the Chinese. The East Turkestan Independence

Movement advocates for an independent East Turkestan State. Fortunately, there has not been an act of violence in the name of this cause since 2016; for the time being it is believed that the movement is hibernating, but its cause is far from over.[52]

On the economic front, the importance of the Aksai Chin and Kashmir regions revolves around the Chinese Belt and Road Initiative (BRI) – a revival of the ancient Chinese Silk Road that aims to boost economic development – that runs through Aksai Chin. One part of the wider BRI is the China-Pakistan Economic Corridor (CPEC) which crosses through the strategically important Gilgit-Baltistan. Although CPEC is a commercial undertaking, the necessary political and strategic communication that has had to occur to facilitate it, has served to strengthen the Sino-India-Pakistan entente. And understanding this strategic context and the symbiotic relationship between CPEC, Kashmir, and the surrounding jurisdictions, is a vital prerequisite for securing peace in the region.

The Indian part of Kashmir

In July 2016, the Kashmir Valley was once again set ablaze after the assassination of Burhan Wani that was followed by some of the worst clashes in decades, leaving 30 people dead. And then, in August 2019, the Indian Prime Minister Narendra Modi decided to abrogate Articles 370 and 35A of the Indian Constitution, and to orchestrate an entire communication lockdown of the Kashmir Valley. Article 370 had granted Kashmir a special status and given them the right to make decisions on their own daily affairs – all except for foreign affairs, defence and communications. It had also given the Kashmir Valley the right to hoist their own flag. Article 35A acted to prevent anyone from outside of Kashmir purchasing land in Kashmir. By scrapping both articles, India argued that it would be more able to control the overall security conditions and fight terrorism. Its aim was also to reduce corruption in Kashmir – enabling women who marry non-Kashmiris to be able to purchase land. Also in 2019, India divided the Indian part of Kashmir into the two Union Territories of Jammu and Kashmir, and Ladakh, the latter being home to a large Buddhist minority.

The people of Kashmir reacted to these decisions with outright anger. The ongoing occupation of the region by Indian security forces has led to increased social unrest, and a new generation of alienated youth who are once again veering toward the taking up of arms. Kashmir, is now one of the most militarized regions in the world.[53] Over the past three decades, between 40,000 (official Indian figures) and 70,000 (official Pakistani and

Kashmiri figures) people have been killed in the conflict, of which an estimated fifty per cent have been civilians.[54]

By around 2012, an estimated total of more than six thousand unmarked graves had been discovered in the Vale of Kashmir. India has claimed that the graves contain the bodies of militants who died in the conflict. The people of Kashmir have demanded a proper investigation and DNA testing. Tens of thousands of children have been raised without a father and, according to a conservative estimate, some 1,500 "half-widows" are waiting for information that could lead to the whereabouts of their husbands.[55] The actual number of "half-widows" is expected to be far higher. Hena is one Kashmiri woman whose husband was taken away by security forces and never seen again:

> Hena was rendered a half-widow in 2003. Her 35-year-old husband Muneer worked as a mason. They lived in their Baramulla house with their four children, Muneer's parents, his two sisters, and four brothers. On 19 July 2003, men of the 2nd Rashtriya Rifles (a paramilitary group) knocked at their door. The male members of the family were separated from the women and children. Muneer, the eldest brother, was escorted out of the house. The family was told he would return the next day, after some questioning. Eight years later, Muneer has still not returned.[56]

Draconian laws that were implemented during the armed conflict of the 1990s remain in place and continue to disrupt Kashmiri society in the Indian part of Kashmir. The security forces have been left to commit abuses of human rights with impunity under the cover of a number of laws: the Armed Forces Special Powers Act (AFSPA) which grants immunity from prosecution for any committed crimes; the Public Safety Act (PSA) which allows detention of a person without trial for up two years; and the Disturbed Areas Act (DAA) which allows security personnel to use whatever force, including lethal, they feel is necessary to maintain public order.[57] More recently yet another such law was implemented in Kashmir – the Unlawful Activities Prevention Act (UAPA). During a visit to Bangkok, Thailand, in spring 2018, I met a retired senior Indian police officer who had dedicated his entire career to the security of Kashmir. He asked to remain anonymous, and while we talked over dinner, he said:

> The Kashmiri police force was trained to battle crime, not to fight militancy. In 1990, we were caught by surprise when thousands of militants coming across the border from Pakistan, stationed themselves in Indian Kashmir. All of a sudden, they stood right in front of us. These

militants were very well-trained. What were we supposed to do? ... At the cost of my family, I made many sacrifices to maintain peace and security in Kashmir, and repeatedly came close to facing death. Many of my colleagues lost their lives in the conflict. The international community and Pakistan as well, need to understand that the Kashmir Valley belongs to us (India), and we will deal with the conflict ourselves, internally. We understand and acknowledge that the people of Kashmir have been suffering a lot, but as long as Pakistan continues to create trouble for us, we will never achieve any sort of normalization in the Valley.[58]

While the Muslim majority has been the main victim of the conflict, tens of thousands of innocent Hindus were displaced at the peak of the conflict in the 1990s. Human rights defender Khurram Parvez said that "an estimated 168,000 Hindus used to live in the Kashmir Valley. The vast majority fled during the conflict, militants killed some four hundred, and about four to five thousand families have remained."[59] A large number of Hindu Pandits who fled during the conflict in the early 1990s, have been living in camps since that time, sometimes under appalling conditions. The Indian government is only now arranging for their return. Parvez highlighted the historical peaceful co-existence of the religious groups in the Valley:

Traditionally, Hindus and Muslims peacefully coexisted in the Kashmir Valley. There are many Muslim families that do not eat beef, and, after generations, this has become a tradition in our Kashmiri society. I don't eat beef, no one in my family does, and many of my Muslim friends do not eat beef either.[60]

But despite this peaceful merging of cultural traditions, the return of the Pandits to the Valley has come with some controversy. The Indian government began an initiative to build settlements specifically for the returning Pandits – and so some sources have claimed that India's intention is to return the Hindus to the Valley in order to alter the demographic balance and to weaken the Muslim majority. In Jammu, there is currently a majority Hindu population, with a large Muslim minority. And Ladakh is home to a predominantly Buddhist population which feels closely affiliated to the Tibetans, as well as to a large minority Shia population. The Hindu and Buddhist populations have virtually no interest in creating an independent Kashmir and favour integration with India.

Azaadi, Freedom and Change in Kashmir

The Predicament of Kashmir

It seems that there are aspects of the status quo that will never change: India is highly unlikely to give up the Kashmir Valley (the Vale of Kashmir), Pakistan is just as unlikely to let go of the strategically important region of Gilgit-Baltistan; and Aksai Chin will remain under China's control for the foreseeable future. The Greater Kashmiri region consists of people with different religions, and diverse ethnicities, languages, cultures and histories. Kashmiri society is not, and has never been, homogenous – but the Kashmir conflict does not have its roots in this lack of homogeneity. Instead, it lies in the daily oppression of the predominantly Muslim population in the Kashmir Valley that suffer on a daily basis with no clear end to the conflict in sight – as well as in the socio-political and economic restraints that exist in the Pakistani part of Azad Jammu and Kashmir and Gilgit-Baltistan. All of these issues have led to widespread dissatisfaction in the whole region. However, this does not mean that a peace process cannot be initiated; and one possible solution is that by effectively maintaining the status quo, the overall situation in Kashmir could be improved provided there is the political will.

Whether or not the Instrument of Accession was signed, the Kashmir Valley is very likely to remain under India's control. The Dixon plan of the 1950s, which divided Kashmir between India and Pakistan and which proposed a plebiscite in the Kashmir Valley only, is very unlikely to work. The Chenab formula, under which all Muslim-majority parts of Kashmir would join Pakistan, is not a solution either. Kashmiris may have declared Maqbool Butt and Mohammad Afzal Guru martyrs in their struggle for *azaadi*, but they do not set the example of peaceful dialogue; India, and the world at large, will continue to consider them (Islamic) terrorists which would add further obstacles to any peace process if this avenue were pursued.

Maqbool Butt was co-founder of the Jammu and Kashmir Liberation Front and was hanged in Tihar jail on 11 February 1984 for the murder of a bank manager in Kupwara (Kashmir), and of a policeman. Mohammad Afzal Guru was hanged on 9 February 2013 for his alleged complicity in the 2001 attacks on the Indian Parliament.[61] Kashmiris observe these days annually to commemorate the deaths of these two men who are considered heroes. But acts of violence, including the hijacking of a plane in 1971, and the killing of the Indian diplomat Ravindra Mhatre in1984, do not help in the creation of dialogue and peaceful resolution.[62]

As long as Kashmiris refuse to denounce violence, and as long as Pakistan continues to appease and support the armed militancy in Kashmir, then increasing instability and enmity will continue. Stone-pelting youths do not offer a solution either. If the Jammu and Kashmir Liberation Front were able to lay down their weapons, then this can be achieved by other groups also. Instead of continuing with a journey of vengeance, the time has come for India and Pakistan to join hands in genuinely addressing the grievances of the people of Kashmir and in outlining a roadmap toward peace and justice.

The majority view in Pakistan – the view that it would have been logical for Kashmir to join Pakistan on religious and ethnic grounds – is valid. And Pakistan is justified in its grievance that the accession of Kashmir to India during the partition of the British Raj was undertaken via means that were likely underhand. The events around the Instrument of Accession no doubt come with a question mark. But the reversal of this accession is extremely unlikely, and dwelling on past grievances will not resolve the Kashmir dispute. Neither will military action, or support for militancy in Kashmir. If no action is taken to improve Indo-Pakistan relations, and as long as the suffering of the people of Kashmir continues to be ignored, then this Paradise on Earth may eventually turn into Hell. As divided as India and Pakistan have been in the past, if they could leave past grievances behind, then a joint indigenous framework for dialogue could be created.

Unfortunately, obstacles with their roots in the past have halted the efforts for peace. Dr. Jean-Luc Racine, author of *Cachemire; au Péril de la Guerre* and one of France's leading scholars on South Asia, has come up with a straightforward analysis of some of these obstacles. He highlights the complexities of Kashmir's history during the decolonization of the British Raj in 1947 – including the fact that the Maharaja of Kashmir was a Hindu while his subjects were primarily Muslim.[63] This fact contributed to the voicelessness of the people of Kashmir who have become prisoners of history and prisoners of silence.[64] While India's rule regarding Kashmir seems to be simple – i.e. the less one talks about Kashmir, the better[65] – Dr. Racine also writes that there are some doubts about the sincerity of Pakistan's efforts.[66]

India has vehemently opposed any outside mediation and does not want any international attention on the dispute – either in the media, among academics, or on the political level. Based on my personal experiences, they also aggressively counter anyone who attempts to work on Kashmir. During the course of writing this book, I repeatedly attempted to engage with my contact at the Indian High Commission. I also applied for an Indian visa, including a visit to Kashmir, but this was all to no avail. This is of course telling – no nation likes the rest of the world to see its most brutal face.

Unlike India, Pakistan has attempted to internationalize the Kashmir dispute by giving Kashmiris the right to self-determination – but they have not achieved any substantial success either. Moreover, some of Pakistan's efforts have resulted in significant setback. For example, Mr. Ghulam Fai of the Kashmiri American Council in Washington, DC, and Barrister Majid Tramboo of the then Kashmir Centre EU in Brussels, were initially thought to be working to internationalize the Kashmir dispute for the common good, but both were exposed for being on the payroll of Inter-Services Intelligence – Pakistan's powerful intelligence agency. Fai subsequently received a jail sentence for alleged tax evasion and making false statements.

I am grateful to the Pakistani authorities for granting me access to Kashmir including to the Gilgit-Baltistan region, but the attitude of Pakistan toward Kashmir is not straightforward. During the course of my visits, I encountered three different general attitudes toward the dispute. Firstly, I met with a number of officials who are committed to a pragmatic resolution. Secondly, there is a fairly large number of people who continue to have sympathy for the implementation of the United Nations Resolutions on Kashmir and bilateral talks, which effectively maintains the status quo. And lastly, there is no doubt a hawkish element, particularly within the armed forces of Pakistan, that have covertly continued to appease and support militant movements against India.

Why this Book on Kashmir?

The essence of this book came out of the main research question, "Can India, Pakistan, and the people of Kashmir can reconcile?" While the historical aspects of a conflict are not always completely relevant to today's developments, understanding the history of Kashmir is nevertheless an important starting-point in finding the means of breaking the deadlock. In this book, I have actively engaged with a large number of Kashmiris – both within Kashmir and the Diaspora – to ascertain their viewpoints. This has been an attempt to start to rectify the problem of the silence of Kashmiri voices. I also interviewed a variety of Kashmiri intellectuals who, although not providing a unanimous voice, need to be heard before the status quo can be broken and discussion can begin; and their voices are all the more important because their viewpoints essentially differentiate from both the official Indian, and Pakistani, stances on Kashmir.

This becomes especially evident in chapter two when exploring the armed struggle in Kashmir, and where I have provided the first-hand account of Farooq, one of the faction leaders of the Jammu and Kashmir Liberation Front, who was actively engaged in the armed struggle from

1989-1994. This chapter explores the root causes of today's terrorism within Kashmir as well as against India, and the reason why Kashmiris staged an armed uprising against India.

Chapter three continues with an exploration of the Gilgit-Baltistan and Azad Jammu and Kashmir regions which are both under Pakistan's control – and the former of which has been put behind an iron curtain to evade international attention on its strategic location.

Chapter four explores the Chinese influence – the implications for regional peace, its viewpoints on Kashmir, and the geo-economic challenges of the Belt and Road Initiative considering that the China-Pakistan Economic Corridor goes through the disputed region of Jammu and Kashmir. While the erstwhile Princely State of Jammu and Kashmir is recognised as disputed territory under the United Nations banner, and despite the fact that the UN Security Council Resolutions only addresses India and Pakistan, the fact that China controls part of the region – Aksai Chin and the Shaksgam Valley – cannot be ignored.

Chapter five describes some of the gross human rights violations that have been committed in the Kashmir Valley and which, without strong condemnation from the international community, are likely to continue. Chapter six identifies the disparities between India and Pakistan, and explores the steps that have thus far been taken (without success) towards resolution. Chapter seven provides two case studies of transitional justice – one from Timor-Leste and Indonesia, and the other from South Africa – as examples of relatively successful and peaceful transitions to democracy following decades of oppression; many lessons can be learned from the methods that were used in these countries to address the human rights violations that took place and to create stability.

Chapter eight forms the conclusion of my research and provides some ways in which the status quo in Kashmir might be broken, dialogue brokered, and peace brought to the people of Kashmir.

Azaadi, Freedom and Change in Kashmir

CHAPTER 2

INDIA AND KASHMIR: THE ARMED STRUGGLE

"There are two chefs who are continuously cooking something in their pots in New Delhi and in Islamabad. They find ingredients, raw material, including wood for the fire in Kashmir." **Raja Muzaffar, who was second in command of the Jammu and Kashmir Liberation Front**

The Youth Take up Arms in Jammu and Kashmir

How should the situation in Jammu and Kashmir be defined? Is it merely an "issue"? Or is it a "dispute"? Or a "conflict"? For the people of Jammu and Kashmir, it is a matter of the restoration of the geopolitical status that they lost on 15 August 1947. Until this time, the different ethnicities and religions in Jammu and Kashmir had been living peacefully together. Like all the princely states, Jammu and Kashmir had not been under direct British rule and they had not been under the occupation of any foreign army. Before partition, the people had hoped to have a democratic and responsible form of government rather than fall under autocratic rule. Both India and Pakistan are responsible for converting Kashmir into a conflict zone and for disrupting the peaceful lives of millions of people; over the span of more than seventy years, both countries have failed to implement the clause of their agreements in the various United Nations Security Council Resolutions that stipulate the demilitarization of Jammu and Kashmir. The future of the common Kashmiri people remains undefined, and the relationship between the establishments in New Delhi and in Islamabad remains hostile.

Violence was brought into Kashmir in different forms, and the people of Kashmir have had little control over these influences.[1] The Kashmiris who have risen against the occupation have been defined in different terms;

should they be defined as guerrillas, freedom fighters, militants or, terrorists? There is no doubt that many political movements in Kashmir resorted to violence once their legitimate right of freedom was denied. Today, it is believed that there is a new generation of Kashmiri youth who are beginning to radicalize. During my meeting with the Kashmiri human rights defender Khurram Parvez in Manila, he spoke about his days of imprisonment, and the fact that the radicalization of dissatisfied and angry young Kashmiri often takes place behind bars.[2]

When I talked with various scholars, they expressed similar concerns about the radicalization of youth in Kashmir. "After all, nothing worked out so far that could have brought about a peaceful solution to Kashmir,"[3] said Farooq. At present, many Kashmiris feel as though their freedoms are being squeezed ever tighter, and the outright oppression and human rights abuses of so many innocent civilians has compounded their anger. Innocent teenage boys come home demoralized – their bodies badly bruised after being terribly beaten by security forces during the night. The vast majority of young protesters do not even carry a gun. However, there are some factions for whom violence forms a central tenet and so a clear distinction should be made between the three main types of militant groups in Kashmir. Firstly, there are the indigenous movements that started the uprising in Kashmir in 1989 and were not religious in nature. Secondly emerged the indigenous movements that were influenced by outside forces and carried an Islamic flag. And thirdly, there emerged the hardcore Kashmiri militant groups whose members are made up mainly of non-Kashmiris. The latter became active in the Valley in the mid-1990s and have changed the narrative of the movement to the present.

Still today, some of these militant forces operate mainly from outside of Kashmir and have the sole aim of destabilizing the Indian Union. These groups originated in January 1990 with the armed uprising that was spearheaded by the Jammu and Kashmir Liberation Front (who were, as mentioned above, the indigenous group of Kashmiris who believed in independence and in the coexistence of all religious groups within Kashmir).

The Jammu and Kashmir Liberation Front (JKLF) was inspired by the *Khalistan* movement in the Punjab. In the 1980s, the people of Kashmir were looking with interest to their neighbouring Punjab, where the Sikhs wanted to liberate *Khalistan* from India. When I interviewed Farooq in Kunming, China, he explained: "Sikh militancy had reached its peak, and there were speculations that Pakistan was supporting them with arms that originated from the war in Afghanistan. We did not like the idea that, unlike the Punjab, the Kashmir dispute was still in cold storage."[4] It is said that at this time, India was being shaken by waves of militant violence as guns from Pakistan were making their way into Punjab.[5]

However, the difference between the *Khalistan* movement in the Punjab, and the armed uprising in Kashmir was that the Punjab was, and is, a constitutional part of the Indian Union, whereas Jammu and Kashmir is disputed territory as outlined under the United Nations Security Council Resolutions. To have more understanding of the rise of militancy in Kashmir, it is important to follow the sequence of events that took place in the decades that followed the partition of the British Raj in 1947 until the rigged elections of 1987 which acted as catalyst for the violence.

After the first Indo-Pakistan war in 1947, the plan proposed by the UN mediator Owen Dixon, known as the Dixon Plan, advocated for what was known as the "partition-cum-plebiscite" solution. This plan proposed that the majority Muslim areas to go to Pakistan (Azad Jammu and Kashmir and Gilgit Baltistan), that Jammu and Ladakh to go to India, and that a plebiscite should be held in the Kashmir Valley (or the Vale of Kashmir) only (rather than in every region). However, India declined this proposal, in part because neither India or Pakistan agreed to remove their troops. Until 1962, many possible solutions were subsequently thwarted such as the Chenab Formula that suggested division along the Chenab River and the accession of all Muslim-majority areas to Pakistan. The ideas of arbitration, and a United Nations-sponsored plebiscite were also rejected. In 1962, after growing tensions between China and India over Tibet, Chinese troops invaded the region of eastern Ladakh – or Aksai China – and the Sino-Indian War was triggered. Wanting to avoid yet another military conflict, India again instituted talks with Pakistan. Between 1962-1963, several rounds of talks between the then Pakistan Foreign Minister Zulfikar Ali Bhutto, and his Indian counterpart occurred, but they ended in stalemate. Then, in August 1965, the Pakistan Army planned Operation Gibraltar which sparked the Indo-Pakistan War. It came to an end only after the UN mediated a ceasefire after seventeen days of all-out war. And in January of the following year, the parties held talks mediated by Soviet representatives in Tashkent, and signed the Tashkent Declaration. But further negotiations at the United Nations in New York did not bring about any further resolution. When Pakistan lost its eastern territory in the 1971 war that created today's Bangladesh, the country was militarily, economically and diplomatically devastated.

In 1972 at Simla, the erstwhile summer capital of British India, the two leaders of the divided (former) colony, Zulfiqar Ali Bhutto and Indira Gandhi, signed an agreement about resolving Kashmir that seemed itself a ghostly remnant of empire in that the Kashmiris were not consulted or involved. As a result of the agreement, although Zulfikar Ali Bhutto secured the release of approximately 90,000 Pakistani prisoners, he had to concede the promise of bilateral negotiation regarding Kashmir rather than insisting on negotiation that involved third parties. Thus, the issue of Kashmir was relegated from the United Nations echelons, to the foreign ministry corridors of New Delhi and Islamabad. This was a blow to the Kashmiri leader Sheikh Abdullah of the Plebiscite Front, the main secessionist party (established in 1955), who had been advocating for the implementation of the United Nations Resolutions. He saw the Simla Agreement as an end to this hope. Nevertheless, some glimmer of hope might have been said to come from it because it paved the way for the Indira-Sheikh Accord that was signed by Sheikh Abdullah and the Prime Minister of India, Indira Gandhi in 1975.

After the disappointment of the Simla Agreement, and perceiving Pakistan's weak position after its loss of Bangladesh, Sheikh Abdullah sought answers from Pakistan. He sent his son Farooq Abdullah, a medical practitioner based in the United Kingdom, to seek an audience with President Bhutto. He hoped to get answers about why Bhutto had changed his policy to accept bilateralism, and why he had accepted the relegation of Kashmir on the international stage and given away the chance of resolving the dispute via United Nations mechanisms. But confused about which political path to follow, Bhutto was evasive rather than up front in his meeting with Farooq. After returning home, Farooq relayed to his father the result of the meeting – that at least for a decade it would be impossible for Pakistan to raise the issue of Kashmir, and so if an arrangement could be made between India and Sheikh Abdullah, then Pakistan would not object.

It should be noted that from 1972 to 1994, India and Pakistan met forty-five times to discuss various issues – yet the Kashmir dispute was discussed only once – between the two foreign secretaries in 1994.[6] President Bhutto's priority during these years was to become a nuclear power in the belief that it would be an effective deterrent against India in the event of a repeat of the incidents leading up to the 1971 Indo-Pakistan War. The way he saw it, the Kashmir issue could be raised again once the elderly Sheikh Abdullah had passed on. Economic assistance for the development of Pakistan was essential, and via the first World Islamic Conference held in Lahore, Pakistan, in 1974, Bhutto successfully opened up a lifeline between Pakistan and the petro-rich Arab world.[7] Armed with petrodollars and Islamic solidarity from countries like Saudi Arabia and Libya, Bhutto embarked upon the path towards a nuclear Pakistan.[8]

There is an unsubstantiated view that President Bhutto made Saudi and Libyan leaders believe that the bomb would also guarantee the security of the latter's countries. Whether this is true or otherwise, his diplomacy worked well during the 1974 Islamic Summit which brought together leaders under the banner of the Organisation of Islamic Cooperation. The summit helped to bring about peaceful cooperation between the attendee leaders such as King Faisal of Saudi Arabia, the Emir of Kuwait, the Libyan Colonel Gaddafi, and the Prime Minister of Bangladesh, Sheikh Mujeeb-ur-Rehman. However, this alliance was tested when King Faisal was assassinated the following year in 1975, and again when Bhutto was, controversially, hanged for the murder of a political opponent in 1979. In 2011, Colonel Gaddafi was, like King Faisal, assassinated – all of these leaders had become unpopular with the United States. The Shah Faisal Mosque in Islamabad and the Gaddafi Cricket Stadium in Lahore stand as testament to the importance that Bhutto placed upon the relationship between Pakistan, and Saudi Arabia and Libya respectively.

During the 1970s, with peaceful attempts at resolution failing, Kashmiris would steadily come to the conclusion that picking up arms to fight for justice would be the only way to affect change. Non-violent protests against India had resulted in brutal suppression, imprisonment and torture – a response that India evidently believed would force the protestors to relinquish their demands for a free Kashmir.

When I interviewed Farooq Siddiqi in 2015, he said, "During my repeated incarcerations, I became increasingly assured that peaceful protests against Indian occupation did not work."[9] He continued, "it was a chilly afternoon sometime in late November 1973 when I saw a woman weeping alone outside the prison gates. She had come alone and was looking for her son."[10] Farooq, then an engineering student, was incarcerated at the time in the *Bagh-e-Mehtab* interrogation centre, in Srinagar in the Kashmir Valley, for one month. The prison was notorious for its torture practices. Heavily guarded by the Indian Army, it lies on a huge piece of land accessible by only one road and fenced-off by three boundaries of barbed wire. Farooq described it as a "concentration camp". The act that had resulted in this imprisonment was the organization of a peaceful student demonstration against the Indira-Sheikh Accord. He had organized the demonstration from the premises of the Regional Engineering College in Srinagar. In the days to come, protests would spread throughout the Kashmir Valley.

When Farooq spotted the weeping woman, he did not know that some young boys had been arrested and shifted to the interrogation centre the previous night. As prison guards opened Farooq's cell in the morning, he saw a young teenager and he asked him his name. "I'm Shabbir Shah," he politely answered. With him was another boy, Ghulam Qadir. It was only later that Farooq heard that the sobbing woman outside the gate had been the mother of Shabbir Shah. "I am not sure if mother and son had a chance to meet,"[11] said Farooq. In the decades to come, Shabbir Shah would become one of Kashmir's most prominent *azaadi* leaders, together with the late Syed Ali Geelani, and Mirwaiz Umar Farooq and Yasin Malik who are today united under the banner of the Hurriyat Alliance (APHC). The other boy that Farooq encountered in the prison, Ghulam Qadir, became JKLF's Press Secretary, and in 1990 unknown gunmen believed to be of Hizbul-Mujahideen assassinated him.

In 1982, the popular head of the government of Jammu and Kashmir, and founder of the National Conference party, Sheikh Abdullah, died. His son, Farooq Abdullah, was subsequently elected, but his leadership ended in 1984 when a faction broke off and his government collapsed. In 1987, elections were widely rigged by the (then still) ruling National Conference party, which side-lined the Muslim United Front from winning a majority of seats. The latter were a party who, alarmed by the decreasing levels of autonomy in Kashmir, were in favour of greater separation from India. The rigging of the election caused outrage and became the final turning point in the decision of many Kashmiris to pick up arms.

Talking with Farooq

This chapter aims to explore the armed struggle in Kashmir from the viewpoints of those who have been, and still are, closest to that struggle. It is primarily based on my interactions and long discussions with Farooq Siddiqi (his real name), alias Farooq Papa (his name known among Kashmiris), alias Zainulabedin (his code name during the armed struggle) (and we refer to him here throughout as both Farooq Siddiqi and Farooq Papa). A draft of this chapter has also been reviewed by prominent leaders and associates of the JKLF, namely Altaf Qadri, Raja Muzaffar, and Amanullah Khan. As one of the faction leaders of the Jammu and Kashmir Liberation Front, Farooq was actively engaged in the military uprising from 1990 to 1994. Since a teenager, he had been repeatedly detained by the Indian security forces, and after the assassinations of Dr. Farooq Ahmad Ashai and Dr. Abdul Ahad Guru in 1993, he was forced to take his family and flee Kashmir. It is believed that Dr. Guru's kidnap and murder was carried out by the Jammu and Kashmir state police in conjunction with an arrested militant of the Pakistani-sponsored Hizbul-Mujahideen.[12] Despite the efforts of the JKLF to liberate Kashmir from Indian oppression, the military effort at this time did not bring about a solution to the conflict.

Today, with the growing gap between the Western and the Muslim Worlds, and with the threat of Al-Qaeda, Islamic State and other Islamic groups spreading throughout the world, international recognition of the conflict has appeared increasingly elusive.

Jammu and Kashmir Liberation Front (JKLF)

Between 1987 and 1988, boys from the Islamic Student League started receiving arms from Ghulam Nabi Butt, the brother of Maqbool Butt who India had declared a terrorist for hijacking a plane and for robbing a bank. In 1984, Maqbool was hanged in Tihar jail, New Delhi, and for many Kashmiris, Maqbool was and still is, a hero who courageously fought against Indian occupation. Members of the Islamic Student League included many individuals who would go on to devote their lives to Kashmiri liberation – individuals such as Yasin Malik, Ashfaq Majeed, Javed Mir, Shoukat Bakshi, Shakeel Bakshi, Hamid, Abdullah Ahad Waza, Bilal Siddiqi, Aijaz Dar and many more.

In 1989, Ashfaq Majeed had a meeting with the JKLF during which it was decided that the Islamic Student League would merge with the JKLF and become the front-running party in Kashmir. However, another member of Islamic Student League, Shakeel Bakshi, disagreed with the merger and continuously presented himself as the leader of the League (and he subsequently never became a member of the JKLF). The supreme council, which was the ultimate decision-making body of the JKLF, consisted of Yasin Malik, Ashfaq Majeed, Javed Mir, Dr. Guru, Dr. Merajudin, Professor Wani, Farooq Papa, and also Professor Ghulam Ahmed Sheikh. Once this supreme council had been established, the JKLF began receiving widespread support from the people for the creation of an independent Kashmir. This development made Pakistan nervous and they began supplying the JKLF with arms through the Jamaat-e-Islami (the conservative Sunni Muslim political organization) in an effort to destabilize Kashmir. At the same time, the Inter-Services Intelligence of Pakistan created the Islamist militant organization, Hizbul-Mujahideen, who favoured, and still favour, full integration with Pakistan. As a result of this injection of arms, the guerrilla fighting, or freedom fighting, did not take long to escalate, and to be transformed into an Islamic extremist movement whose main aim was to weaken the JKLF and its chance of full independence.

The JKLF is a nationalist organization, and can be compared to organisations such as: the Palestine Liberation Organization under Yasser Arafat; the African National Congress under Nelson Mandela; and the armed resistance movement of FRETILIN that fought against the Indonesian occupation of East Timor. Freedom from Indian oppression and self-governance for Kashmir, is the main objective of the organization. In the 1980s, senior leaders in Kashmir did not see any other way out of the conflict than picking up arms. The orchestration of the armed struggle was undertaken by a small group of men including Dr. Ashai, Professor Ghulam Ahmed Sheikh, Dr. Merajudin, and Professor Abdul Rahman Wani, along with Farooq Papa himself. The planning was meticulous. They anticipated that if India was faced with insurgencies in two of its states at the same time – Punjab and Kashmir – it would pressure the Indian government into addressing the issue of Kashmir. They compiled a detailed report which Ashai delivered to Pakistan's President Zia-ul-Haq. The report argued that due to the fact that Pakistan's previous efforts during Operation Gibraltar in 1965 had led only to war with India and no loosening of India's rule in Kashmir – that the time had come to stage an armed uprising from within Kashmir. Furthermore, that military action should be seen to come from within Kashmir, rather than from Pakistan, because any armed incursion from the Pakistani state would be deemed an act of aggression against India and only escalate issues between the two nations, rather than find resolution for Kashmir. Farooq said: "I am pretty sure this dossier was discussed in Pakistan. I am also quite sure that the Pakistani establishment decided to use the Jammu and Kashmir Liberation Front as a vehicle to create an armed struggle in the Kashmir Valley after the Jamaat-e-Islami chiefs, Salahuddin and Turabi, showed reluctance and refused to get involved in the armed struggle.[13]

Pakistan then moved to support the JKLF with arms, training, and support; but it did not take long for them to conclude that the prospect of an independent Kashmir was not in their interests. As a result, Pakistan hastily created the Hizbul-Mujahideen, a militant group consisting of Kashmiris who favour Kashmir's accession to Pakistan. Both the Jammu and Kashmir Liberation Front, and Hizbul-Mujahideen, are comprised of indigenous Kashmiris, but they have different ideological grounds with different agendas. The JKLF was, and still is, an independent organization though some of its leaders and activists have been lured by both India and Pakistan. Hizbul-Mujahideen, on the other hand, is effectively a Pakistani creation. Another difference, is that although all of the members of the JKLF are Kashmiri Muslims, it is a secular organization, whereas Hizbul-Mujahideen has close ties with Jamaat-e-Islami who are a conservative Sunni Muslim political organization believed to preach Islam with an extremist ideology.[14]

Under Yasin Malik's leadership, the JKLF permanently denounced violence in 1994 and then took the Gandhian approach of a peaceful struggle for justice. Today, the JKLF has become less prominent. Although Yasin Malik still receives support in the Kashmir Valley, in recent years he has regularly faced arrest and detention by Indian security forces in an effort by them to limit his influence. In 2022 he was sentenced to life imprisonment. The members of the Jammu and Kashmir Liberation Front are now scattered throughout the world and are no longer as united as they once were. However, members still occasionally come together in different cities to discuss ways and means to find a peaceful resolution to the conflict.

Mirwaiz Farooq's Assassination

In the 1990s, the militant organization, Hizbul-Mujahideen, was the first Pakistani creation to deliberately contribute to the destabilization of the Kashmir Valley. While there was initially widespread support in the Valley for the militarization of the Jammu and Kashmir Liberation Front, the people of Kashmir quickly realized that arms did more damage than good. In May 1990, the father of today's charismatic separatist political leader Mirwaiz Umar Farooq, Mirwaiz Farooq (also a cleric and political leader), was brutally killed – allegedly executed by Hizbul-Mujahideen members.[15] This killing shocked the Valley, "I heard the shots that killed him,"[16] said Farooq Siddiqi, as he continued narrating the story. He emphasized that only a few people know the exact events that revolved around Mirwaiz's assassination.

On 18 May 1990, Farooq Siddiqi was sitting with Sheikh Ghulam Ahmed in Mirza Kamal's house in Nagin. A perturbed Mirwaiz Farooq came running to the house from his own home in his nightgown. He had made his way there via a back street because he was alarmed at the arrival of three boys who had told his guard that they wanted to see him. He didn't know who they were and anxiously relayed, "the guard said they look like militants so I escaped from the back door."[17] Something was obviously wrong; nobody had any idea who the boys could be. The JKLF had no intention of harming anyone. Siddiqi and his friends advised Mirwaiz to ask the men to come back the next Monday, 21 May at 11.00 a.m. "Until then it would give us some time to find out who they were."[18] Mirwaiz asked Farooq Siddiqi and the others if they would be willing to be present at the Monday meeting too; he obviously intuited that something was wrong.

On Monday morning, Farooq Siddiqi and his friends came together. They left home around 9.30 a.m. and headed to pick up the architect Syed Ali Geelani. When they reached his house, he was still getting ready, so by 10.30 a.m. they were still there. Geelani's house was just a three minutes' walk from Mirwaiz' home. Farooq recalled, "All of a sudden we heard gunshots from a not too far distance."[19] They hastily ran outside the house and heard Qasim Billa, a staunch supporter of Mirwaiz Farooq, shouting from a distance of about 200 meters that Mirwaiz had been shot. Apparently, the boys had arrived at Mirwaiz's house at the earlier time of 10.30 a.m. Initially, the visiting boys had said that they were members of the Jammu and Kashmir Liberation Front, but then it is believed that members of the Hizbul-Mujahideen were the ones who shot him.

Mirwaiz Farooq had been a leader of the Awami Action Committee, a well-established organization with a lot of potential. He was known for his moderate values, and it was widely believed that if Mirwaiz had become a prominent political figure, then the influence of Jamaat-e-Islami (sponsored by Pakistan) would have been more limited and it would not have grown into the fundamentalist organization that it later became. The assassination of Mirwaiz has been widely attributed to Hizbul-Mujahideen. Farooq notes that, "these were the days of the beginning of Hizbul-Mujahideen. It has been asserted that a militant who goes by the name Bangaroo killed Mirwaiz Farooq. But his death brought a turning point, and although there was a lot of support among ordinary people for the armed struggle in the Kashmir Valley in its early days, this changed after Mirwaiz's death. Yet, despite this diminishing support, tension between the militants persisted and unfortunately, the armed uprising had only just begun.[20]

Militancy in Kashmir

Three militant groups with origins in Kashmir have been added to the United States' terrorist list. The first two are Jaish-e-Mohammad and Lashkar-e-Taiba which were added shortly after the tragic attacks in the US on 11 September 2001. The third one is Hizbul-Mujahideen. These militant groups were all created by Pakistan's powerful intelligence agency, "Inter-Services Intelligence." After the end of the Afghan-Soviet War, Inter-Services Intelligence created dozens of militant groups which have since been active throughout Pakistan and the wider region. Jaish-e-Mohammad, Lashkar-e-Taiba and Hizbul-Mujahideen are all predominantly aimed at India. However, Jaish-e-Mohammad and Lashkar-e-Taiba should be distinguished from Hizbul-Mujahideen.

The groups effectively share different ideologies and objectives, and their members have different backgrounds. Members of Hizbul-Mujahideen are indigenous Kashmiris whereas Jaish-e-Mohammad and Lashkar-e-Taiba consist mainly of Pakistanis with traumatized backgrounds having either witnessed the brutal slaughtering of people in the Punjab during the partition of 1947, or who were trained to fight as *mujahedeen* in Afghanistan. Jaish-e-Mohammad and Lashkar-e-Taiba are known for their brutal conduct and "non-traditional warfare" otherwise known as terrorism. They were founded in 1989 and joined the Kashmir uprising in 1990. Hizbul-Mujahideen is one of the largest and oldest militant groups operating in Kashmir, and its members consist mainly of disenchanted Kashmiris, whose ideology is based on merging Kashmir with Pakistan.[21]

Although Pakistan, under Pervez Musharraf, withdrew its alleged support for such organizations after the September 11 attacks in the United States, India and the United States argue that Pakistan still continues to have influence in the activities of Hizbul-Mujahideen. This mistrust is a contributing factor to the antagonistic relations between India and Pakistan and in the destabilization of the wider region. In 2017, the United States added Hizbul-Mujahideen to its terrorist organizations list and declared its leader, Mohammad Yusuf Shah, also known as Syed Salahuddin, a global terrorist. Hizbul-Mujahideen has claimed responsibility for several relatively recent attacks, including the explosion in Jammu and Kashmir in April 2014 that injured seventeen people.[22] Hizbul-Mujahideen was also held accountable for the Shopian attack in 2018, that killed four policemen, and the killing of a young woman, Ishrat Muneer, in February 2019. Indian officials said the listing of Hizbul-Mujahideen was a "logical step" after the designation of Salahuddin as a global terrorist – and the issue is of key importance to India as a further step in validating its claim of Pakistan's cross-border terrorism in Kashmir.[23] In December 2021, Indian security forces killed one of its most wanted commanders.[24]

Pakistan's foreign office was disappointed by the US terrorist designation of Hizbul-Mujahideen, and argued that the focus should be brought back instead to Kashmir – and to the fact that Kashmir is the most important issue in India-Pakistan relations. Pakistan reiterated that it should be resolved through dialogue.[25] And Pakistan is right that Hizbul-Mujahideen's objectives relate to Kashmir, and that they do not appear to have any strategies to expand their network beyond the wider Kashmir region. Like the Pakistani leadership, the people of Kashmir, although not generally supportive of this armed militant group, have condemned the fact that Hizbul-Mujahideen was added to an international terrorist list – believing that it was a misrepresentation of what is a locally-focused group. There is no doubt however, that Hizbul-Mujahideen has been responsible for a number of assassinations, and this is one of the differences between its ideology and that of the JKLF. According to Farooq Siddiqi:

We, the Jammu and Kashmir Liberation Front, did not indiscriminately kill civilians; we did not rape women, neither did we target Pandits, nor did we pick up arms in the name of religion. We are secular. Please do not call us Muslim fundamentalists or terrorists. Why would we target the Hindus in the Valley with whom we had peacefully coexisted for generations? We cannot be compared to Lashkar-e-Taiba or Jaish-e-Mohammad, who were inspired by the Afghan *mujahedeen* and were trained to kill. All we wanted was to liberate Kashmir from India's oppression. Today, the world has started to look at Kashmir as a religious conflict infested with terrorism and extremist ideology, disregarding the true nature of the dispute. The vast majority of the Muslims in Kashmir simply never wanted to be part of India, but we are unable to get out of the stalemate of oppression and guns.[26]

Although the JKLF started the armed uprising, it gradually lost its prominence with the passage of time. Over the years, its leadership has either been killed or imprisoned. This gradual decline is another marker of its difference to the other military groups and those organizations who were purportedly linked to Pakistan. With the alleged help from Pakistan, these groups were better trained, funded and equipped. Hizbul-Mujahideen was the first and largest group that was brought into Kashmir, but dozens of smaller groups have also infiltrated the region. However, Pakistan was not the only nation to form such groups; as part of its counter-insurgency programme, India also created militant groups to quell the revolt. In other words, a proxy war began to develop between the two nations in Kashmir, over Kashmir.

The Ikhwan-ul-Muslimeen that became active in 1994 is believed to be the largest counter-insurgency or paramilitary group that India created. Militant groups consisted of surrendered Kashmiri militants as well as some members who were coerced into joining merely to end their torture in captivity. Al-Faran is another militant group believed to have been created by India. In 1995, this group became involved in the kidnapping of six foreigners including two British tourists, two Americans, a German and a Norwegian. The Indian authorities have vehemently denied any support for, or involvement in, any these groups.[27]

The Israeli Hostage in Kashmir

In 1991, the JKLF was involved in the kidnap of a Jewish hostage. In conversation with Farooq Siddiqi, he said: "In June 1991, the Jammu and Kashmir Liberation Front had captured a young Israeli man who was enjoying his holidays on one of the famous houseboats on Dal Lake. The Jammu and Kashmir Liberation Front treated him as an honourable guest, and we had no intention of harming him even though other militant groups insisted we should kill him. They thought he was a Mossad agent."[28] Indian and Israeli officials had said that at least forty Israelis were in Kashmir as part of a vacation group, but insisted there was nothing unusual about this.[29] Farooq continued, "In fact, he was really young and kind and he even supported our plea for independence."[30]

The *New York Times* reported that sometime after midnight on the early morning of 27 June 1991, Kashmiri militants boarded a houseboat on Dal Lake capturing seven Israelis and one Dutch woman:

> The Dutch woman and an Israeli woman were released but the other six men were told they would be killed because they were Jewish. As their hands were tied behind their backs, one managed to untie himself. He helped release the others, attacked one militant, and captured his rifle. Gunfire broke out killing one Israeli and injuring three, while one managed to escape and sought help from local villagers who then attacked him.[31]

His name was Yair Itzhaki. The Jammu and Kashmir Liberation Front only released him after talks with the United Nations military mission in Srinagar, but his safe delivery to the international protection of the United Nations downtown office was no mean feat for the JKLF. "You need to know the real story behind the hostage situation," said Farooq. "Actually, we wanted to release Itzhaki right after his capture but there were some threats involved so we wanted to find the best way out. We were afraid that the Indian government would have killed him and blamed us in order to blemish our reputation in our struggle for independence."[32]

After Itzhaki's capture, two journalists – Shiraz Sadhavi and G.N. Khayal of the *Voice of America* – came to Dr. Merajudin, Altaf, Javed Mir, and Farooq for an interview in their hideouts at Nagin. The Kashmiris told the journalists that they had no intention of keeping or harming him and that all they wanted was his secure release. One of the journalists, Khayal, suggested getting in touch with the United Nations in Srinagar but Farooq relays that they did not have a contact number for that office (it being the time before mobile phones). So instead, Khayal gave Farooq the number of the United Nations Military Observers Group for India and Pakistan (UNMOGIP), and Farooq called them from the neighbouring house which is next to Mirwaiz' house. The house belonged to the sister of Aazam Inqilabis, a veteran militant leader of Operation Balakot.[33] He called and said that he wanted to secure Itzhaki's release: "The military observer on the other side of the phone, I guess he was European, however, told me they did not have the authority to accept the hostage but he continued saying that he would get in touch with the United Nations Headquarters to discuss the situation, and he needed one hour."[34]

After one hour, Farooq called him again and the officer said that he could not receive the hostage unless the United Nations Office in Srinagar would "leave the gate open." This would be the best way to guarantee Itzhaki's security. It was decided that the most secure way to get Itzhaki to the United Nations office would be for him to be escorted by the two journalists in a cab – and they would sit either side of him to reduce the chance of him getting shot. Once they had entered the United Nations office, Khayal would call Farooq to let him know. The plan worked and when, after anxiously waiting beside the phone, Farooq heard the good news he immediately called a press conference with Javed Mir in Nagin. When the journalists asked for the whereabouts of the hostage, the JKLF simply replied that Itzhaki was already safely on United Nations premises. The Indian media, the international media and everyone else attending was astonished by this news. Farooq emphasised:

> We had no intention to kill him. Why would we? Itzhaki was smart and understood the motives of our armed uprising. He said he was, like us, in favour of independence. On his way out to the UN office, he even wore our Jammu and Kashmir Liberation Front T-shirt of "Free Kashmir". Go and check out the articles in the Indian and international media that were published at that time, and you can read that even the Israeli government was impressed with our way of handling the hostage situation.[35]

Farooq's view of this event is supported by various news articles; it appears that Itzhaki did indeed have positive feelings towards his captors. In one article, Itzhaki says:

> I felt quite at home with the JKLF people, with whom I could offer prayers in Jewish style in the same room as they offered prayers in the Muslim way, and Itzhaki warmly embraced his guards before leaving the Jammu and Kashmir Liberation Front hideouts, one of a dozen

places where he had been held during his week in captivity. "They have treated me as friends," he said.[36]

The Armed Struggle Continues: 1990-1995

The years of military upheaval lasted from 1990 to 1995. The Valley was on fire, as India's security forces stepped up the pressure. On a daily basis, residential areas would be cordoned off, houses would be searched, women would be checked for possession of weapons and explosives, and Kashmiri men would be taken away to interrogation centres – some never to return home. Back in those days (and still today) anyone killed was simply labelled a (Pakistani) terrorist and custodial killings were the order of the day during the peak of the armed rebellion in the early 1990s. It is believed that hundreds, perhaps thousands, perished in the interrogation centres (locally known as torture chambers) that were run by the armed forces, though there is no official figure available.[37]

By around 1994-1995 the conflict started to wane. India had, to some extent, succeeded in suppressing the armed militancy by using brutal force. Yasin Malik had been released from jail, but Farooq Papa was, once again, incarcerated. During this time, Farooq's father-in-law died in a car accident. On humanitarian grounds, the Indian security forces released him from prison for a period of six days only, following which he was to report back. "I still have that prison note in which was written I had to report back to jail,"[38] Farooq said. Of course, he did not return. After some weeks, one of his fellow inmates, Idrees, an area commander of the JKLF, was released and came looking for Farooq. When Farooq asked why he had been released from jail, he simply answered, "The Indians released me to assassinate you."[39] Farooq was left with no choice but to flee Srinagar, which he succeeded in doing with the help of his former Saudi boss, Mohammad Al Ribh. Al Ribh had been closely following the news about the increasingly dire security situation in Kashmir, and travelled all the way from Riyadh to get Farooq out of the country; he helped to arrange an Indian passport for him and travelled with him to refuge in Saudi Arabia.

Farooq's wife Suraiya and their two young children were left behind without any travel documents in hand, but they managed to leave Kashmir some months later. I repeatedly asked Farooq for an interview with Suraiya, but like many other Kashmiri women who I asked, she graciously declined. Kashmiri women do speak of the conflict in private discussion, but generally prefer to stay in the background. But his does not mean that they have no voice; they have a strong voice, especially behind the scenes. When

I talked to human rights defender Khurram Parvez in Manila, he said that Suraiya was one of the many resilient Kashmiri women who did not shy away from the conflict. When all the leaders of the JKLF were imprisoned in Kashmir, she took control of the organization while looking after two small children. "She is very brave,"[40] Khurram said. Suraiya and many more Kashmiri women, deserve far more praise than this short paragraph. These women were, and still are, the backbone of Kashmiri society, and have played a central and active role in Kashmir's *azaadi* struggle.

1995: Brutal Modus Operandi

By 1995, the *azaadi* movement had lost its momentum. The JKLF's control had steadily faded as its leaders had either been imprisoned, killed, or had fled the country. The conflict gradually began to transform into far a more brutal modus operandi which changed the essence of the conflict. The armed uprising that had started out as a pro-independence movement against Indian rule, had now become a fully-fledged proxy-war between Pakistan and India. This change occurred around the same time that the Taliban in Afghanistan started taking shape.

Professor Sumantra Bose has outlined a clear analysis of the changing situation in the Kashmir Valley. He points out that "the insurgency did not die out but changed in two ways."[41] Firstly, the insurgency and the guerrillas moved out of the Kashmir Valley and urban areas into the remote areas of forests and mountainous terrain where they found cover, and into tracts of the Jammu region which is multi-religious. By the late 1990s, the topographically rugged areas of the Jammu region, inhabited predominantly by mixed Muslim-Hindu populations, emerged as the new strongholds of the insurgency. Secondly, the origin of the fighters changed; during the first five years of the conflict, most of the fighters were Kashmiri, but then the groups were infiltrated by Islamic extremists from Pakistan who entered the Indian part of Kashmir across the Line of Control.[42] At this time also, the two militant groups, Lashkar-e-Taiba and Jaish-e-Mohammad, that were later added to the US designated terrorist list along with the Hizbul-Mujahideen, were just beginning their new approach of unconventional warfare.

When I asked a retired Indian police officer from Kashmir about Lashkar-e-Taiba, he replied with a short and powerful message, saying, "they were very well-trained."[43] This new dimension complicated the indigenous armed uprising against Indian rule. These *jihadis* introduced "suicidal warfare" to the conflict and targeted military camps, police stations, and government offices, as well as airports, railway stations and Hindu civilians.[44] And they did not limit their targets to Kashmir only – both Jaish-e-Mohammad and Lashkar-e-Taiba have been held accountable for a number of attacks outside the Valley.

The conflict ultimately succeeded in fragmenting an entire society. Apart from the armed militants that were killed, thousands of innocent civilians also lost their lives – many were tortured and others disappeared. Innocent Hindus were targeted by hardcore Islamic extremist forces; they lost their homes, were beaten, raped, children were orphaned and families ended up in refugee camps. The Kashmir Valley, once a Paradise on Earth, had been covered in blood.

Developments in the Kashmir Valley in the Later 2010s

In the years after my meeting with Farooq in China in 2015, we kept in regular contact over the phone. We spoke about today's radicalization of the Kashmiri youth, and the resultant "terrorist" threat. In one of our conversations, we continued our debate about the freedom fighters, guerrillas, militants and terrorists. Pakistan has always claimed that the impulse to pick up arms originated with the indigenous Kashmiri "freedom fighters" in order to liberate Kashmir from Indian oppression. India, on the other hand, has claimed that "freedom fighters", like Burhan Wani who was killed in 2016, are in fact are Pakistani-sponsored terrorists whose main aim is to destabilize the Kashmir Valley.

There is no denying that in the last decade there has been increasing home-grown frustration in Kashmir and that a new generation of Kashmiris have been picking up arms, participating in widespread demonstrations, and engaging in disruptive activities such as pelting the Indian security forces with stones. It is also a well-known fact that Pakistan has supported and trained Kashmiris for years, though this has not always been acknowledged. Today, Pakistan officially supports Kashmir's right to self-determination as outlined in the United Nations Security Council Resolutions on Kashmir. They vehemently deny that any cross-border infiltration, or any support for homegrown militancy in Indian Kashmir, has come across the border from Pakistan. India, however, maintains that Pakistani infiltration as well as the training of Kashmiris in Pakistan, is still occurring, albeit less than in the 1990s.

However, the situation escalated after 5 August 2019 when Articles 370 and 35A of the Indian Constitution were abrogated. India claims that since then, the number of attempted cross-border infiltrations has increased, and the Indian government has once again reiterated that it has adopted a policy of zero tolerance towards terrorism in Kashmir.[45]

As matters stand at the time of writing, scholars agree that it is difficult to evaluate the exact role of Pakistan in the militarisation of young Kashmiris, and the role of the Inter-Services Intelligence in particular. However, a number of terrorist attacks were traced back to Pakistan – of which the ones in Pathankot (Punjab) and Uri (Kashmir Valley) in 2016 were supposed to be investigated by both Pakistan and India, but this did not happen. The unfortunate result of these attacks was that the plan for talks (made in 2015) between Indian Prime Minister Modi and the then Pakistani Prime Minister Nawaz Sharif, were quashed.[46]

Another concerning development in recent years is the hoisting of Islamic State flags in the Valley – an issue around which scholars have identified two points to note. Firstly, the radicalization of the youth in Kashmir remains relatively limited, and the black flag is a symbol of a type of radicalization that criticizes the more established separatists – be they from the Hurriyat or from Hizbul-Mujahideen. The flags also constitute a criticism of Pakistan for its lack of political resolution in Kashmir. Secondly, intellectuals recognize that despite the (at the moment still) limited radicalization, the flags do nevertheless signal an emergence of militant movements who are launching attacks not only at Indian forces but also at soft targets. This development is not limited to Kashmir only and is a trend that has taken place in predominantly Muslim countries.[47] In 2017, the establishment of Ansar Ghazwat-ul-Hind in Kashmir (a breakaway faction which split from the Hizbul-Mujahideen), was announced on an Al-Qaeda radio channel called the Global Islamic Media Front.[48] Their aim is Sharia law in Jammu and Kashmir and *jihad* against India, and they have been invited to join the Islamic State. Another group, IS-Khorasan, who are also active in Afghanistan and Pakistan, have also claimed responsibility for attacks in Kashmir. But these developments, although concerning, have remained relatively obscure and do not appear to be a major challenge at present.

Overall, Kashmiris do not support these groups, nor do Kashmiri separatist leaders have sympathy for any kind of radicalization in Kashmir.[49] It appears, however, that the longer the absence of any sustained dialogue between New Delhi and Islamabad continues, the more likely it is that extremist groups will be able exploit the situation. Whether it be Al-Qaeda, Islamic State, or any other extremist group, they are likely to step into the vacuum left by the lack of dialogue and to exploit the frustration of some Kashmiris that the use of arms seems, yet again, like the only effective solution left.

CHAPTER 3

PAKISTAN AND KASHMIR

The Strategic Importance of Gilgit-Baltistan

Gilgit-Baltistan lies close to Central Asia and borders China, Afghanistan, India and Pakistan. It was referred to by the British as the "Northern Frontier."[1] In 1935 the British leased one part of this state – the Gilgit Agency – from the Maharaja for a period of what was to be sixty years, until they returned it to the Princely State during the partition in 1947.[2] The state of Baltistan, on the other hand, used to be part of the greater Ladakh region, sharing close cultural ties with Tibet.[3] Baltistan was "liberated" by mostly former Balti servicemen during the first Indo-Pakistan War on 1 November 1947. The two regions are very different from each other and the people of Gilgit share close allegiance with China's Xinjiang province. This was seen in 1891 when the ruler of the Hunza region in Gilgit, Mir Safdar Ali Khan, fled (from the British) to China.

Perhaps because of the cultural difference between the whole Gilgit-Baltistan region, and the Kashmir valley, the former has evaded attention on the international stage in stories on the Kashmir dispute. But Pakistan in general considers Gilgit-Baltistan an integral part of the Pakistani nation. Besides the rich water resources coming from five of the world's highest mountain peaks that stand over eight thousand meters high, Gilgit-Baltistan is also home to three of the largest glaciers located outside the polar region.[4] So as well as the region's uniquely strategic location, Pakistan also sees these water resources as vital for its survival.[5]

In the twenty-first century, the disputed region of Gilgit-Baltistan has become even more important after China revived the ancient Silk Road and launched the China-Pakistan Economic Corridor (CPEC), which is the flagship project of Beijing's global game-changing Belt and Road Initiative. The CPEC and the Belt and Road Initiative are not merely game changers but also game challengers, which have reinforced rivalry between the major powers in the region. It has been anticipated that this gigantic infrastructure project worth over US$60 billion will boost the region's economic development and cooperation, and increase multilateral trade. There are now even plans to expand CPEC into Afghanistan. In recent decades, the Chinese have increasingly gained a stronger presence throughout the region. Overall, this project is being appreciated in Pakistan in the same way that the erstwhile Marshall Plan was appreciated in post-war Europe; it has the potential to lift the millions of people living in some of the least-developed parts of Pakistan, out of poverty, and in turn contribute to a more stable security environment. Within Gilgit-Baltistan, the people themselves are also broadly on board with the idea in the hope for increased living standards that will come with economic development.

Traditionally, the inaccessible Himalayan Mountain range served as a natural border defence – protecting the South Asian subcontinent from invasions coming from the north. However, two main roads through the region granted the erstwhile British Raj direct access into China, and played a predominant role in the shaping of today's geostrategic landscape. British historian Alastair Lamb has emphasized the strategic importance of the region during the British Raj, noting that it was the strategic policy of the British between 1846 and 1947 to control the Gilgit Agency as a key observation point into Central Asia and as a defence outpost against any hostile incursions from that direction.[6]

Two main roads were divided during the partition in 1947. In the East, the ancient Ladakh Road, which is now known as the National Highway 1 (NH1), connects Srinagar via Kargil to Leh into Hotan (in Aksai Chin), and further into Tibet. Today, this road is located in Indian Kashmir. In the West, the ancient Gilgit Road, which is today known as the Karakoram Highway (KKH), was completed in 1978 to connect China directly with the Arabian Sea.[7] In the other direction, this road has granted Pakistan direct land access into China and Central Asia over the Khunjerab mountain pass. Pakistan's access into China is seen as being of strategic importance to Pakistan against the backdrop of China's more assertive approach on the world stage. China and Pakistan share a border of six hundred kilometres and yet currently there is only one border crossing between the two nations – located in Gilgit at the Khunjerab Pass. It has been anticipated that a second border crossing – located in Baltistan on the Yarkund-Skardu Road via the Muztagh Pass – may be opened in the future.

Although Gilgit-Baltistan is under Pakistan's control, it has been claimed by India as an integral part of the disputed State of Jammu and Kashmir. As part of the events surrounding the abrogation of Articles 370 and 35A in 2019, India also redrew the maps of the disputed Jammu and

Kashmir region to include Gilgit-Baltistan as an extension of Ladakh and therefore an integral part of the Indian Union. If India were to control Gilgit-Baltistan, this would alter Sino-India-Pakistan dynamics considerably; it would grant India vital strategic advantages, including direct land access into Afghanistan through the Wakhan Corridor. Control over Gilgit-Baltistan would also give India direct land access through the strategically located Khunjerab Pass into West China and also into Central Asia.

China and the China-Pakistan Economic Corridor

Strategically, this region is evidently important to both India and Pakistan, but it is also of vital importance to China's current plans and Pakistan's control over Gilgit-Baltistan has given China some fundamental gains. Historically, the region was hugely important for trade. It was a region through which merchants would go back and forth, crossing valleys, river streams and mountain passes. With the completion of the Karakoram Highway in the late 1970s, China and Central Asia gained access to the warm waters of the Arabian Sea and the Indian Ocean. By opening up direct access to the vast oceans in this way, China not only secured alternative trade and energy routes, it also augmented its airborne and naval capabilities – which posed a new, potentially serious, threat to India's security.[8]

During a seminar on CPEC organized by the Kashmir Institute in Srinagar, the US-China expert Andrew Small said that CPEC had directly, and potentially dangerously, brought China into India-Pakistan cross-border relations: "China would like to use Pakistani ports for both the People's Liberation Army and for the People's Liberation Army Navy," he said.[9] From the Arabian Sea, China would enjoy a short cut into the Indian Ocean instead of needing to travel all the way across the South China Sea, and the Strait of Malacca to enter the Indian Ocean. This is evidently important to China because in recent decades it has been boosting its naval prowess in order to build leverage as an increasingly expanding world power. In 2016 China inaugurated its first naval aircraft carrier. And in December 2019, the second Chinese aircraft carrier and the first domestically-built one, "The Shandong", was inaugurated by the Chinese President Xi Jinping.[10] In June 2022, China inaugurated its third and most advanced aircraft carrier. The port of Gwadar Port, located on the Arabian Sea, is a joint Sino-Pakistan project but managed by China; over the years it has been transformed into one of China's most vital strategic hubs.

Likewise, India has focused on Iran, and has invested in Chabahar port, giving it access to Afghanistan, Central Asia and also the northern parts of the Indian Ocean. In the same way that China manages Gwadar port in Pakistan, India manages Chabahar port in Iran.[11]

Aksai Chin, Kargil and Siachen

Since the 1963 Sino-Pakistan Agreement, the strategically located Shaksgam Valley, or the Trans-Karakoram Tract, located in the wider Baltistan region, has provided China with some vital mountain passes and valleys. Recently, China has constructed roads in close proximity to this region, and proposed a highway through the valley that will ease the journey over the rough and isolated Himalayas from China into India. An important question one might ask, is why Pakistan ceded the region to China in 1963? Was it a decision made merely to finalise the definition of its borders? Or was it a strategic decision? The latter seems likely; in 1999, Pakistan and India fought a war on parts of the Line of Control (LoC) and over Kargil in Ladakh, and in 1984, 1987 and 2003 they fought wars further northeast of Coordinates NJ9842, a point where the LoC ends on the Siachen Glacier. Control of the mountainous regions of Kargil would certainly give Pakistan strategic advances – and Pakistan's control of the Kargil Heights would put India in a more vulnerable position. It would have enabled Pakistan to have a strategic overlook of the important Srinagar-Kargil-Leh Highway in Jammu and Kashmir which could be converted into a military road in the event of war between India and China. Today, the road only goes up to the border with China, but until the People's Republic of China was established in 1949, this road gave India direct land access into Hotan in Aksai Chin (in China's part of Kashmir). Today, Hotan is home to a large Chinese military base.

In 1999, it was the then Pakistani Chief of Army Staff, General Pervez Musharraf, who initiated the Kargil War. But although the Pakistani military successfully advanced into Indian territory, they were compelled to withdraw following the intervention of US President Bill Clinton through Pakistan's Prime Minister Nawaz Sharif. It seems that the international community does not want India and Pakistan to engage in any protracted conflict that could escalate into a bigger war.

On the Siachen Glacier, the simmering conflict began in 1984 when the Indian Army crept onto the glacier. The Line of Control that lies north of coordinates NJ9842, had not been demarcated.[12] The Siachen Glacier is highly inaccessible territory that stretches over sixty-five kilometres and it used to be a no-man's land. When the Indian Army silently penetrated the region in 1984, they caught the Pakistani Army by surprise. But unprepared, and not trained to fight in such an extreme climate (it has become known as

Pakistan and Kashmir

the world's highest battlefield), they had no choice but to retreat almost immediately. Since that time, both India and Pakistan have kept their presence on the Glacier for which men and materials are paying a high price. If India were to capitulate to Pakistan's efforts to reclaim the lost territory, it would mean that India would lose its control of the Srinagar-Leh Road (NH1) – this would considerably weaken India's military strength along the frontiers with China with whom it fought a short but brutal border war in the winter of 1962.

India's control over the Siachen Glacier region is an initial step in its plans for easier access into Gilgit-Baltistan. Through Siachen, they would be able to advance into Skardu, Baltistan's largest city, which, in the event of war would provide great strategic advances. Eric Margolis, author of *War at the Top of the World: The Struggle for Afghanistan, Kashmir, and Tibet* is of the view that when India occupied Siachen, Pakistan became convinced that India had embarked on a grand strategy to forge westward into Baltistan and occupy the city of Skardu. Using Skardu and its large airfield as the main operating base, it was feared that India could then drive into the Gilgit Valley and sever the Karakoram Highway – Pakistan's sole land link with its most important ally, China.[13]

Any attempt by India to gain control over Gilgit-Baltistan would put Pakistan in a vulnerable position. In 1987, Pakistan staged a riposte in the Siachen Glacier when they set up a post on the highest peak, giving the Pakistani forces a clearer vantage point. This made it very difficult for the Indian military forces to ascend the mountain without being noticed. Subsequently, under some of the harshest weather conditions, the Indian Army regained this peak later in the year. Bana Singh, the Indian officer who led the team that battled their way to the summit to achieve this victory, was given the highest military award (*Param Vir Chakra*) for his bravery. A Kashmiri man I spoke with (who wishes to remain anonymous) remembers sitting next to Singh on a flight from Jammu to New Delhi: "Bana Singh held brave Pakistani soldiers in high esteem for their undaunting fight on the Siachen Glacier," he said.[14] In 2003, a ceasefire to the Siachen Conflict came into effect, but, as noted above, both the two nuclear-armed nations maintain a military presence in the area.

Indian and Pakistani soldiers, who are sent to Siachen, receive special training prior to ascending the glacier. Over the years, it is believed that more soldiers have died from the exceptionally harsh weather conditions, and avalanches, than as a result of actual fighting; both the Indian and Pakistani military have discussed the idea of military withdrawal from the area. Unfortunately, a lasting truce has thus far been eluded.

Regional Political Dynamics

Only a few scholars have discussed the issues in Gilgit-Baltistan, and the Indian Professor K. Warikoo of Jawaharlal Nehru University, New Delhi, has said that successive Pakistani governments have effectively put this frontier region behind an "iron curtain".[15] Only a very limited number of published academic articles on the region exist. It is suspected that when talks on Kashmir finally occur, that Pakistan intends to leave the disputed region of Gilgit-Baltistan out of any discussion. Yet, as India's actions in 2019 revealed, when it re-drew the map of the region to incorporate Gilgit-Baltistan into the union territory of Ladakh (after it abrogated Articles 370 and 35A), India views the region as part of Indian territory. But it should also be remembered, that although India views Gilgit-Baltistan as part of the historical Princely State of Kashmir and Jammu, the entire region of Jammu and Kashmir, including Gilgit-Baltistan, was declared disputed territory under the United Nations Security Council Resolutions in 1948. And although Pakistan made claim to Gilgit-Baltistan, it did not consider it a territorial part of the country – which means that for many decades after the second world war, its people lived in a constitutional vacuum.[16] This changed somewhat in November 2020 when Pakistan announced its decision to grant Gilgit-Baltistan the status of full province – but this remains a provisional agreement.[17]

There are also some independence movements who favour autonomy for the region, although they are in the minority. Other groups favour the creation of *Balawaristan,* or what Christopher Snedden calls the "land of the highlanders", comprising of Gilgit, Baltistan and Ladakh located in Jammu and Kashmir, as well as Chitral and Kohistan located in Khyber Pakhtunkhwa in Pakistan.[18] Some intellectuals from Gilgit-Baltistan have claimed that the external intelligence agency of India, the Research and Analysis Wing, has been supporting this movement.

Dr. Martin Sökefeld, Professor of Social and Cultural Anthropology at Ludwig-Maximilian University of Munich, is a frequent visitor to the region. Sökefeld argues that despite the different ethnicities and varied dimensions of religious identity in the region, the people increasingly share a sense of political belonging to Gilgit-Baltistan, as opposed to the rest of Pakistan.[19] He writes:

> The discontent with Gilgit-Baltistan's political status gave rise to a number of smaller political groups which are collectively referred to as nationalists. They demand either greater autonomy of the area or even full independence from Pakistan. He also assumes that in spite of these movements, the majority of Gilgit-Baltistan's population still prefers

full integration of their area with Pakistan as the country's fifth province.[20]

In an email interview, Sökefeld further elaborated:

Still many people prefer full accession to Pakistan because this would be the fulfilment of their fathers' or grandfathers' efforts in 1947, and the "Jang-e-Azadi" that started on 1 November of that year. There is considerable Pakistani patriotism in Gilgit-Baltistan although many people are also very critical of politics towards Pakistan. I think that here we have to distinguish between affiliation with, and affects towards the "nation of Pakistan" and the "government/state of Pakistan."[21]

Conciliation Resources, a UK-based independent non-governmental organization (NGO) that is funded by various European countries, has also been working with the people of Gilgit-Baltistan, and they work around the confidence-building measures that were introduced under the former Pakistan President Pervez Musharraf. One of their reports, *Unheard Voices: Engaging Youth of Gilgit-Baltistan*, published in 2015, concluded that "young people (aged 18-35) generally wish to associate themselves with the larger political and constitutional structure of Pakistan. Almost eighty-two per cent of the youth surveyed prefer to call themselves Pakistanis and disassociate themselves from the larger Kashmiri identity."[22] One gentleman from Baltistan, when asked why the people do not associate themselves with the Kashmiris from the Valley, politely replied "the people from the Valley are different, difficult, and they have a sense of superiority."[23]

Another Balti gentleman, whose forefathers were the rulers of Kargil (in Ladakh) but whose family migrated generations ago north to Skardu (in Baltistan) stated that the majority would like to see Gilgit-Baltistan being incorporated into Pakistan, so that they could enjoy the same rights and the same status. He also argued that, alternatively, the Government of Pakistan should consider granting them the same status as their "brothers" in Azad Jammu and Kashmir – that is, as a nominally self-governing entity administered by Pakistan. In his view, this would alleviate some of the grievances against Pakistan.[24]

Despite this seeming support on the ground for more integration with Pakistan as its fifth province, widespread debates on the topic have been received with scepticism, especially from the leadership living across the Line of Control in Srinagar (on the Indian side of Jammu and Kashmir). If Pakistan were to incorporate Gilgit-Baltistan, it has been said that this would only strengthen India's resolve to maintain the status quo in the Kashmir Valley – creating further complications in moving towards a resolution for Kashmir. However, Martin Sökefeld disagrees:

> I do not think that the Gilgit-Baltistan reforms of 2009 have strengthened India's position because India for decades has regarded its part of Jammu and Kashmir, not only the Valley, as an "integral part of India." India's critique was rather that this reform was a further encroachment of Pakistan on India's rightful territory.[25]

Kashmiris in all parts acknowledge that the people in Gilgit-Baltistan have enjoyed limited political rights, limited education and inadequate development. Pakistan has made some effort in this regard in recent years; it has made an effort to build hospitals, electricity projects, and roads, and it has supported small businesses – not to mention the fact that it is hoped that the anticipated CPEC will also contribute to increased development in the area. Ershad Mahmud, a Kashmiri and an expert on the region, says that "the undefined status of Gilgit-Baltistan has always been unnerving to the Government of Pakistan. The recently concluded CPEC multiplied its [Pakistan's] hidden desire to absorb Gilgit-Baltistan in the larger national polity by making it a formal province of Pakistan."[26]

News of the huge forthcoming Chinese investment in Pakistani infrastructure brought about via CPEC, has stirred a new debate in policy-making circles. One section of the Pakistani government is of the view that Gilgit-Baltistan could be made a formal province under the disguise of legal jargon. Gilgit-Baltistan's future could be re-decided if a plebiscite were to be held in Jammu and Kashmir.[27] If the dispute in Kashmir was settled, then China would invest its resources with more confidence. But not everyone has viewed CPEC in a positive light – many have expressed reservations about the impact of CPEC on Pakistan, while others are sceptical that it will achieve the returns on investment that have been anticipated. In conversation with Martin Sökefeld, he said:

> The impact of CPEC does come with question marks. It appears that nobody knows yet what impact CPEC will have; there has been great uncertainty. Most people in Gilgit-Baltistan simply think about the Karakoram Highway, and they do not consider other aspects of CPEC. Some anticipate that the project will grant them economic benefits, others fear that the trade will actually bypass them. Moreover, many expect environmental damages from growing traffic.[28]

A Brief History

An understanding of the historical events that have shaped today's political landscape between India and Pakistan are essential in understanding the conflict in its wider context. Gilgit-Baltistan and the Kashmir Valley are ostensibly two separate entities within Kashmir that emerged from what is often referred to as the "incomplete partition" that occurred in 1947. However, despite this partition of the region, in the years leading up to when India redrew the map in 2019, it had appeared that India might accept a Kashmiri settlement without the inclusion of Gilgit-Baltistan. Over the years, some political movements in India have advocated changing the Line of Control from a de-facto border into an official international border between the two nuclear powers. Pakistan has strongly opposed this move, and a large percentage of Kashmiris also vehemently oppose the dividing Kashmir in this way.[29] The dispute over Kashmir is a conflict over ideology – and the Kashmir Valley (located in the Indian part of Kashmir) is seen by many in Kashmir as its heart and soul.

The turning point that changed the dynamic between India and Pakistan in Kashmir was the event in which the Governor of Gilgit was overthrown by the Gilgit Scouts under the leadership of the British military officer, William Alexander Brown, in 1947. This coup against the Governor of Gilgit, and ultimately against the Maharaja of Jammu and Kashmir, was the event that led to the Gilgit Agency coming under the control of Pakistan after the first Kashmir war (1947-1948). The Indian and Pakistani views of these events, perhaps not surprisingly, contradict. Some officials in Islamabad and Rawalpindi tend to argue, incorrectly, that Gilgit-Baltistan was never an actual part of the disputed region of Jammu and Kashmir historically and should therefore be dealt with as a separate entity. Since General Zia's rule from 1977-198, Pakistan has, albeit half-heartedly, started taking this stance and treating Gilgit-Baltistan as such.[30]

There is no denying that the people of Gilgit-Baltistan generally share no allegiance to the Kashmiris in the Valley, and the people in both regions share little common ground in relation to religion, ethnicity or cultural heritage. To understand some of today's dynamics, analysis of two time periods is therefore vital. The first is the period between 1819 and 1846, which ultimately resulted in the establishment of the Princely State of Jammu and Kashmir under Gulab Singh. The second important period to understand is that which revolved around the partition period of the British Raj in 1947 and the subsequent uprisings in both Gilgit and Baltistan.

As the Afghan Durrani Empire (1747-1823) was expanding south from parts of Iran, Afghanistan, Central Asia, and West China, into today's

Pakistan, Kashmir, and New Delhi (in today's India), the powerful Sikhs were also expanding their territories north into the region. During one of the Afghan-Sikh Wars and the Battle of Shopian in 1819, the Afghans lost Kashmir and the Sikhs incorporated what is known today as Jammu and Kashmir and also some parts of the Pashtun tribal regions into their empire. This territory extended all the way from the Khyber Pass along today's border between today's Pakistan and Afghanistan which connects Peshawar with Kabul, into Gilgit-Baltistan, reaching all the way into the Kashmir Valley and into Buddhist Ladakh, up to Tibet. As the British East India Company was also competing for territorial ground, this resulted in the First Anglo-Sikh War (1845-1846) which soon led to the dissolution of the Sikh Empire after the Second Anglo-Sikh War (1848-1849).

After the First War with the British Empire, the Sikhs were not in a position to pay the full war indemnity, so as compensation, they gave the Princely State of Jammu and the Princely State of Kashmir to the British, including some mountainous territories.[31] The Sikhs and the British Raj signed the Treaty of Lahore on 9 March 1846, which ceded Sikh control and formalised the British control of Jammu and Kashmir. In turn, as a token of the friendship between the British and Gulab Singh, of the Dogra dynasty, the British sold both Jammu and Kashmir to him for the equivalent of three quarter of a million pounds.[32] This was formalised with the Treaty of Amritsar on 16 March 1846.[33] As a result of the treaty, Singh, although founder of the Princely State, was directly under the command of British governance. With regard to the Gilgit region, although its incorporation into the newly-established Princely State of Jammu and Kashmir resulted in rebellion against the Hindu Maharaja from 1852 until 1860, Gilgit eventually came back under Kashmir's control.[34]

The strategic location of the Gilgit Agency remained of vital importance to the British as the Russian Empire gradually advanced to the Indian subcontinent. In 1935, the British again took Gilgit Agency on lease for a period of sixty years from the Maharaja. Then, during the partition of the British Raj, on 1 August 1947, the British returned the Agency to the Maharaja. In October 1947, the Maharaja posted Brigadier Ghansara Singh as the governor of Gilgit and, as mentioned above, a unit of the Gilgit Scouts then staged a coup; they arrested the governor representing the Maharaja in Gilgit, and set fire to the residency in order to dislodge the Dogras from power.

The liberation of Baltistan was undertaken mainly by former Balti servicemen who, on their own, captured all main mountain passes in Kargil, Dras and Leh overseeing India and the strategic Ladakh Road that leads east to China. The strong morale of Naib Subedar Mohammad Ali, Rustam, and

Ali Haider can be seen in the Padam Parri sector where it has been recalled that less than sixty fighters kept two Indian battalions engaged for another six months even after the Ceasefire Agreement from January to June 1949. The resilience of these Balti and other local fighters is unique in the annals of military war history.[35]

Until this day, these revolts that "liberated" Gilgit-Baltistan, have been surrounded by controversy. The motive of the Gilgit Scouts has been questioned – was it a spontaneous uprising against India's rule in Kashmir? Or was the coup more an act of support for its people? It has also been suggested that the coup was British by design – executed under secret orders to grant Pakistan control over this strategically important northern frontier.

Pakistan staunchly promotes the idea that the uprising of the Gilgit-Scouts was a spontaneous act to liberate Gilgit – as well as the idea that the former Balti servicemen wanted to liberate the majority Muslim Kargil region from the Hindu Maharaja's oppressive rule. India, on the other hand, has been convinced that the Gilgit-Scouts uprising was orchestrated by the British Raj in order to keep some control of the region after partition.[36] When the region was liberated from the Dogra Raj on 1 November 1947, an interim government was established; it lasted a total of sixteen days after which they reached out to Pakistan.

It was not until April 1949, however, when the Karachi Agreement came into effect, that the region, then still called the Northern Areas, formally came under Pakistan's control in the form of the Ministry of Kashmir and Northern Areas Affairs (KANA). It is said that nobody from Gilgit-Baltistan was represented when officials came together to sign the Karachi Agreement. Moreover, the Frontier Crimes Regulations (FCR) was not scrapped; the FCR was a mechanism introduced by the British to exercise control in the tribal regions and it effectively reduced the people's political and civil rights. In 1994 the Frontier Crimes Regulations was finally abolished, giving the people some fundamental rights. In 2009, moreover, the region changed the name of the Northern Areas to Gilgit-Baltistan, and a reform package was introduced in the region, granting the people increased rights but still not the legal status of "province". In 2009, the Government of Pakistan introduced the Gilgit-Baltistan Empowerment and Self-Governance Order, which allowed the people of the region to democratically elect their own chief minister.[37]

Through these reforms, the region was given a status similar to that of the other provinces of Pakistan. However, still without any representation in the parliament and senate, there is ongoing confusion among the people about whether the region is effectively a part of Pakistan as a fifth province, or whether the region remains disputed territory. Aiman Shah, Chief Editor of *Daily Ausaf*, a local newspaper from Gilgit, expresses his dissatisfaction about the undefined status of Gilgit-Baltistan. He believes that the people of the region have been made scapegoats of the Kashmir conflict which has prevented them from getting equal rights within the Pakistani state. He said "of course we feel for the people of Kashmir and the ongoing oppression that they have to endure on the Indian side. But, having said this, we also want our voices to be heard and we want our fundamental rights of equality and fair representation."[38]

The Gilgit-Baltistan Region

Although Gilgit-Baltistan has remained poor and largely underdeveloped, the "Northern Frontier" is rich in history and culture, and is home to diverse ethnic groups living in the mountainous regions where the Karakoram, Hindu Kush and the Himalayas converge. Today's Gilgit-Baltistan comprises of a number of erstwhile princely states with rulers or *mirs*. The two main regions are Gilgit and Baltistan. Hunza and Nagar are the largest princely states while Gizher, Diamer, Astore, Gilgit, Baltistan and Ghanche are the smaller ones. The *mirs* of Hunza used to enjoy grazing, trade and cultivation rights on the Chinese Sinkiang (today's Xinjiang) lands and, until today, the people closely identify themselves with the Chinese on the other side. Although traditionally home to a predominantly Shia Muslim population, Gilgit-Baltistan has been strongly influenced by traditions from the Muslims in Sinkiang (erstwhile East Turkestan), and by Tibetan Buddhism.

The Baltistan region has also been referred to as Little Tibet. The people have closely identified themselves with this cultural heritage and are proud of it. Ancient Buddhist rock carvings and stone inscriptions can be found throughout Gilgit and Baltistan and are unique to this region. It is believed that there are some fifty-thousand rock carvings and five to six thousand inscriptions of a dozen scripts dating back to the late Stone Age that are found in Gilgit-Baltistan and are among the world's largest epigraphic records.[39] Close to Gilgit, the Kargah Buddha, possibly dating back to the seventh century or earlier, is carved in the walls high up in the mountains. In Skardu, the Manthal Buddha Rock represents a ninth century meditating Buddha relief surrounded by small Bodhisattvas and two standing *Maitreyas* (future Buddhas).

Baltistan was part of Ladakh until the partition of 1947, and the cultural ties between these two regions have remained closely intertwined. Historically, Ladakh was divided into the three administrative districts of

Leh, the capital, Kargil, and Skardu, Ladakh's historical winter capital. Today, Skardu lies in Baltistan while Leh and Kargil are located in the Indian part of Kashmir. The main language spoken in Baltistan is Balti, which is similar to Ladakhi, and which is a western Tibetan archaic dialect spoken in areas which were part of the Tibetan kingdoms.[40] Ali Changezi is a Kashmiri intellectual originally from the Kargil region who reiterates the strong ties with Tibet – especially in the language. In conversation in 2017 he said, "history records that the Balti language is an offshoot of Tibetan, and Tibetan researchers on ancient civilizations are not only surprised but also fascinated to learn of the many more branches of their languages."[41] He continued:

> Until the arrival of Islam in the region, the people of Baltistan and Ladakh were closely attached to Tibet and students would go to Tibet in pursuit of education that would last some thirty years until they returned home. When Amir Kabir Syed Ali Hamdani came to the region to spread Islam between 1373-84, Islam started influencing the region and, consequently, Persian and Arabic terminology was also introduced, ultimately burying some of the socio-cultural heritage of Tibet.[42]

Gilgit-Baltistan is sparsely populated, with just around 870,000 people according to the 1998 census (the last to be held). Today, it is estimated that the region is home to some two million people in a conglomeration of numerous ethnic groups and tribes.[43] Traditionally, the Shia were the predominant religious group until their numbers started dwindling when the Sunnis from Punjab and from the tribal areas began migrating into the region (in what is believed to have been state policy). Today, just like in other parts of the Muslim world, there are some imbalances between the Sunnis and Shias in the region. For example, the Mosques in the region have been influenced by Persian architecture such as that traditionally found in Isfahan, Iran.

The policy that changed the demographics started during the tenure of former President Zia-ul-Haq (1976-1988) and resulted in sectarian violence. Although Gilgit-Baltistan remains predominantly Shia, the percentage of Shias has reduced from around eighty per cent in 1947 to about fifty-five per cent in the early 2000s.[44] Ismailis (in Hunza, Gilgit) and Nurbakhshis (in Baltistan) are in the minority. Ismailis are followers of the Aga Khan, while Nurbakhshi is a blend of Sunni and Shia religious practices. While the region has been kept relatively peaceful compared to other provinces of Pakistan, sectarian violence has increased somewhat in the past few decades. The history of the ongoing sectarian violence in

Gilgit-Baltistan dates back to the 1960s and 1970s, when the religious leaders of Sunni and Shia sects started a campaign of mutual invective. The international scenario in the form of the Iranian Revolution and the Afghanistan War contributed to further sectarian trouble in the late 1980s and 1990s.[45]

Gilgit-Baltistan, however, is not the only Kashmiri region under Pakistan's control. While Gilgit-Baltistan is predominantly Shia Muslim, the vast majority of Kashmiris in Azad Jammu and Kashmir are Sunni. It is widely believed that Pakistan divided the two regions for political purposes. Over the past decades, hardly any direct interaction has taken place between the two regions. For example, one man from Gilgit who I interviewed, named Aiman Shah, has no real interest in having any interaction with the Kashmiris from Azad Jammu and Kashmir.[46] Martin Sökefeld's research supports the fact that this sentiment is relatively widespread.[47] However, Muhammad Najib, a Kashmiri from Poonch, in Azad Jammu and Kashmir, and an expert on the region, would like to see more people-to-people contact between Gilgit-Baltistan and Azad Kashmir.[48] But in an email interview he also reiterated that "historically, culturally, and religiously, there are considerable differences between the different Kashmiri regions. While people of Gilgit-Baltistan are more closely linked to the Chinese and the Tibetan cultures, the people of Azad Jammu and Kashmir share a lot of similarities with the people from the South Asian subcontinent.[49] He added, "the only common point Gilgit-Baltistan and Azad Jammu and Kashmir share is that both regions were under the same government of Maharaja Singh before the division of the subcontinent in 1947." [50]

Azad Jammu and Kashmir

While Gilgit-Baltistan has not received attention on the international stage, Azad Jammu and Kashmir has been widely talked about on various regional and international forums. Historically, an extended part of the Kashmir Valley, and home to a population of approximately four million people, Azad Jammu and Kashmir was divided between India and Pakistan after the frontier tribal invasion in 1947. The Karachi Agreement of April 1949 granted Azad Kashmir a special status with its own constitution and government. Successive prime ministers, presidents and other government officials from Azad Kashmir have travelled to various parts of the world to advocate for Kashmiris' right to self-determination and for the implementation of the United Nations Security Council Resolutions. These officials have not hesitated in bringing the human rights abuses committed by the Indian security forces in the Kashmir Valley to international attention. Farzana Yaqoob was Minister of Social Welfare and Women's Development in Azad Jammu and Kashmir from 2011 until 2016. She is considered to be one of the most thought-provoking leaders in the region on issues of conflict, women's empowerment, and social security networks.[51] When I asked Farzana about the future of Kashmir, she replied:

> Kashmir has shown perseverance. The Kashmiri youth are now leading the cause. The new generation is as involved in their struggle for freedom as their forebearers. They desire basic rights, and free movement. Recognition of the conflict is leading to increased discussion about Kashmir. Kashmir has become more relevant and the youth of Kashmir are finding new ways to interact with the world. They are connected to the Internet and social media. The youth will decide the future of Kashmir.[52]

Farzana continued to say that she believed that the *azaadi* movement would ultimately increase in importance in the future and that it would also be increasingly recognized on international forums. She believes that this recognition will lead to discussions and workable solutions that will lead to greater peace and regional security. In the past, nothing has been achieved and the status quo has continued because the various solutions on the table have affected either the territorial integrity of India or of Pakistan.[53] She added, "I hope the international bodies will show more interest and fairness towards the people of Kashmir and uphold their basic human rights as well."[54]

The Political System in Azad Jammu and Kashmir and its link with Gilgit-Baltistan

Muhammad Najib (the expert on the region, from Poonch, in Kashmir) who I interviewed in 2017, said:

> While Azad Jammu and Kashmir exhibits a fine statehood with a President, Prime Minister, Supreme Court, State Assembly and a constitution called the Interim Act 1974, the act in practice creates plenty of hurdles which results in a poor record in Azad Jammu and Kashmir for basic human fundamental aspirations. For instance, it is mandatory for the people of Azad Jammu and Kashmir to ensure their determination to believe in the accession to Pakistan. This is vital for

taking part in general elections. The second by-product of the 1974 Act is providing leverage to the government of Pakistan by deploying lent officers [officers deployed by the federal government of Pakistan] in Azad Jammu and Kashmir. These officials from the Pakistan government control the region. The twelve allocated seats for migrants settled in Pakistan is another crucial factor engineered to control the deployment of the government in favour of the interests of the government sitting in Islamabad. Moreover, the hierarchy of the Kashmir Council and the Ministry of Kashmir Affairs foster a double-thick layer of control factors over its resources. Evidently, the most crucial factor is that both Gilgit-Baltistan and Azad Jammu and Kashmir are a legitimate part of the conflict but they are each controlled by Pakistan in a different manner. The former is being controlled by an Executive Order (a simple letter from the federal government), and the 1974 Interim Act controls the latter.[55]

Najib emphasized once again that he wanted to see more interaction between Azad Jammu and Kashmir and Gilgit-Baltistan which is for him a crucial factor in moving forward, and one that has increasingly become part of the discourse on Kashmir. He believes that bilateral ties between the two disputed regions are essential, and he not only advocates for the reopening of the traditional trading routes connecting Gilgit-Baltistan and Azad Jammu and Kashmir, but also for the establishment of a public service commission to handle the affairs of both regions. The two regions have effectively been separated from each other since 1947, and so he believes that conflict resolution institutes should be established as a vital starting point in moving toward peace and building effective dialogue. When I interviewed another local from the Azad Jammu and Kashmir Region, Ershad Mahmud, he said that there is a great yearning in Azad Jammu and Kashmir for integration with other areas of the erstwhile Jammu and Kashmir State – particularly with Gilgit-Baltistan. But he added that the reciprocity of this sentiment from the Gilgit-Baltistan side is somewhat missing,"[56] Mahmud continued:

> The popular demand in Azad Jammu and Kashmir, both in the nationalist and mainstream political circles, is of integration with Gilgit-Baltistan, and what suits most is the creation of one autonomous government comprising the two provinces. But this prospect now seems difficult in view of the international political climate after the initiation of the China-Pakistan Economic Corridor. The Government of Pakistan holds sway over public opinion in both regions which can be channelled

into a futuristic strategy on the Kashmir conflict. If the creation of one unit is not possible here, the second option is the provision of an empowered political structure in Gilgit-Baltistan and in Azad Jammu and Kashmir, with more connectivity between the two regions through the civil society and people-to-people contact.[57]

Nevertheless, different schools of thought are being represented in Azad Jammu and Kashmir and strong institutions, like the decades-old political parties and student organizations, have their presence in Azad Jammu and Kashmir. The patronage of government institutions has always been one-sided, favouring the mainstream ideology of accession to Pakistan. The culture of youth and student politics has good capacity and such institutions are quite vibrant. They actually have the capacity to set the ideological learning of the political parties but due to unstructured efforts, this capacity has seldom been translated into sound political action. The institutions of civil society have always been on the back burner as the political climate of Azad Jammu and Kashmir has less space for civil society involvement. And ideas that govern the systems of civil society activism are considered alien in Azad Jammu and Kashmir.[58]

Azad Jammu and Kashmir has been going through a political transition since its inception; many factors contribute to this transition and after seventy years of prolonged conflict, many divergent narratives have come forward in the state. Aspirations in Azad Jammu and Kashmir have always been in flux but the dominant aspiration over the years is accession to Pakistan. However, a number of people, particularly the young generation, seem quite critical towards the government of Pakistan's role in the affairs of Azad Jammu and Kashmir. Issues like lack of autonomy and legislative powers and administrative, and the financial control of Pakistan over mega infrastructural and development projects are points of contestation between the Government of Azad Jammu and Kashmir and Pakistan. The fact that political identity of the region has been in disarray for more than seventy years has given rise to an identity crisis in the youth.[59]

However, one year after my interview with Najib, in a landmark decision on 1 June 2018, the Government of Azad Jammu and Kashmir promulgated the Azad Jammu and Kashmir Interim Constitution Act, 1974. This was an immensely empowering act that has enabled Azad Jammu and Kashmir to begin taking major decisions in the area of its own economic planning and in the running of day-to-day matters.[60] While some have remained sceptical of this decision, the vast majority have celebrated the devolution of power from Islamabad to Muzaffarabad (the capital of Azad Jammu and Kashmir).[61]

But credit must also be given to the Pakistani state for developing Azad Jammu and Kashmir. Across the Line of Control on the Indian side of Kashmir, Srinagar and its surroundings were traditionally known as the most developed and cultured parts of Kashmir. Srinagar is home of the world-renowned shawl-making industry, as well as home to the art of the richly-decorated and hand-painted papier-mâché artifacts, colourful embroidery, silk carpet weaving, and many other cultural traditions and innovations. Azad Jammu and Kashmir, on the other hand, was traditionally relatively underdeveloped with limited infrastructure and industry. But this changed after 1947 when Azad Jammu and Kashmir gradually became more developed. It has now turned into a relatively prosperous region. Moreover, Kashmiris tend to be of the opinion that compared to Pakistan, there is more economic equality in Azad Jammu and Kashmir than in Pakistan. In Azad Jammu and Kashmir, there are not many huge landowners, and land passes down from one generation to the next, while in Pakistan, the bigger land owners suppress the people and expect them to vote for them blindly. Perhaps as a result, real poverty is rarely seen in Kashmir.

The Azad Jammu and Kashmir Region

Chakothi is a border town located on the heavily fortified Line of Control that divides Kashmir between India and Pakistan. Chakothi is one of the border crossings where commercial trucks cross the Friendship Bridge into Indian Kashmir to exchange goods. A military briefing recently elaborated on the ongoing hostility between the two countries where innocent civilians on both sides of the de-facto border have become victims of the cross-border shelling despite both countries having pledged to adhere to the Ceasefire Understanding that came into effect in 2003 after the Siachen War. Parts of the Line of Control are fenced-off and in some areas mines have been laid to prevent armed militants from crossing from Pakistan's Kashmir into the Valley. For India, cross-border infiltration by the militants has remained a serious concern. Unfortunately, civilians living in the area have occasionally become victims of land mines – leaving the scars of the conflict forever visible on innocent Kashmiris.

Following the armed uprisings in the 1990s, thousands of Kashmiris from Indian Kashmir crossed the border into Azad Jammu and Kashmir to avoid persecution and now live in refugee camps. Although some claim that the camps are being kept in operation as anti-Indian propaganda, the financial restraints of both the Pakistani and the Azad Jammu and Kashmir governments have prevented the displaced people from leaving the camps. Today, an estimated seven thousand Kashmiri families are scattered throughout various camps in Muzaffarabad, Bagh, Kotli, Mirpur, and Rawalakot.[62] When visiting the camps, families tell stories that have mostly been untold or forgotten in the outside world. Each family member has a story to tell about when they crossed the Line of Control into Pakistan.

As the years went by, the armed conflict gradually lost its momentum and a new generation was born. Although the new generation have never witnessed bloodshed in their lifetimes, their parents' trauma is being is passed down to them. The Pakistani government established the Kashmir Model School to give some assistance to the underprivileged children who are living in the camps. Parents often have limited ability to raise their children. In 2015, I interviewed the then school principal, Mamoona Tayyab:

> The majority of the children have been unable to have good focus in the class, and an overall strong sense of distrust prevails among them. The children do not want to share any of their pencils, notebooks, or any study material. The children keep it all to themselves. And when the children are sick, the parents often still send them to school. They believe that the teachers at school will look after their children better than they themselves are capable of taking care of them at home.[63]

It is evident that the people of Kashmir are the main victims of the conflict and, as the struggle of the Kashmiris' right to self-determination continues, a resolution has remained elusive. There does not seem an easy solution in which both Gilgit-Baltistan and Azad Jammu and Kashmir get their indigenous voices heard, and in which the region gains more self-determination and stability. An effective dialogue in which all the aggrieved parties come together seems the only way to ease the tension in this region where three nuclear powers are competing for influence and control. Lastly, the effect of the development of CPEC in the coming decades should not be underestimated; as argued above, CPEC will be either a regional game changer or a game challenger which could ultimately alter the geopolitical and geostrategic landscape of the entire region

Azaadi, Freedom and Change in Kashmir

CHAPTER 4

CHINA'S GEOSTRATEGIC CONTEXT

Introduction

Understanding Sino-India-Pakistan relations since the establishment of the People's Republic of China in 1949, is vital in gaining an in-depth understanding of Kashmir's geostrategic and geopolitical context. And when understanding India's stance on Kashmir, an understanding of US-India relations is also crucial – so a brief analysis of US-India relations will also be included in this chapter. During the last few decades China has largely remained a silent observer in its relations with Kashmir. This changed in August 2019 with India's abrogation of Articles 370 and 35A after which China called for a closed-door meeting to discuss Kashmir at the United Nations Security Council. This was the first time since 1965 that the Security Council held a meeting on Kashmir.[1] In December 2019, China requested another closed-door meeting at the United Nations Security Council.[2] And in January 2020, they made a third attempt. As a bordering nation, and one that controls Aksai Chin, China will need to be included in talks and negotiations once India and Pakistan move towards a renegotiation of the boundaries and a final resolution.

Little is known about the sparsely populated region of Aksai Chin, and only a few have been granted access to this part of Kashmir that lies on the Chinese side of the "Line of Actual Control" (the name of the de-facto border that lies between Ladakh and Aksai Chin). In 1951, China began the construction, through Aksai Chin, of the China National Highway 219 connecting Xinjiang with Tibet. The road was completed in 1957, and used to be the only year-round access road into the Tibetan region. Aksai Chin is very isolated from the rest of the world, and India only discovered that the road had been built (or newly tarmacked) when it saw it on China's new maps.

Historical grievances between India and China about the demarcation of the boundaries date back to the British Raj. The Johnson Line, created under the British-led survey team between 1847 and 1865, places Aksai Chin in India. In the 1890s, after China began to show an interest in the area, the Macartney-MacDonald Line was proposed (by Britain to China), and it placed most of the Aksai Chin region in China. However, no agreements were finalised at the time, and so now, unsurprisingly, India continues to place Aksai Chin within its boundaries, while China firmly asserts that Aksai Chin will remain under its control.

Today, the geo-economic implications of the Belt and Road Initiative and CPEC in particular – where regional peace is recognized as the main ingredient to success – brings Aksai Chin, and Jammu and Kashmir as a whole, into greater international focus. China's increasing military presence on its side of the Line of Actual Control proves the strategic importance of the region to China.[3] In June 2020, the Sino-India border dispute in the Kashmir region reached an unprecedented momentum between the two nuclear powers in the Galwan Valley. At the time, *The New York Times* reported that it was the "deadliest clash between the two nuclear-armed nations in decades," and said that it was coming at "a fraught moment ... with the nationalist leaders of both nations eager to flex their muscles."[4] The fight left twenty Indian soldiers dead, and Indian officials say that dozens were captured. At the beginning of 2021, *The New York Times* again reported that Indian and Chinese troops "clashed along their disputed Himalayan border," and continued, "as many as 100,000 troops from the Indian and Chinese armies are now facing off across inhospitable mountain passes in subzero temperatures in the Ladakh region alone."[5] It is said that four Chinese soldiers died in this border clash.

In January 2022, a new Chinese land border law came into effect which increased Chinese military presence and surveillance along the border in order to curtail illegal crossings.[6] India opposed the move, and analysts in New Delhi see it as a sign of the hardening stance of China on the boundary dispute.[7] India and China have experienced relatively peaceful relations in the past decades, but the border clash created the "most difficult phase" for three to four decades.[8] Pakistan and China on the other hand have enjoyed what has become widely known as an "all weather friendship" since 1963. It may be helpful at this point to look at China's basic foreign policies, from the 1950s onward, to provide further insight into its stance on Kashmir.

Sino-India Relations

After the founding of the People's Republic of China, India was one of the first countries to recognize the new Republic on 1 January 1950. During the outbreak of the war on the Korean Peninsula (1950-1953), India mediated with the United States on China's behalf. Premier Zhou Enlai and Indian Prime Minister Jawaharlal Nehru enjoyed a good diplomatic relationship. Zhou's profuse thanks for India's attitude on the Korean War contributed to a feeling that the two countries might create a solid friendship which would be to the greatest benefit for Asian solidarity.[9] In the 1954 Sino-Indian Agreement, the two countries laid out a framework for China's basic foreign policy principles known as the "five principles of peaceful coexistence." These were agreed as follows:

- Mutual respect for sovereignty and territorial integrity
- Non-aggression
- Non-interference in internal affairs
- Friendship and equality
- Peaceful coexistence

These basic foundations of Chinese foreign policy were presented at the first Asia-Africa Conference in Bandung, Indonesia in 1955. In the years that followed, however, the dynamics between China and India altered, and although they enjoy fairly stable relations today, the following developments have affected the Sino-India entente:

- Grievances over Tibet and over the 1962 Sino-India border war
- Unresolved border disputes over Arunachal Pradesh and Aksai Chin
- China's geostrategic assets believed to encircle India
- Sino-India economic power competition
- US strategies to contain China
- The "all weather friendship" of China and Pakistan

In some areas, the boundaries between India and China had been arbitrarily drawn by the British, and there were British encroachments when the British-Indian troops twice invaded Tibet in the late nineteenth and early twentieth centuries. In the twentieth century, the Indian government appeared to have inherited from its erstwhile colonial masters certain attitudes of possessiveness toward Tibet which the Chinese greatly resented.[10] In 1954, Nehru and Zhou avoided discussing the boundary disputes which Zhou stated were problems "left over from colonialism."[11] However, after the founding of the People's Republic of China in 1949, China gradually began exerting control over the Tibetan plateau. In 1959, as political and social unrest increased, the young Dalai Lama saw no choice but to flee his Tibetan homeland. He settled in Dharamsala, India, where he established the Tibetan government in exile. India's hosting of the Dalai Lama has been a bone of contention between India and China ever since. In 1962, China fought a short but brutal border war with India over the disputed regions of Arunachal Pradesh and Aksai Chin. India considered this war a betrayal of the friendship that had been built up between the Jawaharlal Nehru and Zhou Enlai.

The 1962 war left a permanent scar on the relationship between the two nations which is still visible to this day. As a result, India came to view China as its foremost regional rival.[12] Until 1978, China had engaged in revolutionary diplomacy towards India and the rest of the world. Then, in 1976, it became evident that, after a quarter of a century, China's revolutionary diplomacy was about to go into reverse when the leaders of the revolution began dying off. First, Kang Sheng, head of the public security bureau and the mastermind behind the Cultural Revolution, died on 16 December 1975. Then, on 8 January 1976, Premier Zhou Enlai died of cancer, and on 9 September 1976, Chairman Mao Zedong passed away.[13] The vacuum left by these losses opened the door for reform, and in 1978, when China started opening up, relations between the two nations began to improve a little.

From the early 1980s, China began normalizing relations with all other countries but particularly emphasized the building of friendly relations with its nearest neighbours. In 1993, both India and China signed an agreement to respect each other's boundaries and ensure peace along the Line of Actual Control. Although China successfully resolved almost all of its other land border disputes, the border conflicts over Bhutan, and those over the territories of Arunachal Pradesh and Aksai Chin are still disputed in the early 2020s.

During China's revolutionary years, Mao had already embarked on an impossible mission to resolve its border disputes with the erstwhile Soviet Union, but this was to no avail. After the collapse of the Soviet Union in 1991, China, together with Kazakhstan, Kyrgyzstan, Tajikistan and Russia – collectively known as the *Shanghai Five* – sat down together and peacefully resolved the long outstanding boundary issues. China has been relatively willing to give up territory in order to stabilize relations with its neighbouring countries. For example, in key bilateral relations with Southeast Asia and India, China has been willing to make compromises to create what its diplomats, adopting the Western lingo, call "win-win" outcomes.[14] It should be noted however, that its maritime territorial disputes have been more difficult to settle.[15] Its maritime strategy has been focused on securing its energy supplies, and China is now the world's largest oil and gas importer.[16]

In China's effort to expand its commercial interests, it has been widely hypothesized that China's geostrategic assets, also known in the West as its "string of pearls" strategy, has been created with the aim of circling India. Gwadar port, on the Arabian Sea in Pakistan, is one of those ports that undoubtedly has strategic value as well as economic. Traditionally, China's sea routes pass through the Indian Ocean and the Strait of Malacca which both India and the United States could block in the event of war, or if tensions over the South China Sea were to escalate. China has also been building ports surrounding India in Myanmar (a deep-water port), Bangladesh (a container shipping facility) and Sri Lanka (a commercial shipping centre). India has been especially alarmed by Chinese investments in Sri Lanka, which New Delhi views as part of its own backyard.[17]

China and India are both members of the five emerging economies – Brazil, Russia, India, China and South Africa, collectively known as BRICS – who are all close trading partners. It is often felt, however, that rather than cooperating, China and India are competing. China expert and author of *China and India Prospects for Peace*, Jonathan Holslag, writes, "China and India's engagement in international commerce has contributed to competition, rather than cooperation, in neighbouring regions, and such engagement [in international commerce] cannot ameliorate the strategic sources of their enduring conflict."[18] They have also competed over water resources. Moreover, China is one of the (only) five nations worldwide who has a permanent seat on the United Nations Security Council – a vetoing position that India has been actively lobbying for.

So evidently, despite a relatively stable relationship between the two Asian giants in the past decades, there are hurdles that need to be overcome, and these hurdles have ongoing and direct impacts on the everyday lives of Kashmiris. For example, from 2008-2012, visa authorities in the Chinese Embassy in New Delhi would issue visas to Kashmiris on a separate sheet stating that Kashmir is disputed territory and hence not part of the Indian Union.[19] In 2009, China invited Kashmir's pro-independence leader Mirwaiz Farooq for a visit in order to discover his perspective on Kashmir and on Muslim issues in the area.[20] Although India has been distrustful of China's regional intentions, China has been far more concerned, from a security perspective, with the stability of the Korean Peninsula, Taiwan, and the disputed islands over the East and South China Sea.

US-India Relations

The US relationship with India is an importance factor in the relationship between China and India. The US and India are clearly interconnected; the United States has been active in containing the "China threat" as a growing global power and India has been an important asset in achieving that goal. If the China-India connection were to become closer, this could diminish some of the US containment strategies against China. But as things stand, the strategizing between the US and India has meant that the US has turned a blind eye to violence and human rights abuses within India, yet condemned China for similar actions.

In particular, the United States has closed its eyes to India's oppression and military occupation of the Kashmir Valley, but also to similar oppression in other parts of the country. Yet the United States has continued to condemn China for its human rights violations, oppression, and the lack of political freedom experienced by the minority Muslim population in Xinjiang and the Buddhists in Tibet. When China violates human rights against the Uighurs in Xinjiang, the international media (rightly) condemns it and accuses Beijing for its lack of political freedom and for suppressing secessionist movements. But when India brutally kills "militants" in the Kashmir valley – who are often desperate youth – the global media mostly stays quiet, or accuses those killed of belonging to one of Pakistan's alleged terrorist organizations.

In a further effort to build closer ties with India and to boost its energy sector, the United States has signed a pact allowing American companies to supply India with civilian nuclear technology. As a counter measure, China has been condemned for boosting nuclear cooperation with, and investment in, Pakistan. India's Prime Minister Narendra Modi, who was held accountable for the killing of two thousand Muslims in the State of Gujarat in 2002, was removed from the US blacklist when it became clear he would be elected Prime Minister in 2014. In 2020, during President Donald Trump's state visit to India, the two leaders finalized a US$3 billion defence deal that included the sale of the combat AH-64E helicopters – considered the world's most advanced.[21] The United States is now one of the largest foreign direct investors in India – and this growing economic relationship has been a fundamental element of the strategic partnership between the two. To fulfil its strategic intentions, India has been one of the world's largest importer of weapons; until 2019 it was the largest importer for eight consecutive years.[22] And in 2022, due to their continued concern about China's growing influence, India and the US took further steps to deepen their defence and military ties.[23] India's military modernization has the potential to generate billions of dollars' worth of business for American companies and it also helps to strengthen the nations' strategic role in the region at a time when the Indian and US militaries are conducting more and more joint exercises.[24] But unlike India, China has its own fast-growing indigenous weapons production industry. And, its naval expansion has been rapid; in fact, China's naval fleet may now have surpassed that of the US Navy.[25]

The Sino-Pakistan "All Weather Friendship"

Where the United States and India have shared concerns about China's growing worldwide influence, China and Pakistan have shared similar grievances against India. After the Sino-India border war of 1962, it did not take long for China to understand that a strategic alliance with Pakistan would be a vital asset. Over the past decades, China and Pakistan have embraced their "all weather friendship" which includes close cooperation in the fields of economy, defence, nuclear issues and security. The former Pakistani Ambassador to China, Masood Khan, described the robust friendship between the two countries as "higher than the mountains, deeper than the oceans, stronger than steel, dearer than eyesight, and sweeter than honey."[26]

China supported Pakistan in its 1965 and 1971 wars against India, and Pakistan mediated the rapprochement of China and the US when it facilitated Henry Kissinger's secret trip to China. During his visit to Pakistan, Kissinger, the then US national security advisor, promptly vanished from the public scene under the pretext of "being sick." In fact, he had boarded a Pakistan International Airlines aircraft on a mission to China to meet with Premier Zhou Enlai and re-establish diplomatic relations after decades of deadlock.

Pakistan has been the primary recipient of China's arms exports since 1991.[27] It has been said that China's dealings with Pakistan have always been conducted with one eye on India. In 2011, Beijing chose to supply Pakistan with two new civilian nuclear reactors, even though the deal appeared to violate Chinese non-proliferation commitments. It was a boon for Pakistan's energy-starved economy. It was also a way for China to counterbalance a controversial nuclear deal reached earlier between the US and India.[28] In February 2015, China opened its largest embassy in Islamabad, Pakistan. A stable and secure Pakistan is in China's interest for a variety of reasons. Firstly, following the NATO and US withdrawal from Afghanistan, securing China's borders in the region is essential for regional peace. Xinjiang has remained a serious headache for the central authorities in Beijing. It is also widely believed that some Uighur militants have received training in Pakistan's volatile tribal areas along the Afghan border. China has anticipated, however, that CPEC will contribute to stability in this volatile border region that lies between West China, Pakistan, and Afghanistan.

The Uighur Communities and China

Solving the problems of terrorism, separatism, and extremism have been top priorities in China's political agenda in recent decades. The issues of Tibetan and Uighur separatism have repeatedly reached international headlines, and in recent years, it is the Chinese treatment of the Uighurs that has especially caught the attention of the international media. The Xinjiang region borders both Afghanistan and Gilgit-Baltistan, and it is believed that over the years, thousands of Uighur religious militants have left the region to join international terrorist organizations in Afghanistan, Syria and Turkey.[29] The Turkic-speaking Uighurs are scattered around China, Kazakhstan, Tajikistan, Uzbekistan, Kyrgyzstan, and a small number also live in Afghanistan. They form the ethnic majority in China's northwest Xinjiang province, and share no common ethnic, linguistic or religious culture with the Han Chinese (who comprise an estimated ninety per cent of China's population). The vast majority of the Uighur population have never had any aspiration to be part of greater China.

There is a strong sense of alienation among the Uighurs in Xinjiang. The East Turkestan Independence Movement was founded by separatist militant Uighurs who favour the creation of an independent state.[30] This group argues for an independent state covering an area that includes parts of Turkey, Kazakhstan, Kyrgyzstan, Uzbekistan, Pakistan, Afghanistan, and the Xinjiang Uighur Autonomous Region.[31] In 2003, its founder, Hasan Mahsun, was assassinated by the Pakistani military, but it is widely believed that on the ground, the Uighur militants have close ties with Pakistani militants in the volatile tribal regions of Pakistan.

Xinjiang province is connected with Gilgit-Baltistan via the border crossing at Khunjerab Pass through which the tribal regions of Pakistan can be reached. This makes regional security issues and the need for peace and stability all the more important. Initially, the social unrest between the Uighurs and the government in Beijing was confined to the Xinjiang region only, but the violence thereafter became deadly and started spreading throughout China. Ethnic tensions reached an unprecedented culmination in July 2009 when peaceful protests escalated into violence and an estimated two hundred Han Chinese were killed. In October 2013 a suicide attack on Beijing's Tiananmen Square killed two bystanders and three inside a vehicle. The East Turkestan Independence Movement claimed responsibility for the attack and security in and around Tiananmen Square has since been tightened. In March 2014, a group of attackers dressed in black with large blades, killed twenty-nine innocent people and injured 140 at Kunming Railway Station. A few months later, in May 2014, Uighurs orchestrated a suicide attack in Xinjiang's capital Urumchi. Since 2016, however, the terrorist attacks have ceased.[32]

Despite the efforts of Beijing to include the Uighurs in mainstream society and address their social, economic and political grievances, Beijing is yet to win over their hearts and minds. In its efforts to crack down on terrorist-related incidents and to integrate the Uighurs into mainstream Han society, it has been alleged that as many as 1.5 million Uighurs and other Muslims are held in camps in China's Xinjiang region in what the Chinese authorities call "vocational training centres."[33] China believes that in the longer term, economic development will be a significant factor in creating a more stable and secure environment in the region. It also believes that the vocational training centres will provide the Uighur youth with the necessary skills, including language skills, to undertake jobs and thereby reduce their risk of their being exploited by violent extremists.

The upswing of separatist violence in the Uighur population, and the desire to improve economic development in Xinjiang, is another reason why the Belt and Road Initiative (BRI) has been such an important item on China's foreign agenda. In 2022, President Xi declared the emergence of a more (globally) assertive China; China's "new normal" of slow and sustainable economic growth (announced in 2017) puts pressure on it to open new markets for its consumer goods and excess industrial output. So, the BRI will help open up new trade routes as well as secure long-term energy supplies that will benefit the Xinjiang region and China as a whole.[34]

The Belt and Road Initiative (BRI) and the China-Pakistan Economic Corridor (CPEC)

The BRI will help to bring China, Central Asia, Russia and Europe (the Baltic) together; and it will link China with the Persian Gulf and the Mediterranean Sea through Central Asia and the Indian Ocean. The 21st Century Maritime Silk Road (also known as the MSR) is the maritime part of the BRI. It is designed to go from China's coast to Europe through the South China Sea and the Indian Ocean in one direction, and from China's coast through the South China Sea to the South Pacific in the other.[35] Chinese authorities claim that cooperation on the BRI could involve some sixty-five countries and some sixty-three per cent of the current world population – and moreover, contribute to a large share of the world's gross domestic product (GDP).[36] However, many countries in Asia and elsewhere are concerned about the geopolitical impact of the Belt and Road Initiative. Although Beijing has sought to allay these concerns in its latest plan by stressing the "win-win" potential of the initiative, its efforts will have important foreign policy implications for a number of key regional players including Japan, India, and Russia.[37]

CPEC, as the China-Pakistan part of the BRI, states that its primary objective is to contribute to the region's economic development and peaceful future. The plan, is that it will be developed over a period of fifteen years along three corridors – western, central and eastern – connecting Kashgar in China's Xinjiang Uighur Autonomous Region with Pakistan's deep-water Chinese-built Gwadar Port, four hundred kilometres from the Strait of Hormuz. Twenty per cent of the world's oil currently passes through the Strait, and much of it is destined for China.[38] During conversation, Ali Changezi, a political analyst of Balti origin, said, "CPEC in fact will not only emancipate the people of Gilgit-Baltistan, but the whole of Pakistan, including Khyber Pakhtunkhwa, Balochistan, and Punjab. Historically, access to the warm waters was a dream of the Czars. The Karakoram Highway [running from China through Gilgit-Baltistan to Pakistan] which replaces the ancient Silk Road serves both socio-economic objectives and also those of the military."[39]

But while many believe that CPEC will be of economic benefit, the importance of Pakistan's geographic position – connecting Central Asia, South Asia, China and the Middle East – means that the economic corridor will also unarguably be of strategic importance to China.[40] China will gain from closer relations with Afghanistan which is rich in natural resources, as well as from the easier access to the Arabian Sea and the Indian Ocean. In 2015, during Xi's visit to Pakistan, President Xi and Pakistan's then Prime Minister Nawaz Sharif, formed closer ties by signing a Memorandum of Understanding.

India however, strongly objected, and one month later in May 2015, during Prime Minister Narendra Modi's visit to China, Modi made his objections to CPEC clear. As mentioned, CPEC and stronger ties between China and Pakistan, would take away the strategic advantage of India and the United States of being able to block China's crucial trade routes (that currently run through the Indian Ocean and the Strait of Malacca) in the event of war. CPEC would also reduce the strategic importance of the South

China Sea – which has continued to be a flashpoint of tension between China and the United States. And oil and gas pipelines, railways, and roads from Kashgar in China to Gwadar Port would also all be of great strategic advantage to China during a conflict.

Undoubtedly, the implementation of CPEC will alter the regional power dynamics. Dr. Sajjad Ashraf, adjunct professor at the Lee Kuan Yew School of Public Policy, National University of Singapore, has stated:

> For India, a major economic engagement between two of its adversaries – China and Pakistan – is a double dilemma. The economic reality of rising China compels India to support the various sections of road connectivity, like in Central Asia, East Asia and also connecting China with Myanmar, Bangladesh and India through the Southern Silk Road. Yet, India could not overcome its deep anathema towards Pakistan by objecting to the project on the question of its passage through the disputed territory of Jammu and Kashmir, during Mr. Modi's China visit in May (2015). These Indian prejudices do not contribute to rapprochement between the two.[41]

But India's attitude toward CPEC seems to fluctuate. For example, on 12 August 2015, *The Economic Times* reported on a Chamber of Commerce meeting in Pakistan, that seemed to indicate a softening of India's attitude toward CPEC. At the meeting, India's High Commissioner to Pakistan Mr. T.C.A. Raghaven stated, "India is not worried over the US$46 billion economic corridor between Pakistan and China as an economically strong Pakistan would bring regional stability." He further added that there is a "need to remove mis-perception between Pakistan and India for the restoration of mutual trust."[42]

However, in 2019, India again raised concerns about CPEC in response to China and Pakistan's joint statement about the deteriorating conditions in the Indian part of Kashmir. India argued that the construction of CPEC was already changing the status quo of Jammu and Kashmir – a territory that is viewed by the Indian authorities as Indian territory. Raveesh Kumar, the spokesperson for India's Ministry of External Affairs (MEA) said: "India has consistently expressed concerns to both China and Pakistan on the projects in the so-called 'China Pakistan Economic Corridor,' which is in the territory of India that has been illegally occupied by Pakistan since 1947."[43]

It should be noted that due to New Delhi's protest against CPEC, India has not joined the umbrella Chinese government BRI project.[44] But regional stability is vital to India's economic growth as well as China's, and the key to regional peace is a resolution of the dispute between India and Pakistan over Jammu and Kashmir. This means that balancing diplomacy between the India-China-Pakistan triangle has become even more vital.

China and Kashmir

In general, there is limited literature available on China's historical stance on the Kashmir dispute. From 1951 onward, when China gradually took control over Aksai Chin at the same time that it began exerting control over Tibet, it effectively put the disputed region behind an iron curtain. Currently, the region appears to be under strict military control.

US Professor John W. Garver, is one of the few western scholars, who has explored China's perspective on Kashmir in his book *Protracted Contest, Sino-Indian Rivalry in the Twentieth Century*. In the 1960s, China was a staunch supporter of the United Nations Resolutions and of the plebiscite promised to the people of Kashmir. In February 1964, Zhou Enlai signed a joint communiqué during his visit to Pakistan stating that both China and Pakistan "expressed the hope that the Kashmir dispute would be resolved in accord with the wishes of the people of Kashmir as pledged to them by the people of India and Pakistan."[45] This remained China's stance from 1964 until 1979.[46]

However, in the early 1980s during Deng Xiaoping's opening up of China after its decades of isolation, the country sought to build friendly relations with neighbouring countries including India. This shift had started already in the 1970s when Beijing's view of the world became less revolutionary.[47] Yet, despite taking a more neutral stance by respecting the terms of the bilateral Simla Agreement between India and Pakistan (1972), China still also supported the widening out of the resolution in Kashmir via the 1948 United Nations Resolutions.[48] But this changed after the armed uprising broke out in the Kashmir Valley in the 1990s – from then on, China no longer pushed for the implementation of the United Nations Resolutions on Kashmir, and it also no longer supported Pakistan's policies to internationalize Kashmir. In fact, interviews that Professor John W. Garver conducted among Chinese diplomats in Islamabad in the mid 1990s, reveal that China advised against any effort to bring Kashmir before, or to convene a special session of, the United Nations. They argued that, "there was simply too little international interest in the issue."[49]

Then, in 2019 after the Indian abrogation of Articles 370 and 35A, the Chinese stance changed again; China's response was not only to call three United Nations Security Council meetings on Kashmir, but also to issue a joint press release with Pakistan stating that China would pay close attention to the current situation in Jammu and Kashmir. It reiterated that Kashmir was a dispute left over from history and that it should be properly and peacefully resolved from all angles possible – that is, via the UN Charter, relevant UN Security Council Resolutions and via bilateral agreements.[50] The statement reiterated that China was opposed to any unilateral action (that is, India deciding anything on its own) that might complicate the situation.[51]

This might seem somewhat paradoxical considering that China has harshly condemned foreign meddling in its own affairs – for example when it received international criticism of its treatment of the Uighur community or on the independence of Tibet. China has taken an uncompromising stance on any activity that it deems related to terrorism, separatism, or extremism, and it has taken great pains to avoid any loss of control over these issues at any cost. China has also taken a tough stance on Taiwan and on the dispute in the South China Sea. In 2016, China vehemently rejected an international arbitrary court ruling in The Hague over the South China Sea dispute with the Philippines. Under Xi Jinping's rule, China has increased the pressure on Taiwan to accept the 1992 "One China" consensus. China's measures have ranged from dispatching bombers, fighter jets, and warships to circle the island, conducting live-fire military exercises in waters close to Taiwan, and squeezing Taiwan's diplomatic space by cutting off its diplomatic ties. China has also limited Taiwan's access to international organizations and undertaken various economic measures.[52] The 1996 Taiwan Strait Crisis also caused military upheaval between the two nations. Shortly after the inauguration of Joe Biden as the forty-sixth president of the United States in January 2021, Chinese bomber planes flew into Taiwan's air defence identification zone – and this type of intimidation of Taiwan has continued to increase in recent years. In other words, although China advocates for dialogue and a peaceful resolution on Kashmir, it does not always address its own internal and foreign disputes in this way.

Interview with former Vice President of the Republic of Indonesia, Try Sutrisno. We enjoyed a lively and informal discussion and I was very fortunate to receive such an in-depth briefing on the Indonesia-East Timor conflict. He was accompanied by his son Cheppy (left), and Mr. Priyatno Sulisto (right). **Jakarta, Indonesia (2018)**

Last minute preparations to present my keynote speech at the National Defence University. The author (far left) and Shujaat Bukhari (far right). I felt very grateful to get the chance to meet Shujaat. His assassination in 2018 came as a huge shock to me. He was an excellent journalist and a dedicated friend to us all. **Islamabad, Pakistan (2015)**

A proud day to interview former Pakistan President Pervez Musharraf at his residence. He is someone who I personally greatly admired for his efforts in bringing peace to Kashmir while he was President. **Dubai, United Arab Emirates (2018)**

A special day to remember. Invited for afternoon tea at the residence of the late Major General Jamshed Ayaz Khan (Retd.). Photograph with my parents James Schuurmans (left) and Cuny Schuurmans (middle) who joined me on this short visit to Pakistan. On our way from the airport to Islamabad my mother turned silent while looking out of the window. All of a sudden, she exclaimed, "where are all the women in Pakistan, I don't see any." **Islamabad, Pakistan (2015)**

A visit to the "Working Boundary" where villagers have come face-to-face with the ceasefire violations and cross-border shelling between Indian and Pakistani border security forces. **Sialkot, Pakistan (2015)**

While making a brief stop in Doha on my way home from Johannesburg to Jakarta, I was non-stop invited to the homes of kind Kashmiri families from both Indian and Pakistani Kashmir who prepared lunch, traditional snacks and Kashmiri tea. **Doha, Qatar (2015)**

In memory of Mahatma Gandhi's non-violent resistance and the burning of identity passes in 1908. Mahatma Gandhi sets a unique example for anyone in the struggle for peace and justice anywhere in this world. **Johannesburg, South Africa (2015)**

Interview with Mr. Essop Pahad, former Minister in the Presidency of South Africa from 1999-2008. He actively participated in the anti-apartheid struggle, and he was also actively engaged in the transition period from apartheid to democratic reform. **Johannesburg, South Africa (2016)**

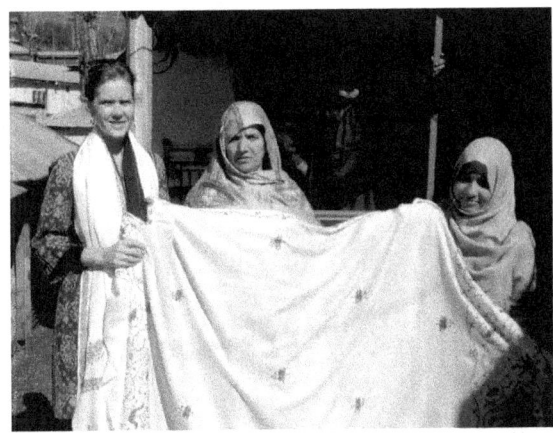

Working visit to the designated camps – usually referred to as refugee camps – where displaced Kashmiris have been living since the insurgency broke out in the 1990s. Kashmiri women demonstrated the art of the traditional shawl making. **Muzaffarabad, Azad Jammu and Kashmir, in the Pakistani part of Kashmir (2015)**

Working visit to the designated camps – refugee camps – for the displaced Kashmiris who fled from Indian Kashmir into Pakistan's Kashmir during the height of the armed insurgency in the 1990s. The scars of armed conflict are clearly visible in the eyes of the people. Kind Kashmiri women did not hesitate to invite me into their homes. **Muzaffarabad, Azad Jammu and Kashmir, in the Pakistani part of Kashmir (2013)**

Informal lunch with Nobel Peace Laureate Jose Ramos-Horta (right), his younger brother Arsenio Ramos-Horta (left), the author and her father James Schuurmans. I am grateful to Dr. Ramos-Horta for his warm hospitality during our visits to Timor-Leste. He and his family always made us feel at home. **Dili, Timor-Leste (2017)**

Arsenio Ramos-Horta drove me to the border region between Timor-Leste and Indonesia where we were warmly welcomed by some Indonesian soldiers who had freely crossed the peaceful border into Timor-Leste. **Border region with West Timor (province of Indonesia), Timor-Leste (2015)**

Meeting with Farooq Papa during my interview with him in China. I always felt the immense pain in his heart when he spoke out about the armed struggle in Kashmir – a home so far away and to which he is unable to go back. I felt I was opening old wounds. After our visit to China, we had lengthy discussions on the phone but Farooq often diverted the topic of conversation. Chapter two is a vital historical analysis about the armed struggle which cannot be omitted. It took, however, almost three years to be completed. **Kunming, People's Republic of China (2015)**

Having coffee with human rights defender Khurram Parvez. Khurram provided me with the latest updates on the deteriorating security conditions in the Kashmir Valley following the assassination of Burhan Wani, a year earlier, in 2016. In 2021, he was arrested and incarcerated in the notorious Tihar Jail in New Delhi, India. In January 2023, while still incarcerated, he won the Martin Ennals Award for his work as a human rights activist.
Manila, Philippines (2017)

The author with Farzana Yaqoob, Minister of Social Welfare and Women Development (2011-2016) of Azad Jammu and Kashmir. We participated in an international seminar on Kashmir at the European Parliament. Ms. Farzana is an outspoken kind lady in whose company I was always made to feel comfortable. **Brussels, Belgium (2013)**

My security during my visits to Pakistan, well… only part of the entourage which usually accompanied us during our visits. I am grateful to the Pakistani government for their warm and welcoming hospitality, and for arranging my visits to the Kashmir region which always needed considerable planning. I consider myself very fortunate to have visited this beautiful country with such kind people and such delicious cuisine everywhere I went. **On the way to Muzaffarabad, Azad Jammu and Kashmir, in the Pakistani part of Kashmir (2015)**

Working visit to Baltistan. From Khaplu we drove towards the Siachen Glacier and to the border of the restricted area past which it is prohibited for foreigners to enter. **Road to Siachen Glacier, Gilgit-Baltistan, in the Pakistani part of Kashmir (2018)**

The Kargah Buddha is carved out of the rocks. It is located some ten kilometres from Gilgit and dates back to the seventh century. These ancient rock carvings are unique to the region of Gilgit-Baltistan. **Gilgit, Gilgit-Baltistan, in the Pakistani part of Kashmir (2018)**

"The Friendship Bridge" located on the Line of Control. Part of the bridge is controlled by India and the other part by Pakistan. **Chakothi (Line of Control), Azad Jammu and Kashmir, in the Pakistani part of Kashmir (2013)**

CHAPTER 5

SILENCE IS A CRIME IN TIMES OF CONFLICT

The Human Cost of Conflict in Kashmir

"Silence is a crime at times of conflict," Ali Mohammad Mir used to remind his grandson, Khurram Parvez, who would later become the prominent human rights defender. Ali Mohammad was a kind, honest, and hard-working man who lived by his principles; like many fellow Kashmiris, he raised his voice against the injustices perpetrated by the state and in 1990, he was killed for it by Indian police during the Gaw Kadal massacre. Khurram was only thirteen years old at the time. The massacre occurred when police opened fire on unarmed Kashmiris who had come out onto the streets of Srinagar to protest the re-appointment of the controversial Governor Jagmohan who was known in Kashmir for his authoritarian control, lockdowns and military force. The trigger point for the protest came after the night of 20 January 1990, when over 400 people were dragged out of their homes after house-to-house raids during which it also emerged that women had been raped by the arresting security forces. When the citizens came out in protest, they were fired upon indiscriminately by the authorities. Many estimates put the toll above fifty and over 200 people were injured.[1]

The police officer responsible for the shootings against the stone-pelting Kashmiris on that day happened to be Khurram's next-door neighbour. This meant that after the event, Khurram was reminded of the nature of his grandfather's death on a daily basis. It changed the direction of Khurram's life, and his previously ordinary school days turned into days of agony that would start in the early mornings. "Each morning as I would leave for school, the police officer would leave for work," said Khurram. After a quarter of a century, Khurram's grief at the loss of his grandfather whom he so admired is still tangible.[2]

In the first couple of years after his grandfather's death, he continued to feel a strong sense of resentment against the neighbour, and like many of his classmates, he grappled with the idea of picking up arms and joining the militants to take revenge against those who had shot his relative. However, during this time he also engaged in long discussions with relatives and friends; he read religious books and he repeatedly met with Islamic intellectuals. And so in 1993 he dropped the idea of becoming a militant and joined the peaceful struggle in the cause of Kashmir.[3]

But unlike Khurram, many other teenage witnesses and victims of violence in the Kashmir Valley did go on to take up arms against India. Burhan Wani, who was born in 1994, is just one example. He came from an educated middle-class family and took up arms at the age of fifteen after he witnessed his brother being beaten by Indian security forces – a brother who would also be killed a few years later.[4] In 2015, at the age of twenty-one, Wani had become the face of the "new age militancy" of alienated Kashmiri youth (from the Valley) and was named as one of India's most wanted commanders of the Pakistani-sponsored Hizbul-Mujahideen. He was very active on social media. On 8 July 2016, following a tip-off, the Special Operations Group assassinated Wani together with two of his associates in Kokernag, in south Kashmir.[5] His perceived association with Pakistan was strong; India had labelled him a Pakistani-sponsored terrorist and when he was buried, he was wrapped in a Pakistani flag. Although the vast majority of Kashmiris no longer identify themselves with Pakistan, many Kashmiris have declared Burhan Wani a hero, martyr and a freedom fighter. It is said that tens of thousands of sympathizers attended his funeral. Gowhar Geelani stated in his book *Kashmir Rage and Reason* that more than two hundred thousand common Kashmiris participated in his funeral on 9 July 2016.[6]

His killing reminded the Kashmiri people, once again, that they had had enough of India's occupation. After his death, mass protests broke out, innocent youth were killed, violence escalated, and an entire lockdown of the Valley occurred as a result. Shopkeepers had no choice but to close their businesses and curfews were imposed; in some areas, mobile services were shut down, internet and social media were blocked, and *azaadi* leaders were put under house arrest with no access to outside communication. Hospitals became overloaded with injured people.

Shujaat Bukhari, Chief Editor of *Rising Kashmir*, posted on Twitter "twelve days of curfew, information blockade, no newspaper for four days, forty-six killed, two thousand injured that is today's Kashmir."[7] A day earlier he had posted on Facebook "in my twenty-six-year long career in journalism and reporting from Kashmir, I have not seen such a high number of injured in a particular phase of unrest."⁸ Bukhari also stated that peace in the Kashmir Valley had always been deceptive – that it had been fragile and that no lessons had been learnt.⁹ The response to the protests by the Indian security forces was violent and many of those injured were seriously injured. Bukhari wrote that many Kashmiris who "were undergoing treatment in various hospitals, may not even be able to lead normal lives anymore," and that "scores of young boys who had been hit by pellets may have lost their eyesight."¹⁰ Within a few days, social media was overloaded with articles related to the social unrest in the Valley and, in particular, with news on the youth who had lost their sight as a result of being hit by pellets.

I interviewed a student, Khan (not his real name) who had left Kashmir before this spate of violence occurred, to return to university. I asked after his well-being and he replied, "I am fine, my family and friends are fine, we are all safe," but he continued saying, "many Kashmiris have fallen victims of a bloodbath to which there seems no end in sight." ¹¹ Khan, who comes from Pulwama, a district in southern Kashmir where the militancy has deep roots, also said that he regretted that "nobody on the international front has expressed any concerns about the loss of innocent souls in the land of Kashmir."¹² For him, just like for many other Kashmiris, Burhan Wani was a martyr, a hero who was killed in the name of the Kashmiri struggle for *azaadi*. And so, for Khan, militancy seemed a legitimate response in the face of what seemed an inexplicable international silence.

In an unusual move, the Chinese Ministry of Foreign Affairs issued an official statement on its website in response to the violence in July 2016. The Chinese Foreign Ministry Spokesman Lu Kang stated that "the Kashmir issue is left over from history. China holds a consistent stance and hopes relevant parties will address the issue peacefully through dialogue."¹³ The *New York Times* and *The Guardian* published articles related to the social media restrictions. In a *New York Times* editorial titled "Kashmir in Crisis" published on 21 July 2016, India was criticized for the oppression, violence, use of pellet guns and the "black laws" of the Indian security apparatus that act against civilians with impunity.¹⁴ The article concluded that any failure to take steps would only push more young Kashmiris into militancy, and make impossible the political solution that alone might bring an end to the desperation that has, once again, gripped the region.¹⁵ No western country issued any political statements related to the crisis in Kashmir. Sajjad Karim, member of the European Parliament, wrote a letter to the then EU's Foreign Policy Chief, Federica Mogherini, requesting to find ways to end the violence in Kashmir and asking for the European Union to work with India in addressing the widespread human rights abuses – but no action was taken.¹⁶

When Pakistan, on the other hand, did express its concerns about the human rights abuses in the Valley, including the killing of Burhan Wani, in a news program on Indian national television, *The Newshour Debate*, the presenter was of the opinion that Pakistan had no right to comment. According to the Indian intellectuals on the programme, Burhan Wani was a Pakistani terrorist; they pointed out that Pakistan had also violated human rights – in the Kashmir region as well as in Balochistan. This televised debate between Indian and Pakistani intellectuals did not take long to spiral out of control, resulting in the representatives of both countries aggressively finger-pointing and the debate falling apart.[17] What the programme did make clear however, was that this was a conflict being played out between India and Pakistan, while the victims of the conflict themselves were being ignored. In the weeks that followed, the situation in Kashmir remained tense; thousands more were injured and scores of innocent youths were either blinded or killed.

In 2018, two years after the use of pellet guns in Kashmir, the international community finally started paying some attention to the suffering of the Kashmiris and the first ever United Nations Human Rights report on Kashmir was created. It stated:

> One of the most dangerous weapons used against protestors in 2016 – and which is still being used by security forces – was the pellet-firing shotgun. According to official figures, seventeen people were killed by shotgun pellets between July 2016 and August 2017, and 6,221 people were injured by the metal pellets between 2016 and March 2017. Civil society organizations believe that many of them have been partially or completely blinded.[18]

However, despite the report, there is still ongoing silence on the situation in Kashmir which has granted Indian security forces blanket amnesty over the human rights abuses that they have committed. The violence of 2016 is just one example of the simmering conflict between India and Pakistan over Kashmir. In 2004, Khurram, who had witnessed his grandfather's killing in 1990, also became a victim of the conflict; he was badly injured and lost a limb when an Improvised Explosive Device exploded while he and his colleagues were monitoring parliamentary elections to prevent coercion and rigging by Indian security forces. Aasia Jeelani (1974-2004) who was a close friend of Khurram and his colleague in the Jammu and Kashmir Coalition of Civil Society (an organisation who advocate for peace and disarmament in the Valley) and the driver, were killed in the attack.

Khurram's Narrative of the Attack in 2004

By 2004, the boycotting of elections was an established phenomenon in Kashmir. There had been calls for election boycotts during most of Kashmir's election campaigns and in some previous elections huge boycotts had resulted in punitive repressive policies (by the Indian state) that coerced people to vote. When the 2004 Indian parliamentary elections came around, many Kashmiris again wanted to boycott and the Indian Army were again using coercive tactics to force people to cast their ballots. On the morning of 20 April 2004, various activists and volunteers from human rights organizations and civil society groups set out from Srinagar in nine different teams travelling to different areas in the Kashmir Valley. They set out early in the morning. Although Aasia had fallen sick the previous day, she was still determined to do her part, and she arrived with the others at the office at 5.30 a.m. She had not been listed in any of the teams and so when she arrived, she said that she wanted to join Khurram and his colleagues.[19]

As they left Srinagar they drove to Kupwara district, located some hundred kilometres northwest of the summer capital, where they visited various towns and villages asking people whether or not they had a free choice to vote. The last place they visited was a small town named Sogam, and as their vehicle left the town, Khurram noticed four army vehicles ahead of them, so he told the driver to reduce their speed and keep a distance. After they continued driving for about two kilometres, the army vehicles suddenly made a U-turn.[20]

Khurram's car stopped to avoid overtaking the army vehicles and after a few tense minutes an explosion hit the car. Although Khurram had remained conscious, he initially found himself in darkness and could not open his eyes. Once he was able to see clearly through the dust, he noticed that the driver was dead, and Aasia who had been sitting right next to him, was stuck in her seat and badly injured. All the others had luckily been either unharmed or sustained only minor injuries. They quickly managed to get out of the car and pulled Aasia out. Meanwhile, Khurram felt a terrible pain, and when he looked down at his leg, he noticed a deep wound and it seemed that a bone was also missing. Trying to get out of the car, he had to lift his leg with both hands and pull himself out of the car while carrying his injured leg. As he got out, he saw that the army personnel were already standing outside their vehicles not far from their car; they were standing still, silently watching, and did not reach out to help any of the victims.[21]

There were two casualties on the ground, one was the driver who had been instantly killed, and the other was Aasia who was still alive but crying out in anguish to Khurram for help and pain relief. "Badly injured as she was, she remembered her mother," Khurram said, "another twenty more minutes passed while the army officers silently looked at us from a distance. They might have called the hospital to request for an ambulance, as our mobile phones did not work." Sure enough, an ambulance unexpectedly arrived which drove them some three kilometres to the nearest emergency centre. Aasia was still alive. Besides Khurram's badly injured leg, his head was also bleeding profusely from a wound that needed immediate care. "Aasia is dying, and we want to save your life," doctors told Khurram as they were treating him. "The first ambulance will take you to Srinagar hospital which is a two and half hours' drive, and the second one, which is still on the way, will take Aasia." But Khurram refused to go first, and asked the doctors to take Aasia first instead.[22]

Somehow both were simultaneously taken in different ambulances to SMHS Hospital in Srinagar. He had remained conscious and while driving he noticed that his mobile phone had started working again. He called his mother who had meanwhile been informed by the police about the incident. "Are you all right?" she asked anxiously, to which Khurram firmly responded firmly that although he was suffering from some minor injuries she need not worry.[23]

When he reached the hospital, however, his mother was shocked to see her son in such a poor condition. She later told Khurram she could not believe he actually had the strength to call her from the ambulance. When doctors arrived to treat him, Khurram right away told them to amputate his leg but doctors said they would do all they possibly could to save it. Aasia had reached the hospital half an hour earlier and Khurram enquired about her. "She is doing fine and is undergoing treatment," doctors said, after which they hastily left the emergency room. Khurram had not been informed yet that Aasia had sustained multiple injuries and that she had been declared dead even before reaching the hospital.[24]

For two weeks surgeons did all they could to rescue Khurram's leg, but on 5 May 2004 they were left with no choice but to amputate. A few weeks after the first amputation, his wounds did not heal, and to avoid further complications, he was airlifted to New Delhi for further treatment. Surgeons conducted a second amputation. While Khurram was in the hospital in New Delhi he received an anonymous call from a man in Kashmir who offered condolences and told him that militants were responsible for the bomb blast, which had meant to kill him.[25]

However, earlier when Khurram was still in the hospital in Srinagar, police officers from Sogam came to meet him and told him that those who planted the bomb were from the army but that they, the police, did not have authority to arrest them. The police did not say much and quickly left saying that they only wanted Khurram to know the truth. Khurram was surprised that someone was now holding militants accountable for the attack and so he decided to start investigating the matter on his own. The Indian government authorities suggested that the Pakistan-sponsored Laskhar-e-Taiba had been behind the attack, but they denied responsibility.[26]

When Khurram managed to get in touch with a representative from Laskhar-e-Taiba, they said that they do not use Improvised Explosive Devices, and suggested that Khurram should enquire with Hizbul-Mujahideen. The Hizbul commander he talked to also denied involvement in the attack, and stated that he would be foolish to stage an attack against him – after all, Khurram had been working for the good cause of *azaadi*. After some months of research, Khurram reached a deadlock in his investigation, and although he remained distracted about the motivations of those responsible for the attack staged against him, he felt he had no choice but to leave those vital questions unanswered for the time being. It would take Khurram a few more years to get closer to the truth about who had been behind his assassination attempt.[27]

In the years that followed, Khurram became a renowned human rights defender, during which time he began to work more closely with one of his relatives, Parvez Imroz. Parvez and Khurram had both been founding members of the Jammu and Kashmir Coalition of Civil Society. Parvez Imroz is now one of Kashmir's leading human rights lawyers and civil activists. In 2006, he was awarded the eleventh Ludovic-Trarieux International Human Rights Prize. The first time this prize was awarded had been to Nelson Mandela in 1985 who, at that time, was a forgotten man in jail and considered a terrorist by many.[28] Parvez Imroz has dedicated most of his career to the oppressed people in Kashmir. In 2017, he was also awarded the prestigious Thorolf Rafto Memorial Prize for his human rights work.

Imroz has worked with victims of systematic torture and rape, and it is he who "discovered" the unmarked graves in the Kashmir Valley. When Khurram and Parvez planned to travel to the United Nations in Geneva to address the human rights violations in the Valley in September 2016, Khurram was banned from boarding the plane in New Delhi. As he returned to Kashmir, security forces arrested him under the Public Safety Act and put him behind bars. In November 2021, Khurram was arrested once again under the Unlawful Activities Prevention Act and was incarcerated in the notorious Tihar jail in New Delhi, far away from his family in Kashmir. It is evident that anyone who works against the Indian government faces the risk of arrest and incarceration.

Human Rights Abuses in Kashmir

Jezza Neumann, a multi-BAFTA-winning (British Academy of Film and Television Arts) director worked with Parvez Imroz when he produced *Kashmir's Torture Trail* (2012). This is one of the few western documentaries on Kashmir that provides a detailed account of the ongoing human rights abuses and reveals the on-the-ground realities of the political and social unrest in the Kashmir Valley. The documentary starts in 2010 with the unarmed protests in the Kashmir Valley that erupted after Indian security forces killed three innocent civilians. In the protests that followed, four thousand Indian security forces were injured (likely by thrown stones) and 180 Kashmiris were killed, including scores of children. Thousands were detained in the aftermath and when they were released, they told chilling tales of brutal torture.[29] India claimed that the stone-pelting youth were funded and organized by terrorist organizations from Pakistan.[30] Over the past two decades, tens of thousands of Kashmiris have been arrested and detained for two years without trial under the Public Safety Act, and they are frequently re-arrested after their release. Mr. A.S. Dulat, former chief of the Research and Analysis Wing, wrote in his memoir, *Kashmir, The Vajpayee Years*, "when detention under the Public Safety Act had ended, one would be re-arrested just outside the gate of the prison and sent back in."[31] Indian police have often claimed that invoking the Public Safety Act against stone-pelters is the only option they have in effectively controlling the incidents in the Valley.[32]

International organizations like Amnesty International and Human Rights Watch have repeatedly condemned India for these undemocratic laws. In 2006, in its report *India: Impunity Fuels Conflict in Jammu and Kashmir*, Human Rights Watch pointed out that Indian law has enabled the authorities to act with impunity. There are cases where Indian security forces have shot civilians under the authority of laws such as the Jammu and Kashmir Disturbed Areas Act (DAA) and the Armed Forces Special Powers Act (AFSPA).[33] Only very few cases of police and military personnel killing innocent civilians have been prosecuted. Human Rights Watch also stated that the work of both the National Human Rights Commission and the State Human Rights Commission in Jammu and Kashmir is severely hampered by laws that prohibit them from directly investigating abuses carried out by the army or other federal forces. Although government officials claim that disciplinary measures have been taken against some security personnel, it is unclear that this ever happens as details are almost never made public.[34]

In Amnesty International's report of July 2015, the organization expressed serious concerns about India's draconian laws, in particular with regard to the Armed Forces Special Powers Act which was extended to Jammu and Kashmir in 1990. This Act allows security officers to fire upon or otherwise use force, even to the extent of causing death, not only in cases of self-defence but against any person contravening laws or orders prohibiting the assembly of five or more persons.[35] Although Amnesty International was one of the few international organizations actively reporting on Kashmir, Amnesty International India was forced to close its operations in September 2020 after Indian authorities froze its bank accounts. Amnesty's report claimed that this "occurred shortly after Amnesty International India had published briefings demanding accountability for grave human rights violations carried out by the Delhi police and the government during the Delhi riots and in Jammu and Kashmir."[36] The United Nations has also expressed concerns about these laws. In March 2012, Christof Heyns, the United Nations Special Rapporteur on extrajudicial, summary or arbitrary executions, visited India. In his report to the United Nations Human Rights Council, he highlighted the immense powers given to the state in these laws; he stated that "the powers granted under AFSPA are in reality broader than that allowable under a state of emergency as the right to life may effectively be suspended under the Act and the safeguards applicable in a state of emergency are absent."[37]

Moreover, the widespread deployment of the military creates an environment in which the exception becomes the rule, and the use of lethal force is seen as the primary response to conflict. Calling for the repeal of the law, he said that "retaining a law such as AFSPA runs counter to the principles of democracy and human rights."[38] India has a long history of human rights violations in the Kashmir Valley, and many Kashmiris have been the victims of brutalities such as being beaten, being forced to drink urine, being burned with cigarettes, having nails pulled off, and being given electric shocks. And the documentary *Kashmir's Torture Trail* tells of even more brutal stories of human rights violations in the Valley.

Farooq Siddiqi avoids talking about the torture practices conducted by Indian security forces. He once revealed, while pointing to his knee, "until today – after more than a quarter of a century – I still have a problem with my knee. It still hurts."[39] In another conversation, he recounted a time in the early 1990s when he and Yasin Malik were close to being captured during a random police check of rickshaws passing through the streets of Srinagar. To avoid capture and the inevitable torture, one of them held a hand grenade tightly in their hands in readiness to pull the trigger if they were caught. It could have killed them instead of saving them from arrest, but Farooq said that had they been arrested, "Yasin and I knew the exact location of the weapons and ammunition and we would have gone through extensive torture. It would have been unbearable."[40]

The Kashmir Disappearances

Jason Burke of *The Guardian* is one of the few western journalists who has reported on human rights violations in Kashmir. In 2010, he published an article titled *WikiLeaks Cables: India Accused of Systematic Use of Torture in Kashmir*. The article revealed that, according to the leaked diplomatic cables, US officials had evidence of widespread torture by Indian police and security forces and were secretly briefed by Red Cross staff about the systematic abuse of detainees in Kashmir.[41] In his article, *Kashmir Unmarked Graves Hold Thousands of Bodies*, he writes about the frequent accusation against the Indian security forces in Kashmir – that they have staged gun battles, in which innocent civilians have repeatedly been killed, and passed the battles off as separatist militant gun fights in order to earn rewards and promotions.[42]

As mentioned previously, more than six thousand unmarked graves have been discovered in Kashmir in recent years. India has often stated that these are the bodies of (Pakistani sponsored) militants. The people of Kashmir, however, have demanded an official enquiry. In 2009, the Srinagar-based International People's Tribunal on Human Rights and Justice in Kashmir (IPTK) headed by Parvez Imroz, published a report titled *Buried Evidence* on the first batch of the 2,700 unmarked graves. A community elder in Srinagar stated that "my son was killed in a fake encounter and was buried by the police as a 'Pakistani terrorist'. We want justice. We want his name restored. We want his memory healed."[43]

Of the 2,700 graves, 154 graves contained two bodies each and twenty-three graves contained more than two corpses. Within these twenty-three graves, the number of bodies ranged from three to seventeen.[44] The bodies buried in the 2,700 graves investigated by IPTK were routinely delivered to gravesites at night, and many bore the marks of torture. Reportedly, photographs of the dead were sometimes documented by local police stations but not made available to the public or relatives. Gravediggers and caretakers developed a system of identification by tagging bodies prior to burial. Identification occurred through clothing, distinguishing characteristics and marks, and/or numbering. The process of identification was dependent on literacy, the threats facing the gravediggers, and other factors, and so they were usually orally recorded and remembered, although some were recorded in writing.[45]

Human Rights Watch and other human rights groups have called for an independent investigation into the alleged killings and enforced disappearances by the Indian security forces.[46] The 2009 report recommended that the commission should call for immediate DNA sampling and other forensic tests in order to match the victims with living relatives.[47] Atta Mohammed was a gravedigger and buried 203 bodies on a hillside adjacent to the Jhelum River between 2002 and 2006. The police delivered most of the bodies to him after dark.[48] Traumatized by this tragic episode, Atta Mohammed stated that the bodies he buried "appeared in his nightmares, each in graphic, gruesome detail."[49] He said:

> I have been terrorized by this task that was forced upon me. My nights are tormented and I cannot sleep, the bodies and graves appear and reappear in my dreams. My heart is weak from this labour. I have tried to remember this all…the sound of the earth as I covered the graves…bodies and faces that were mutilated…mothers who would never find their sons. My memory is an obligation. My memory is my contribution. I am tired, I am so very tired.[50]

In 2008, the European Parliament in Brussels passed a Resolution on the mass graves in Indian Kashmir that stated:

> It is a call on the Indian government and the state authorities to investigate all allegations of enforced disappearances; we urge jurisdiction of all cases in which military, security or law-enforcement agents are suspected of being involved to be assigned to a civilian prosecutor's office, and a single public database of all persons who have gone missing and all bodies that have been recovered to be created; calls on Member States to facilitate and support all possible cooperation between the Indian and Pakistani governments in relation to this investigation.[51]

Besides the Resolution, the European Parliament has not taken any further concrete action to address the unmarked graves in the Valley.

A report titled *Half Widow, Half Wife?* published in 2011 and authored by the Association of Parents of Disappeared Persons examined the situation of women in Kashmir who have been labelled "half widows". These women, whose husbands have disappeared but not yet been declared deceased, number at around 1,500 in Kashmir but the actual number is thought to be much higher.[52] Women in this situation face economic, social, and emotional insecurities. Children of half widows are often particularly traumatized, and are vulnerable to loneliness, impoverishment, and exploitation.[53] The mothers too, often suffer from post-traumatic stress disorder (PTSD), sleep deprivation, and other anxieties, adding to further complications and fragmentation of an already traumatized society.[54]

While the Indian government technically provides some financial relief, this is mostly only received after a lengthy legal process that many women cannot afford. And the impunity enjoyed by the Indian security forces has resulted in a sense of powerlessness that has prevented people from speaking out and seeking justice. But the issue of the disappeared and the unmarked graves in the Kashmir Valley remains a serious concern that is still affecting people's lives today. In an email in 2018, Parvez Imroz wrote:

> Not even a single perpetrator of human rights violations was punished for the crime. It appears highly unlikely that the government will conduct investigations into the presence of mass graves or allow any international institution to carry out probes into the graves. Even the International Committee of the Red Cross, which has a presence in Kashmir, cannot do anything, as the organization is operating with a limited mandate. The domestic legal remedies have been exhausted and only the international organizations and institutions could mount pressure on the government for doing exactly what the governments in other conflict areas have done in mass grave issues. The Association of Parents of Disappeared Persons has approached the State Human Rights Commission to take up the matter with the High Court and the matter is pending before the Commission.[55]

Violence Against Women in Kashmir

In 2015, Laura Kyle of the programme Inside Story on *Al Jazeera English* invited a group of researchers and politicians to give their viewpoints on the report released by Amnesty International on the human rights violations in Kashmir. The group consisted of the British historian and author on Kashmir Victoria Schofield, human rights defender Khurram Parvez, and Rakesh Sinha, Director of the India Policy Foundation. During the debate, Rakesh Sinha represented the official Indian government view – denying the allegations of human rights violations in Kashmir in general, as well as flatly denying the mass rape that occurred in Kunan Poshpora in 1991. This incident occurred in Kupwara on 23 February 1991 when, after fighting with militants, the Indian Army cordoned off two villages, separated the men from the women, and raped dozens of girls and women during the course of the night.⁵⁶ An investigation by the Indian government into the incident rejected the allegations as baseless.⁵⁷ In response to criticism of the government's handling of the investigation, the army requested that the Press Council of India investigate the incident. The team of investigators concluded that the charges against the army were "a well-concocted bundle of fabricated lies and a massive hoax orchestrated by militant groups and their sympathizers and mentors in Kashmir" and they recommended that the soldiers be cleared of all charges.⁵⁸

Human Rights Watch reported that in Kashmir, rape has been used as a means of targeting women whom the security forces accuse of being militant sympathizers; in raping them, the security forces attempt not only to punish the individuals but moreover to attempt to humiliate the entire community.⁵⁹ In the 1990s, rape occurred frequently during reprisal attacks on civilians following militant ambushes. In these cases, anyone residing in the area became the target of retaliation.

Anyone within range may have been shot; homes and other property burned, and the women raped. In some cases, women who had been raped were accused of providing food or shelter to militants or, they were raped when they refused to identify their male relatives as militants. In other cases, the motivations for their abuse were not made explicit. In many attacks, the selection of victims was seemingly arbitrary and the women, like other civilians assaulted or killed, were targeted simply because they happened to be in the wrong place at the wrong time.⁶⁰ The armed militant organizations in Kashmir also targeted civilians, although not to the same extent as the security forces.⁶¹

In 1994, in Hyhama, a small village in Kashmir, seven women were allegedly gang raped by security forces. In 1997 in Wavoosa village near Srinagar, seven women were reportedly raped during a routine cordon and search operation.⁶² The story of Asiya and Neelofar is well-known among the Kashmiris. In May 2009, Asiya and Neelofar mysteriously disappeared when they went out to their family's apple orchard. When the bodies of these young women were discovered a few days later, they were initially told that they had been drowned. Further investigations concluded that the two women had been gang raped and brutally murdered. Justice is yet to be done for Asiya and Neelofar.⁶³

Notwithstanding very few testimonies, accepted witness accounts, and concerted campaigns on the part of human rights organizations (such as Amnesty International and Human Rights Watch), the armed forces have denied all the instances and allegations of rape.⁶⁴ Sexual violence against women in Kashmir has been inadequately addressed. One reason for this is the stigma that female victims face when talking about their ordeals. There are also financial restraints and a lack of government support. Parvez Imroz is one of the activists who actively engages with the victims of sexual violence in Kashmir and who works to bring these cases to the attention of the Indian authorities. Imroz has emphasised the need for advocacy:

> In 2018, the Support Group for the Kunan Poshpora mass rapes, filed a petition before the State Human Rights Commission asking the state government to provide a status report on the progress of 143 cases of sexual crimes committed between 1989 and 2017. But unfortunately, there are no organized groups working for women's rights due to different reasons but mainly the lack of resources. The NGO's with resources and special privileges are busy with soft issues that do not cause embarrassment to the government.[65]

A Summary of Events

The shootings at Gaw Kadal Bridge in 1990, where Khurram's grandfather was killed, has not been the only massacre, and over the past few decades, the Kashmir Valley has witnessed a number of tragic events. On 6 January 1993, Border Security Forces (BSF) killed an estimated fifty-five innocent civilians in Sopore, Baramulla district, after members of the Jammu and Kashmir Liberation Front attacked a BSF patrol post. The Indian security forces opened fire on a bus, killing its driver and at least fifteen passengers, and they set offices, homes, and shops on fire, killing scores of people. On 10 April 1993, an arson attack on the business centre of Lal Chowk in downtown Srinagar was set on fire, killing over 125 civilians. Indian authorities pointed a finger at the militancy, but many others allege that the BSF started the fire. On 22 October 1993, at least thirty-seven people were killed when the Border Security Forces opened fire to disperse more than ten thousand people marching on the National Highway in Bijbehara. The protestors were demonstrating against an earlier incident of firing on protestors near the Hazratbal Shrine in Srinagar.[66] An eyewitness recalled the events to Human Rights Watch:

> The people had gathered on the National Highway which passes through Bijbehara town. It was like this even then, narrow, with shops on both sides of the road. There were thousands of people shouting slogans. But it was peaceful... The BSF just opened fire without any warning. It was terrible. There were so many people lying on the ground. Others were running in panic...This road, this very road, was full of blood.[67]

In 2014, The Jammu and Kashmir Coalition of Civil Society published *The Anatomy of a Massacre: The Mass Killings at Sailan*, in which it revealed the massacre of 3 August 1998, when nineteen people of one family, including eleven children and five women, were shot to death at point black range in their homes in Sailan. After they had been killed, their bodies where horribly dismembered and, in one case, almost decapitated with axes and sharp instruments.[68]

Pakistan's Role in Kashmir

Despite the poor human rights record of the Indian security forces, India has not been the only perpetrator of atrocities in the Kashmir Valley; there is also plenty of evidence to support the accusation that Pakistan has supported the armed militancy in Kashmir. Militancy has been a major contributary factor in the growing instability of the South Asian region as a whole. As the armed insurgencies began to wane from 1993 onwards, Pakistan created Lashkar-e-Taiba to stage brutal attacks in the Valley against the Indian state. These attacks resulted in the killings of many innocent civilians, including those of minority religions. Lashkar-e-Taiba not only created regional instability in Kashmir and the wider region, it also contributed to the fragmentation of a society of different religions and ethnicities who had previously cohabited peacefully for centuries.

Moreover, Pakistan's creation of, and support for, the armed militancy in Kashmir also permanently blemished the image of the indigenous *azaadi* struggle including that of the Jammu and Kashmir Liberation Front who would later also come to be labelled terrorists. This was demonstrated in March 2019 when the Indian Ministry of Home Affairs banned the Jammu and Kashmir Liberation Front under anti-terror law, claiming that it incited terrorism.[69]

In 2004, the then US Deputy Assistant Secretary of State, Michael G. Kozak, appeared before the Government Reform Subcommittee on Human Rights and Wellness in Washington, DC and reported that militant groups active in Kashmir were responsible for execution-style killings of civilians, including several political leaders and party workers. These groups, who consist of Pakistanis and other foreign nationals, were, and are, also responsible for kidnappings, rapes, extortion and other acts of random terror that have killed hundreds of Kashmiris. These militants have also regularly executed alleged government informants. In 2003, the Indian Home

Ministry said that militants had killed 808 civilians, and for 2002, the figure was 967.[70]

Kashmiri militant and terrorist groups have also undertaken numerous execution-style mass killings of Pandits (Hindus), Sikh and Buddhist villagers in Jammu and Kashmir. They have also engaged in random acts of terror, using time-delayed explosives, landmines, hand grenades, rockets and snipers.[71] Over the past decades, there has been much debate about the displaced Kashmiri Pandits who became targets of frequent attacks orchestrated by Kashmiri militant groups in the Kashmir Valley. In 2003, when twenty-four Hindus were massacred in Kashmir, the then US Congressman Joe Wilson released a statement condemning the attacks: "The fact that the terrorists who committed this act would kill two young children and eleven women demonstrates what a heartless, despicable act this truly was."[72] He added, "since the armed insurgency in Kashmir began in 1989, more than four hundred thousand Kashmiri Pandits have been forced from their homes in Kashmir."[73] This number is debated, and the human rights defender Khurram Parvez has stated that the true figure is less. He estimates that around 168,000 Pandits used to live in the Kashmir Valley (approximately four per cent of the entire population in the Valley) and that in 2017, only an estimated four thousand remained.[74] Writing in 2003, Professor Sumantra Bose estimated that between 1989 and 1990, around 130,000 to 140,000 Pandits were living in the Valley and that approximately one hundred thousand Pandits were forced to flee to New Delhi and Jammu.[75] Bose argues that:

> Organised groups representing Pandit migrants have since claimed that they were forced out of the Valley by a systematic terror campaign of "ethnic cleansing" and even "genocide", [whereas] pro-*azaadi* Muslim opinion in the Valley tends to argue that the migration was encouraged and even actively facilitated by Indian officials, particularly Governor Jagmohan, in a deliberate attempt to stigmatize the *azaadi* movement as sectarian and fundamentalist.[76]

He furthermore points out that "the displacement of Pandits from the Valley has been the prime tool of Indian officials, politicians, and media in the propaganda war over Kashmir since 1990."[77]

Nevertheless, it is indisputable that in the early 1990s, within a relatively short span of time, the vast majority of the Pandit community in the Valley was forced to leave their homes. Many relocated to New Delhi and Jammu, while tens of thousands of others ended up in displacement camps, often living in appalling conditions. In the late 1990s, attacks on Pandits in the

Valley again increased; there is a long list of brutal attacks against the Pandit minority, allegedly undertaken by either Lashkar-e-Taiba or other Pakistani-affiliated terrorist groups.

In January 1998, twenty-three Hindus were killed in the Wandhama massacre.[78] Disguised in Indian Army uniforms, gunmen opened fire upon innocent Hindus after having a cup of tea with them.[79] Four children and nine women were among the victims. In April 1998, the Prankote massacre cost the lives of twenty-six Hindus when they refused to convert to Islam, and the Chapnari massacre in June of the same year killed another twenty-five Hindus during a marriage celebration. In 2000, thirty people were brutally massacred while on their yearly pilgrimage to Amarnath Temple. Laskhar-e-Taiba was blamed for this ferocious attack. In 2002, two suicide bombers entered the Raghunat Temple in Jammu killing eleven people.[80] Another fourteen people were killed when two suicide bombers entered the same temple again in the November of that year. Earlier, in May 2002, terrorists attacked a tourist bus carrying mainly army families, killing thirty-one people. In 2003, continuing with their ethnic-cleansing rampage, terrorists entered the village of Nadimarg, dragged families out of their homes late at night, and killed twenty-four people. In Jammu in 2006, in what became known as the Doda massacre, another nineteen innocent Hindus were killed. On that day, two separate attacks took place in which innocent Hindu villagers became the victims of bloodbaths.[81]

Over the past few years, there have been ongoing debates about the return of Pandits to the Valley, and around the creation of Palestinian-style settlements that may lead to ghettoization and further complications. Kashmiris from the Valley, however, would all unanimously reiterate that for generations Kashmiri Muslims and Pandits had been living peacefully side-by-side, and that it would never be in the interest of the Muslim majority in the Valley to attack their neighbours based on religious grounds.

Following the tragic September 11 attacks on the United States, the then Pakistani President Pervez Musharraf was left with no choice but to support the United States in their "War on Terror," after which Pakistan's support for the militancy in Kashmir gradually waned. However, although Pakistan officially banned several militant groups, including those operating in Kashmir, it is widely believed that some of these groups have continued to operate in the Valley, albeit under different names. In 2006, Human Rights Watch reported that Pakistan appeared to be keeping its options open, should peace talks collapse, by continuing to support militant groups.[82] It also stated that Pakistan remained accountable for abuses committed by militants that it had armed and trained.[83] But despite this regional volatility, the native Kashmiris have not given up their *azaadi* struggle, and the Kashmiri youth has become even more determined than before.

As mentioned in previous chapters, although violence dwindled in the first decade of the twenty-first century, in the second decade, an increasing number of Kashmiris began picking up arms again. In 2016, an article published in *Foreign Affairs* (magazine of the Washington, DC-based Council on Foreign Affairs) titled "Valley of the Brawls" stated:

> Members of the Jammu and Kashmir police, army officials, a former chief of India's foreign intelligence agency, and a former Indian national security adviser, have expressed fears that the region could once again see major conflict, pointing to its rising religious radicalism, communal tensions, and as they called it, a significant increase in militant violence.[84]

The article also stated that the revival of militant organizations, particularly in southern Kashmir, posed another alarming threat; for example, Hizbul-Mujahideen has been resurrected due to a swell in recruits.[85] And after 2019 and the events around the abrogation of Articles 370 and 35A, it has become even more critical that, within Kashmir, a close eye is kept on the development of homegrown militancy.

But not all young Kashmiris see violence as the way forward. Kareem (not his real name), a Kashmiri student I interviewed, is one of the young Kashmiris who will never give up on the struggle for *azaadi* in Kashmir and has chosen the power of the pen instead of the barrel. When I interviewed him in 2016, he said:

> Neither India nor Pakistan want to resolve Kashmir according to the aspirations of the people of Kashmir which has resulted in Kashmiri youth taking up arms and this has created unrest in the Valley. For the past seven decades, Kashmiris have been denied their right to self-determination which has become the main cause of uprisings. Kashmir is not a bilateral issue between India and Pakistan, but one that includes the people of Kashmir.[86]

As long as the people of Kashmir remain excluded from formal peace talks and the struggle for *azaadi* continues, the vast majority will continue pelting stones, the human rights abuses will continue, yet more innocent Kashmiris will be killed, and the deadlock will not be lifted

CHAPTER 6

THE INDIA-PAKISTAN DISCORD

Kashmir and the Shifting Balance of Power in Asia

The antagonism between India and Pakistan that began with the partition of the British Raj in 1947 and the disputed accession of parts of Kashmir to India, has resulted in geopolitical implications that have now reached far beyond Kashmir itself.

Despite India's non-alignment policy during the Cold War, it was nevertheless a close friend of the erstwhile Soviet Union and is still today on friendly terms with Russia. However, in recent decades, India has also increasingly drawn closer to the United States and its allies – joining the camp that seeks to temper China's rapidly growing economic power. Since the Cold War, the competition that both the US and India feel toward China, has opened the door for greater US-India cooperation.[1] India has been increasingly portrayed as the world's largest democracy with secular values. It has a solid, rapidly growing economy, and is a member of the BRICS. Over the past seventy years, India has been successful in developing its image as a serious player on the world stage – and this development has been backed by the US who have also, for example, backed India's aspirations of getting a permanent seat in the United Nations Security Council.[2] It is generally accepted that partnership between India and the US contributes significantly to peace, stability and prosperity in the Indian Ocean and in the Asia-Pacific region as a whole.[3]

In the face of these alliances, China and Pakistan have cultivated their "all weather friendship" in an attempt to balance regional power politics. The main difference between the US and China today lies in the conflict between their ideologies that was created with the establishment of the People's Republic of China in 1949. Some of Pakistan's Islamic ideology has also been incompatible with that of the west, and its harsh condemnation on the international political stage has lead to an increasing divide. Pakistan is an Islamic state where religious extremism and the support for armed militancy and the *mujahedeen* has been deeply rooted in the military establishment that began with the Afghan-Soviet War (1979-1989) under President Zia-ul-Haq.

Yet this was not always the case. In 1947, Muhammad Ali Jinnah, the founding father of today's Pakistan, took Kemal Ataturk as a role model and sought to establish an Islamic state based on modern, progressive and secular values. Over the decades however, this moderate ideology faded away in the minds of sections of the Pakistani population, and with the tragic events of September 11 2001, the Muslim world and the west were to drift even further apart.

In the United States, the attitude towards Islam and Muslims became an especially important subject after Donald Trump was elected president in 2016 on a right-wing popular platform that explicitly called for a ban on Muslim immigration.[4] In 2019, India also introduced anti-Muslim legislation when Prime Minister Narendra Modi and the Indian government passed the Citizenship Amendment Bill that bans Muslims from acquiring Indian citizenship. This formed part of the increasing Hindu nationalist ideology in India which Prime Minister Narendra Modi has been suspected of actively propagating; *Hindutva* is a right-wing nationalist agenda that considers Muslims a threat to the Indian nation on one hand, but also believes that the Kashmir region is an integral part of the Indian Union.[5] As Christophe Jaffrelot has quoted in his book *Hindu Nationalism*, "we [India] say that Kashmir is a part of India."[6]

The passing of the anti-Muslim legislation resulted in mass protests throughout India.[7] Protests occurred again when Donald Trump visited India in February 2020. On 26 February 2020, an article in *The Washington Post* stated that "New Delhi became a battlefield for the worst communal violence the city has seen in decades."[8] So the policies of Donald Trump have resulted in increasing tension between the United States and the Muslim world, while anti-Muslim tensions in the South Asian subcontinent have also been on the rise.

Discrimination against Muslims in India is not a new phenomenon; Basharat Peer is a Kashmiri journalist and author of *Curfewed Night*. He wrote in his memoir that when he moved to Delhi around the year 2000, he was looking for a place to stay but each time the landlord found out that he was a Muslim, and also a Kashmiri, he was told that they could no longer rent the room to him. After searching for a long time and feeling discouraged, he finally found a place to stay at the house of an elderly Kashmiri Hindu. She warmly welcomed him and offered him a place to stay. He wrote, "I fought my tears; after months of suspicion, I was being welcomed."⁹

Although the Biden administration has taken a different approach towards Islam, such tensions are not easily reversed. The attack by Malik Faisal Akram on the Texas synagogue in January 2022, and his demands to release the Pakistani Aafia Siddiqui, who is said to have become radicalised after the September 11 attacks, have not contributed to healing between the communities. Although Pakistan and the US were allies during the Cold War, the strength of this relationship faded after the defeat of the Red Army (1989) in the post-Cold War era. Since then, Pakistan and the US have been at odds with each other over a number of issues including: the US sanctions to counter Pakistan's nuclear weapons program in the 1990s; Pakistan's support for the Taliban; ongoing militarization in Pakistan; and the US strategies pursued in the post-9/11 "War on Terror."

In January 2018, US President Donald Trump took an even tougher stance against Pakistan when he suspended nearly all security-related assistance to Islamabad until it could prove its commitment to fighting terrorism and cut its ties to militant groups such as the Taliban.[10] In July 2019, in an effort to crack down on terrorism, and a few days prior to Pakistan Prime Minister Imran Khan's state visit to the White House, Pakistan arrested Hafiz Saeed. Saeed was the founder of Lashkar-e-Taiba and is believed to be the mastermind behind the 2008 Mumbai attacks.[11]

When, on 22 July 2019, the US and Pakistan leaders met in Washington, DC, President Donald Trump made a controversial move and offered to mediate between India and Pakistan to resolve the Kashmir dispute. While Imran Khan warmly welcomed the offer, it angered India which was still insisting that it wanted to resolve Kashmir bilaterally as per the Simla Agreement. In August 2019, when Trump met Indian Prime Minister Narendra Modi on the side-lines of the G7 summit in Biarritz, France, President Trump had softened his stance somewhat and expressed the hope that something positive would come out of the talks between India and Pakistan.[12] The Biden Administration has not changed the US approach towards Kashmir; in a statement made shortly after Biden's inauguration, the US Department of State clarified that there had been no change in America's Kashmir policy and that Washington still considers Kashmir a territorial dispute between India and Pakistan.[13]

The relationship between the United States and Pakistan, is at a clear crossroads after the Taliban takeover of Afghanistan in August 2021, but the outlook is concerning.[14] The US does not seem to have an interest building a strong relationship with Pakistan, and Pakistan's poor reputation on the international stage has served to benefit India's reputation as well as

India's economic interests.[15] As long as the international community remains quiet on the issue of Kashmir, this will continue to work in India's favour. Any criticism of state-sponsored terrorism would be justified, but Pakistan claims that the militants in Kashmir are indigenous freedom fighters. These accusations and denials on both sides are common; for example, India holds Lashkar-e-Taiba accountable for the November 2008 Mumbai attacks, while the Pakistani establishment vehemently denies any involvement. The former Pakistan President Pervez Musharraf also cast doubt on Pakistani involvement, saying, "the ISI, – Pakistan's spy agency – would not have left me in the dark, I would have known about it."[16] In conversation, Musharraf also asserted that corruption can occur at the highest level of global politics, "intelligence is a *dirty* world, and they operate in strange ways. Sometimes they [countries] can even harm themselves to convince the public and the world to play things in their favour."[17]

In September 2016, militants attacked Uri, a military base in Indian Kashmir, right across from the Line of Control, killing eighteen Indian soldiers. Pakistan has denied any involvement. In June 2018, militants killed Shujaat Bukhari, the Editor in Chief of *Rising Kashmir* in Srinagar as he left his office. Lashkar-e-Taiba was held accountable by the Indian authorities who even released the names of the four militants involved in Shujaat's assassination.[18] However, Lashkar-e-Taiba themselves denied any involvement and pointed the finger instead at Indian security agencies.[19] These are just two more examples where India and Pakistan have been at odds with each other – each throwing accusations and counter-accusations. In February 2018, Pakistan was put on the grey list of the Financial Action Task Force (FATF) watchdog – the global anti-money-laundering and anti-terrorist-financing watchdog that was set up to try and tackle these issues. Any country put onto the grey list is given a set of recommendations with the aim of improving those issues. Although initial progress started off slowly, it is said that Pakistan's continued political commitment has led to considerable progress in the implementation of its action plan.[20]

India has repeatedly stated that its main threat comes from Pakistan and its terrorist networks, and that this should always be the top priority for any talks between the two nations. The two nuclear-armed nations were on the brink of war after the terrorist suicide attack of 14 February 2019 that killed forty Indian police officers. Although the security conditions in the months that followed stabilized somewhat, this changed again after India's abrogation of Articles 370 and 35A in August 2019 when relations between the two countries once again reached an all-time low. When India declared

Jammu and Kashmir, and Ladakh, two separate Union Territories, as part of the Indian state, this complicated matters even further. Pakistan reiterated that the abrogation of the two articles was not only a violation of the United Nations Resolutions on Kashmir but that it also went against any bilateral agreements of the Simla Agreement (1972) and the Lahore Declaration (1999) between India and Pakistan.[21] In the United Nations General Assembly in 2019, the Pakistani Prime Minister Imran Khan reached out to the world community, suggesting that a (nuclear) war was imminent if the Kashmir conflict was not resolved. Both former US Presidents Bill Clinton and Barack Obama, have dubbed Kashmir the world's most dangerous place.[22]

But there are always voices who emphasize peace, and in 2018 Pakistan's Foreign Minister Shah Mehmood Qureshi joined those voices, emphasizing that there was no military solution – and that the only solution is dialogue with India.[23] And although relations between the two nuclear powers have endured repeated setbacks since 2019 (with the Pulwama attacks, the Balakot airstrike, and abrogation of Articles 370 and 35A), in February 2021 they both agreed to adhere to a ceasefire along the Line of Control. A month later, talks started again over issues related to the Indus Water Treaty after a hiatus of two years.

Since the Second World War, the conflict between India and Pakistan over Kashmir has led to three full wars – in 1947, 1965, and 1971. It is often forgotten that the 1971 war that led to the secession of East Pakistan (when it became Bangladesh) also started in Kashmir. In 1999 the two countries again fought a war, albeit a relatively contained war, in Kashmir over Kargil and on several occasions, they also fought on the Siachen Glacier. Most South Asian experts agree that the instability in Kashmir could ultimately lead to a nuclear dispute if Kashmir is not adequately addressed. Cross-border skirmishes are likely to continue while no resolution has been reached, and there is always the risk that these could escalate.

The fact that much terrorism against India is linked to Kashmir, is often neglected in the media; but this fact shows that the cessation of terrorism in India and a resolution for Kashmir go hand in hand. If both of these issues were to be addressed simultaneously, it could generate a more stable security environment and improve India-Pakistan relations. Pakistan's reputation since the Cold War – as a place that harbours and supports terrorism – forms a significant part of the problem. Although worldwide attention has widened from Al-Qaeda and the Taliban in Pakistan and Afghanistan – to the ideology of the Islamic State that has rapidly been expanding its brutalities throughout the world – the threat of Pakistan's state-sponsored terrorism has also remained a serious cause for concern on the international front. The militancy in Kashmir against India needs to be tackled, whether it be Lashkar-e-Taiba, Jaish-e-Mohammad, or Hizbul-Mujahideen – to the benefit of Kashmir, India, Pakistan, as well as the wider region.

Although India and Pakistan have repeatedly restarted talks over Kashmir, all attempts at long-lasting dialogue have ended in stalemate. The November 2008 Mumbai attacks ended the last rounds of an effective dialogue that the then Pakistani President Pervez Musharraf and his Indian counterpart Prime Minister Vajpayee had initiated during the Agra Summit in 2001. Initial talks had started off with some hesitation, partly because it had been Pervez Musharraf who had instigated the Kargil Conflict in 1999 which had inevitably resulted in distrust on the Indian side. But India eventually opened negotiations with the military leader, and in 2006 Pervez Musharraf was actively engaged with India over his four-point proposal to move towards a practical resolution, or what he called the "out-of-the-box" solution on Kashmir. In his last press conference in January 2014, the Indian Prime Minister Manmohan Singh said that "the two countries came close to clinching a solution during the period from October 2006 to March 2007 but could not close the deal; and by the following year, Musharraf had not only lost authority but also power."[24]

These talks may have borne fruit if a few things had not happened: if President Musharraf had not been forced to step down in the summer of 2008; if the Mumbai attacks had not taken place in the November of that same year (for which Lashkar-e-Taiba was held accountable); and if Pakistan's leadership had not re-started advocating for the implementation of the United Nations Resolutions on Kashmir (which includes a plebiscite for the people of Kashmir).

Former Pakistani President Pervez Musharraf's "out-of-the-box" solution on Kashmir was greeted with scepticism among the opposition in Pakistan. It seemed to many in Pakistan at the time that he had abandoned Pakistan's previous stance on the implementation of the United Nations Resolutions – but he has since reiterated that he in fact never did so. He declares that he was, instead, taking a dialogic approach whereby he was prepared to give up his stance on the UN Resolutions if India were also willing to reciprocate. In conversation in 2018, Musharraf said, "unless there is a quid pro quo and India agrees to something, we will stick to our point of the United Nations Resolutions on Kashmir."[25]

Despite Pakistan's ongoing efforts to implement the UN Resolutions on Kashmir, it has been widely acknowledged at this stage that a plebiscite will never be implemented – simply because India has vehemently opposed any referendum on Kashmir. Therefore, as it stands today, advocating for the

United Nations Resolutions effectively results in the maintenance of the status quo in Kashmir. Hypothetically, a United Nations-sponsored plebiscite in which the Kashmiris are given the choice to join either India or Pakistan, has also come with some controversy because it appears that the aspirations of the majority of Kashmiris no longer lies with either of those nations. An anti-India sentiment has always run high among the Muslim majority in Kashmir, but support for Pakistan has also gradually faded over the decades. In the twenty-first century, the on-the-ground realities of life in Kashmir are very different to those in 1948. And today, a large number of Muslims in the Valley would want a third option to be included in any plebiscite – an option that the United Nations-sponsored plebiscite does not include – that is, the option to vote for independence.

The Simla Agreement vs. the UN Security Council Resolutions

The conflicting approaches of India and Pakistan toward Kashmir lies largely in the difference between the Simla Agreement and the UN Security Council Resolutions. While Pakistan has been advocating for the implementation of the various United Nations Security Council Resolutions, India has stipulated that the Simla Agreement is the only starting point for any bilateral talks, including the Kashmir dispute. India's former Prime Minister Indira Gandhi and her Pakistani counterpart Prime Minister Zulfikar Ali Bhutto signed the Simla Agreement, which is considered a comprehensive blueprint for good neighbourly relations between India and Pakistan, in 1972.[26] The Simla Agreement contains a set of guiding principles, mutually agreed to by India and Pakistan, to which both sides agreed to adhere in their relations with each other. These principles emphasized the need for respect of each other's territorial integrity and sovereignty, non-interference in each other's internal affairs, respect for each other's unity, political independence, sovereign equality, and the renunciation of hostile propaganda.[27]

The following three points of the agreement are especially noteworthy. Firstly, it was agreed that the two countries share a mutual commitment to the peaceful resolution of all issues through a direct bilateral approach. Secondly, it was agreed that both countries would be committed to building on the foundations of a cooperative relationship with special focus on people-to-people contacts. And lastly, both countries pledged to uphold the inviolability of the Line of Control in Jammu and Kashmir, which was to be an extremely important confidence-building measure between India and Pakistan, and a key to durable peace.[28]

After the Simla Agreement was signed in 1972, India rejected any possibility of mediation from the United Nations. Robert G. Wirsing, author of *India, Pakistan, and the Kashmir Dispute*, supports this viewpoint and points to the absence in the Simla Agreement of any reference to United Nations having any mediation or peacekeeping role in Kashmir.[29] He argues therefore that the Kashmir conflict, and any other outstanding issues between India and Pakistan, should be resolved through bilateral means without any interference of the United Nations and its Security Council Resolutions.

However, Dr. Muhammad Khan of the National Defence University in Islamabad disagrees and argues that the United Nations was in fact mentioned in the Simla Agreement. In conversation in 2018, he reiterated that the "Pakistani Prime Minister Zulfikar Ali Bhutto was very smart in negotiating the Simla Agreement as it clearly stipulated that relations between both countries would also be governed according to the United Nations Charter which includes the Kashmir dispute."[30] In support of this argument, two points that are included in the Simla Agreement require attention. Firstly, it states that "the principles and purposes of the Charter of the United Nations shall govern the relations between the two countries."[31] Secondly, it states that:

> Both Governments agree that their respective Heads will meet again at a mutually convenient time in the future and that, in the meanwhile, the representatives of the two sides will meet to discuss further the modalities and arrangements for the establishment of durable peace and normalization of relations, including the questions of repatriation of prisoners of war and civilian internees, a final settlement of Jammu and Kashmir and the resumption of diplomatic relations.[32]

Although both nations agreed to a peaceful resolution in 1972 according to the Simla Agreement, in 1984, Indian troops caught Pakistan by surprise when they infiltrated the Siachen Glacier and stationed themselves in the un-demarcated areas of Siachen. Perhaps it was this event that emboldened Pakistan to infiltrate Kargil in 1999 – a classic tit for tat that completely took India by surprise. The situation between the two nations remained tense until 2003 when they agreed to a ceasefire. Until today, whenever tensions break out between the two nuclear powers, both are reminded to adhere to the 2003 "Ceasefire Understanding" – despite that fact that this "understanding" has its own failures and was never actually signed.

The killing of the 21-year-old Hizbul-Mujahideen commander Burhan Wani by the Indian Security forces in 2016, brought the Kashmir issue to the fore again between the two nations. After the event, Pakistan's Foreign Secretary reached out to India, and handed over a letter addressed to his Indian counterpart, inviting him to visit Pakistan for talks on the Jammu and Kashmir dispute. The letter highlighted the international obligation of both the countries to resolve the Jammu and Kashmir dispute in accordance with the United Nations Security Council Resolutions.[33] India, however, continued to insist that it would only engage in bilateral talks as it sees them outlined in the Simla Agreement. As part of India's response to Pakistan's invitation to hold peace talks on Kashmir, the Indian Foreign Secretary Mr. S. Jaishankar wrote that terrorism (that is, Pakistan's support for, or laxity on, terrorism) should be the basis of the proposed dialogue. He then also called for discussion on "the earliest vacation of Pakistan's illegal occupation of the Indian State of Jammu and Kashmir" referring to Gilgit-Baltistan and Azad Jammu and Kashmir.[34] Jaishankar accepted the invitation to visit Islamabad, but listed the following five points as the first and most pressing points of discussion: Cessation of cross-border terrorism by Pakistan aimed at Jammu and Kashmir; Ending incitement to violence and terrorism from Pakistan; Detaining and prosecuting international recognized Pakistani terrorist leaders who have been publicly active in exhorting and supporting violence in that state; Closing down Pakistan terrorist camps where terrorists such as Bahadur Ali continue to be trained; and lastly, denying safe havens to terrorists in Pakistan.[35] In response to these preconditions, Pakistan ignored the call to hold talks on cross-border terrorism, and once again Jaishankar was invited to Islamabad to discuss the Kashmir dispute as per the United Nations Security Council Resolutions.[36] So, the talks ended in deadlock before they had even started.

In August 2019, after the abrogation of Articles 370 and 35A of the Indian Constitution, the Kashmir conflict entered a new and deeper phase of uncertainty. In an article written in *The New York Times* in September 2019, the Indian High Commissioner to the United States, Harsh Vardhan Shringla, wrote that Indian actions regarding Article 370 had no implications outside of India. He argued that India's external boundaries had not changed, and nor had the Line of Control with Pakistan been affected.[37] Pakistan on the other hand, argued that in the abrogation of the articles, India had violated both the Simla Agreement and the United Nations Security Council Resolutions on Kashmir. It is for this reason that Pakistan has continued to refer to the implementations of the United Nations Security Council Resolutions on Kashmir. At the time of writing,

Pakistan sees no way forward with India through bilateral dialogue because as what they claim that India simply does not want to talk.

Part of the reason that India has continuously regarded the United Nations Resolutions obsolete, is that Pakistan did not comply with the preconditions set to withdraw its forces from the Valley in 1948 and in the early 1950s. Another reason is that India claims that the United Nations Resolutions were non-binding because they were passed under Chapter VI instead of Chapter VII of the UN Charter. Moreover, India has been disappointed with the United Nations' lack of intervention in Kashmir with regard to Pakistan's refusal to withdraw its troops. In 2002, the former Indian Foreign Secretary J.N. Dixit wrote:

> The manner in which the United Nations handled the Kashmir issue from 1948 onwards is a dismal story from India's point of view. Instead of taking action on the merits of the issue, on the basis of the constitutional and legal accession of Jammu and Kashmir to India, and instead of asking Pakistan to withdraw from its aggression, the United States over the years converted what should have been the issue of "invasion of Jammu and Kashmir, a part of India, by Pakistan" into "an Indo-Pakistan dispute."[38]

As a result, and although successive United Nations Secretary Generals have repeatedly offered to mediate, some have questioned the sincerity of the United Nations to resolve the dispute in Kashmir. While the debate – about whether it is the Simla Agreement or the United Nations Resolutions that should take precedence – seems to go round in circles, little emphasis is placed on the fact that the Simla Agreement holds within it the stipulation that both nations should be governed according to the United Nations Charter. Technically, this means that involvement of the United Nations is a legitimate option either way.

Some Pakistanis believe that India's continuous refusal to grant the people of Kashmir a plebiscite shows that India was never genuinely committed to implementing the United Nations Security Council Resolutions. During the period when the first UN Resolutions on Kashmir were passed, the vast majority of Muslims on the Indian side would indisputably have voted to join Pakistan. And as Pakistanis often point out, Jawaharlal Nehru, the Indian Prime Minister between 1947 and 1964, did not even attended *one* meeting of the United Nations Security Council in New York on Kashmir.[39]

Besides their views on the United Nations Security Council Resolutions, India and Pakistan also have conflicting views on the mandate of the United

Nations Military Observers Group for India and Pakistan. UNMOGIP is part of the United Nations peacekeeping mission. It is a military unit that was set up under the Karachi Agreement in 1949 to supervise the Ceasefire Line.[40] Under the Simla Agreement of 1972, the Ceasefire Line was replaced by the "Line of Control" and some of the boundaries were redrawn. India has argued that in theory, because the "Ceasefire Line" was replaced, under the Simla Agreement, by the "Line of Control", this should have made UNMOGIP obsolete.[41] However, the UN Secretary-General argued that it should remain because it has not been officially terminated by a new resolution.[42] Robert G. Wirsing's perspective, that "the Simla Agreement had nothing at all to say about the UN's peacekeeping mission," at the very least emphasizes the need for dialogue and the creation of a new, redrawn agreement.[43] In conversation in 2018, Dr. Muhammad Khan stated that the creation of the "Line of Control" was a tactical move on India's part, and that, "India changed the Ceasefire Line into the Line of Control to fall short of an international border – to appease the Indian people." In this way, the Indian people got something that was close to an international border, and Pakistan were able to defer it.[44] So as it stands in 2022, UNMOGIP still operates a small number of soldiers on both sides of the Line of Control, albeit a lesser number on the Indian side. And although the existence of UNMOGIP continues, it is viewed as holding a more symbolic, rather than active, role.

Terrorism vs. *Mujahedeen* or Freedom Fighters

In his Independence Day speech in 2016, the Indian Prime Minister Narendra Modi openly accused Pakistan of state-sponsored terrorism. He indirectly implicated Pakistan as responsible for the radicalization of Burhan Wani whose death on 8 July of that year resulted in mass protests against the Indian government, and a resultant entire shutdown of the Kashmir Valley. Early the next year, the then Pakistani Prime Minister Nawaz Sharif praised Burhan Wani as a martyr in the name of *azaadi* in Kashmir.[45] Former Pakistan President Pervez Musharraf explained this eulogization as follows:

> Pakistan does not consider them terrorists or militants but *mujahedeen* – freedom fighters – who are fighting against Indian state-sponsored terror in Kashmir by denying the people their right to self-determination as per the United Nations Security Council Resolutions. India has killed thousands of innocent civilians in the Valley. There is widespread public

support in Pakistan against the oppression in Indian Kashmir, and it has been easy to mobilize many supporters throughout Pakistan who mostly come from the religious madrassas and pick-up arms to fight against Indian oppression.[46]

However, while Pakistan sees the actions of individuals such as Burhan Wani as part of a legitimate fight against Indian oppression, it also sees talks on Kashmir with India as "the 'international obligation' of both the countries to resolve the issue." India on the other hand argues that Pakistan has "no locus standi in addressing any aspect of the situation in Jammu and Kashmir." India's position is that apart from working together to end the infiltration of Pakistani terrorists into Indian territory, Kashmir is an "internal matter." Its confidence that the world supports its view is evident in a statement given by a representative of its Ministry of External Affairs in 2016 who said, "The world is aware that Pakistan has a long history of violence and terrorism against India, as also in the broader region," before adding, the "Indian state of Jammu and Kashmir has been its particular target."[47]

This is certainly evident in Pakistan's handling of terrorists. For example, in 2011, the world witnessed the killing of the world's most wanted terrorist Osama Bin Laden who had been living with his family in Abbottabad, Pakistan. Yet in the same year in Pakistan, Zaki-ur-Rehman, commander of the Lashkar-e-Taiba, and allegedly one of the masterminds behind the Mumbai attacks on 26 November 2008, was granted bail. He was finally sentenced to five years in jail in January 2021 by a Pakistani anti-terrorism court in Lahore – but not for the Mumbai attacks – rather, in a terror financing case amidst mounting international pressure on Islamabad to bring to justice terrorists roaming free in the country.[48] Hafiz Saeed, the founder of the Lashkar-e-Taiba, received sanctuary in Lahore, Pakistan, and was only arrested a few days prior to Imran Khan's state visit to the White House in July 2019. Dawood Ibrahim, one of India's most wanted criminals linked to terrorism who may even have had ties with Osama Bin Laden, is believed to be hiding in Pakistan, a claim that Pakistan has continued to deny (although Pakistan did add him to a sanctions list in 2021). Maulana Masood Azhar, leader of Jaish-e-Mohammad (mainly active in Kashmir) has openly declared jihad against India. As many as 126 individuals and twenty-four terrorist entities, sanctioned under the UN Security Council 1267 and 1988 Committees' Lists, are associated with and thought to be living in, Pakistan.[49]

It should then come as no surprise that India continues to reiterate the need to address terrorism in Pakistan. However, some progress has been made and Pakistan has been successful in cracking down on militancy in some areas. The Haqqani network in the mountainous and lawless tribal regions of North and South Waziristan located on the Frontier with Afghanistan is one example. In recent years, security conditions have improved throughout the country, and it is likely that Pakistan has achieved far more success than the international community has been willing to acknowledge. It appears, however, that it has been unsuccessful, or unwilling, to take adequate or concrete steps against the militancy that attacks India.

South Asia's Nuclearization

While the status quo between India and Pakistan has remained, the ongoing nuclear proliferation has continued to endanger the peace and security of the Asian subcontinent. And although Kashmir has traditionally been the predominant trigger point for potential war in South Asia, the nuclearization of the region has had much wider repercussions on regional stability. This is worth further analysis especially after US President Biden said in a more recent speech that Pakistan has "nuclear weapons without any cohesion," and referred to the South Asian country as being "maybe one of the most dangerous nations in the world."[50]

Pakistan developed its nuclear weapons programme after India undertook its first nuclear test in 1974. George Perkovich, author of *India's Nuclear Bomb* (1999), wrote that international security considerations played little role in the shaping of India's nuclear policy.[51] Pakistan's acquisition of nuclear weapons, to which the western media has at times referred to as the "Islamic bomb," being the *only* Islamic state that has a nuclear bomb, has come with some concern and controversy. Moreover, the late A.Q. Khan, who is widely referred to as the father of Pakistan's nuclear bomb, has done substantial damage to Pakistan's reputation. Khan was a German-educated metallurgist. He was not only accused of spying for Pakistan by stealing the blue prints to build a bomb while he was working for URENCO in the Netherlands, it is also believed that he illegally sold nuclear technology and fissile material to Iran, North Korea, and Libya.

While the Kashmir factor has not been the *raison d'être* of India's nuclear deterrent, it has granted both India and Pakistan leverage in the conflict. In the aftermath of India's 1998 round of nuclear tests, Mr. Advani (Indian Deputy Prime Minister 2002-2004) stated that "the nuclear tests have ushered in a new era in India-Pakistan relations," and warned

Islamabad that New Delhi would respond to provocations in Kashmir in a manner "costly for Pakistan."[52]

The US-based Council on Foreign Relations has stated that the subcontinent's nuclear era has been marked by chronic crises and close calls – India and Pakistan have come close to war three or four times since 1990 and edged toward nuclear war at least twice. The disputes have grown more intense and more frequent with time.[53]

The Non-Proliferation Treaty (NPT) of 1968 and the Comprehensive Test Ban Treaty (CTBT) of 1996, to which both India and Pakistan are not signatories, have been central to understanding the genesis behind the South Asian nuclear doctrine, including its potential dangers. Naeem Salik, author of *The Genesis of South Asian Nuclear Deterrence* writes that "India refused to sign it [NPT] on the grounds of its inherent inequity and discrimination between the nuclear 'haves' and 'have nots' while Pakistan considered it a political suicide to sign it as long as India did not do so."[54] For similar reasons, Pakistan did not become a signatory to the CTBT in 1996. As a result, both South Asian nations overtly projected their nuclear arsenal in tests in the May of 1998 in a display that shocked the world. The acquisition of nuclear weapons by both India and Pakistan also highlighted geopolitical fissures that date back to the Cold War.[55] Perkovich wrote: "Despite the United States' strict non-proliferation policy, leading US State and Defence Department officials at this time were secretly considering whether to make arrangements to provide India and other friendly Asian countries with US nuclear weapons in the event of serious military threats against them from China."[56]

The strengthening of ties between India and the United States is also evident in the fact that in the aftermath of India's nuclear tests in 1974, US sanctions remained conspicuously absent. Pakistan's response meanwhile, remained faithful to the famous line by the Foreign Minister, Zulfikar Ali Bhutto, who had stated in 1965: "If India makes an atom bomb, then even if we have to feed on grass and leaves – or even if we have to starve – we shall also produce an atom bomb as we would be left with no other alternative. The answer to an atom bomb can only be an atom bomb.[57]

Pakistan began its nuclear weapons programme in 1971 after the war with India and their defeat in East Pakistan. Although Pakistan's strategic thinking is primarily focused on national survival against India, for which they believe that nuclear weapons are their only deterrent and guarantee, the following factors have also played a major role in their nuclear doctrine:

- International discrimination against Pakistan's nuclear programme because of its Muslim population.

- Ongoing discrimination against Pakistan as a Muslim state while India constantly seems to escape blame when violating global non-proliferation norms.
- Pakistan's belief that India, the US, or Israel, might use military force to stop Pakistan's nuclear program.[58]

In 1981, Israeli and Indian joint intelligence considered conducting a preventive strike – using Indian airspace – on Pakistan's nuclear facilities.[59] Indira Gandhi approved the plan, but a US warning forced both India and Israel to abandon it.[60] The disparity between the international response to India's nuclear programme on the one hand, and Pakistan's nuclear programme on the other, only seems to get further apart – as have the political motivations of both countries. The US is so keen to support India's nuclear programme that it has supported India's bid to get membership to the prestigious Nuclear Suppliers Group (NSG).[61] Pakistan considers this move a blatant attempt by the US to gain strategic benefit in South Asia.[62]

In turn, China has continued to block India's entry to the NSG – apparently in support of Pakistan. What is often not noted however, is that Beijing also opposes Pakistan's candidature on the same grounds as it opposes India's – because both India and Pakistan are non-NPT states and therefore both ineligible for NSG membership. But either way, Pakistan argues that if India were to get membership to the Nuclear Suppliers Group, then Pakistan should be granted that same status. As long as India decides to build up its military conventional capacity (with US support), Pakistan sees it has no choice but to follow suit. Islamabad vehemently dismisses the West's ongoing failure to recognize it as a serious nuclear-armed nation on the international stage. Ambassador Masood Khan, Director General of the Institute of Strategic Studies in Islamabad (ISSI) said that Pakistan is a legitimate nuclear power.[63] Zahir Kazmi, a nuclear expert and a Director at Pakistan's Strategic Plans Division, has said that instead of the discriminatory attitude toward Pakistan, "it is the nonproliferation regime that must be normalized, not Pakistan."[64] Moreover, the Pakistan Foreign Minister Bilawal Bhutto Zardari (son of the late Benazir Bhutto) considers Biden's criticism unjustified and recently emphasised to reporters that Pakistan's nuclear weapons meet "'each and every international standard' of security and safety outlined by the UN's nuclear watchdog, the International Atomic Energy Agency."[65]

Musharraf's Out-of-the-Box Solution

In 1999, in an effort to defuse the tension after the nuclear tests of May 1998, the Indian Prime Minister Atal Bihari Vajpayee extended an olive branch to Pakistan; he boarded a bus to Lahore, met with Prime Minister Nawaz Sharif and together they signed the Lahore Declaration. This declaration reiterated that both countries would resolve their differences through bilateral dialogue as outlined in the Simla Agreement. In relation to the nuclear doctrine, the declaration stated that both India and Pakistan would take steps to reduce the risk of accidental or unauthorized use of nuclear weapons. They would also discuss concepts and doctrines with a view to elaborating measures for confidence-building in the nuclear and conventional fields, aimed at the prevention of conflict.[66] However, in May 1999 when the Kargil Conflict broke out, it resulted in a struggle for power between the Pakistani Prime Minister and the Chief of Army Staff that ended in a military *coup d'état* that ousted Prime Minister Nawaz Sharif from power on 12 October 1999. Despite the widespread international condemnation of a military takeover in an era of global democratization, Sharif's successor, President Musharraf, opened doors to negotiations over Kashmir. While Musharraf was the Commander in Chief, he stated that "the Indo-Pakistan dispute is a hindrance to socioeconomic cooperation and development in South Asia …[and] without a solution to Kashmir, permanent peace in the region will remain elusive."[67]

Although drafting workable solutions was difficult at the start – especially over the idea that India wanted to make the Line of Control an international border – the two countries eventually agreed to holding a series of peace talks in 2004. Musharraf described his approach to the talks at the time as "moving along two parallel tracks: one track is confidence-building measures, and the second one is conflict resolution."[68] He summarized his approach to the talks in what he called his "four-point proposal". Although not a new idea, as it had already been discussed during Track II dialogues with the United States, the proposal listed the key points of discussion that he thought would result in the most fruitful dialogue. The four-point proposal was as follows:

- Identify the geographic regions of Kashmir that need resolution. At present the Pakistani part is divided into two regions: Northern Areas (Gilgit- Baltistan) and Azad Kashmir. The Indian part is divided into three regions: Jammu, Srinagar, and Ladakh. Are these on the table for discussion, or are there ethnic, political, and strategic considerations dictating some give and take?[69]

- Demilitarize the identified region or regions and curb all militant aspects of the struggle for freedom. This will give comfort to the Kashmiris, who have had enough of the fighting and killing on both sides.[70]
- Introduce self-governance or self-rule in the identified region or regions. Let the Kashmiris have the satisfaction of running their own affairs without having an international character and remaining short of independence.[71]
- Fourth and, most important, have a joint management mechanism with a membership consisting of Pakistanis, Indians, and Kashmiris overseeing self-governance and dealing with residual subjects common to all identified regions and those subjects that are beyond the scope of self-governance.[72]

During the interview that was conducted with Pervez Musharraf in 2018, he summarized his current views on Kashmir:

- The core of the problem is rooted in the Kashmir Valley where the vast majority of Muslims never wanted to join the Indian Union. Moreover, during the partition it would have been logical for Kashmir to accede to Pakistan instead of India. Take, for instance, the geographic location. The fastest road from Srinagar to New Delhi does not go through India, but goes via Muzaffarabad, Islamabad, and Lahore. India's denial in granting a plebiscite has created long-time problems for us.[73]
- Today, as a result, the Kashmir Valley is heavily militarized. The people of Kashmir have been fed up with such a large military presence. Innocent Kashmiris are being killed at random, and nobody has been put on trial for their deaths. Under the leadership of Narendra Modi, the situation has gone from bad to worse. India and Pakistan need to demilitarize the Line of Control, and send its soldiers back to the garrisons. The Indian Army also needs to vacate the cities in Kashmir. This will give Kashmiris some breathing space.[74]
- I [Pervez Musharraf] met with Omar Abdullah, former Chief Minister of Kashmir, in Manchester. He agreed to my points and to self-governance of Kashmir. He reiterated, however, that two elements are extremely important for peace to prevail, which is firstly the establishment of an independent supreme court, and also an independent election committee. These two institutions are essential if India wants peace in Kashmir.[75]

- The most difficult part is the Line of Control. India would agree to change this into an international border but what have we, Pakistan, been fighting for? We cannot just change the Line of Control into a hard border. In negotiations, you have to give something, and take something, and there should also be a double benefit in any resolution that can be sold to our peoples to our advantage. If we open border crossings along the Line of Control, we can say that we have eradicated the border to allow cross-border travel, and India can say that the Line of Control has been made a permanent border.[76]

Moreover, he emphasized the importance of demilitarization, "we need to keep the demilitarization for fifteen years, and after that we revisit the situation again, and see if we should make any amendments or continue on the same path. Peace building requires a long period of time. This does not just happen overnight.[77]

Musharraf emphasised that during his tenure as president (2001-2008), the Indian Prime Minister Manmohan Singh had been very flexible in his negotiations with him, and had facilitated his meeting with the leaders of the All Parties Hurriyat Conference both in the High Commission of Pakistan in New Delhi and by giving permission to travel to Islamabad in 2005. However, agreement was not ultimately reached:

[Syed Ali Shah] Geelani [member of Jamaat-e-Islami and of Hurriyat] was the hurdle ... he disagreed to my plan. Initially Yasin Malik also opposed the idea, as you know, he favours the creation of an independent nation. But I told Yasin that independence is no option, and we need to join hands to work for peace in Kashmir. He agreed, and over the years we have become very close.[78]

Speaking with a lot of respect for both Indian Prime Ministers – A.B. Vajpayee and Manmohan Singh – Pervez Musharraf has regrets that although an agreement was drafted and the signing ceremony had already been planned when he met with Mr. Vajpayee for the first time in 2001, in the end no official agreement was ever signed between the two nations. Apparently Hindu-nationalist hardliners such as L.K. Advani and other Indian ministers who opposed Pakistan, had opposed the signing. Later on however, Advani and President Musharraf came to reach greater understanding. Musharraf considers both of the Indian Prime Ministers who he worked with during his time as president (Vajpayee and Singh) as "men of peace" who were "committed to a Kashmiri resolution." And he lamented that today, the issue seems to have moved further away from the dialogue that had occurred during the noughties. He said:

> Today, [interview held on 27 April 2018] a lack of sincerity and a lack of flexibility has caused hurdles to move ahead in the peace process. Moreover, Pakistan's geostrategic position in the world is very important which also leads to friction between India and Pakistan with Kashmir in the background, especially with today's China-Pakistan Economic Corridor.[79]

India has strategic concerns about the China Pakistan Economic Corridor because it will grant China access to the markets of the world and to the navigation of the Indian Ocean, as well as give it easier access to the energy and natural resources of the Middle East and Africa. Nevertheless, Musharraf believes that CPEC will ultimately be of tremendous benefit to the whole region. He recognizes however, that in the meantime, the tensions around geo-political alliances between Pakistan and China, and India and the United States will impact on finding resolution in Kashmir: "There is friction in the region between different nations competing for power and interests where geo-economics plays a leading role. This consequently, also impacts Kashmir."[80]

Regional Conflicts and Dynamics

On the regional level, the conflict between India and Pakistan has also extended into neighbouring Afghanistan which is considered Pakistan's strategic backyard, and where both India and Pakistan are competing for influence. Both Pakistani military and intellectuals talk of "Pakistan's strategic depth," which refers to Pakistani policies in Afghanistan that aim to counter the perceived threat from India. Pakistani leadership has repeatedly said it has hard evidence that India has been using Afghanistan to encircle Pakistan on both its eastern and western borders with the aim of weakening Pakistan. They claim that there are Indian consulates located in Afghanistan, close to the border of Pakistan in the cities of Jalalabad and Kandahar, which Pakistan alleges are being used to create problems in Pakistan. However, these consulates were closed after the Taliban takeover of Kabul on 15 August 2021.

Traditionally, Afghanistan and India are united in their opposition to Pakistan, but with India having US backing this complicates things further.[81] Afghanistan was the only country in the world to vote against

Pakistan's admission to the United Nations in 1947. After the Taliban took over and declared the establishment of the Islamic Emirate of Afghanistan in 2021, however, the regional geopolitical landscape has been altered. Pakistan has supported the Taliban in Afghanistan. It cannot afford to have hostile neighbours on both its eastern and western borders. The roots of the Taliban date back to the Cold War and the Soviet-Afghan War (1979-1989) when the United States, together with Saudi Arabia and Pakistan under then Pakistan President Zia-ul-Haq, trained, armed, and funded the *mujahedeen* to defeat the Red Army during the Cold War.

India, on the other hand, has traditionally maintained close relations with the Taliban's antagonists – the non-Pashtun tribes known as the Northern Alliance, which consists of Tajiks, Uzbeks and Hazaras, the last a Shia minority. These tribes are living in the northern belt of Afghanistan. In addition to these links with northern Afghanistan, India also has easy access, via Afghanistan and Iran, to the volatile Baloch region that lies in southwestern Pakistan. Balochistan, of which Quetta is the capital, is a historical region that is now divided between Iran, Afghanistan and Pakistan (although its largest portion lies in Pakistan). It has been prone to social and political unrest and insurgents have been fighting against the Pakistani state there for decades. Traditionally, its tribal leadership aligned itself with India and they favoured accession to India during the partition in 1947 but there are also elements within Balochistan that aspire to create an independent nation.

In 2016, an Indian naval officer, Kulbhushan Jadhav, alias Hussain Mubarak Patel, was arrested in Quetta, and admitted that the Research and Analysis Wing (of India) had indeed been actively engaged in Balochistan to destabilize Pakistan. A Pakistani military court accused him of spying and sentenced him to death in 2017. India countered by claiming that the confession was obtained under duress and filed a case, with the International Court of Justice, to block the execution in 2019. Both Pakistan and India have accused each other of spying and espionage. It is widely asserted that Indian intelligence have also spearheaded movements in Karachi, where the Muttahida Quami Movement (MQM), one of the leading political parties in Pakistan's Sindh province, have been involved in political violence. The majority of members in the MQM are *Muhajirs* who migrated to Pakistan from India during the partition. Moreover, Pakistani authorities have asserted that India has actively engaged in terrorist attacks not only in Karachi but throughout the country. In 2018, Maleeha Lodhi, then Pakistan's Permanent Representative to the United Nations in New York, strongly condemned India's covert activities in Pakistan during a Security Council meeting. Referring to India's state-sponsored terrorism against Pakistan she said, "our capture of an Indian spy has amply demonstrated and proved beyond any shadow of doubt."[82]

In Pakistan, many are frustrated that the Pakistani state is continuously accused of state-sponsored terrorism while India seems to evade criticism on the international stage. It is widely believed, as Pervez Musharraf has said, that "India does not want to annex Pakistan but they want to split the country into different pieces."[83] With this in mind, some doubt India's sincerity around its insistence on wanting to resolve Kashmir without outside interference (that is, bilaterally as per the Simla Agreement); why, when India is so against outside interference, did they bring the case of Kulbhushan Jadhav to the International Court of Justice in The Hague? The accusation by some Pakistani intellectuals is that India only agrees to third-party mediation as long as it serves India's national interests. And sure enough, although both India and Pakistan claimed victory after the Kulbhushan Jadhav case, Pakistan's original ruling was blocked when the court ruled that, "the Islamic Republic of Pakistan must take all measures at its disposal to ensure that Mr. Kulbushan Sudhir Jadhav, of Indian nationality, is not executed pending a final judgment of the court in the Jadhav case."[84] At the end of 2022, Kulbhushan Jadhav is still on death row in Pakistan.

Bilateral Disputes over Water Resources and Boundaries

Another dispute of a different kind between India and Pakistan, is the dispute over access to water. The Indus River flows from various tributaries that begin in Himalayan springs and run through Ladakh, Jammu and Kashmir, Himachal Pradesh, and Punjab, before flowing through Pakistan and into the Arabian Sea near Karachi. The Indus Water Treaty was signed in 1960 after nine years of negotiations between India and Pakistan with the help of the World Bank, which is also a signatory.[85] Seen as one of the most successful international treaties, it has survived frequent tensions, including conflict, and has provided a framework for irrigation and hydropower development for more than half a century.[86] Both countries, which heavily depend on these river flows, have implemented the treaty relatively peacefully despite India having claimed that the deal is unfair. During the 2016 political unrest and uprising in the Kashmir Valley, India threatened Pakistan with the revocation of the Treaty – a move that would have had a serious and negative impact on Pakistan. There have also been various disputes around India's building of hydro plants – for example

Azaadi, Freedom and Change in Kashmir

around the Wullar Barrage (Pakistan's terminology) or the Tulbal Project (India's terminology). This is a dispute over a proposed dam on the Jhelum River in Kashmir. Pakistan has claimed that the dam is a violation of the Indus Water Treaty, they also charge India of having geo-strategic motivations in the building of the dam because it would enable India to control the flow of the river in times of conflict. India, on the other hand, claims that the dam is being built to enable the navigation of the rivers in the summer for the easier transportation of goods and people. Either way, it is believed that any withdrawal of the Indus Water Treaty would alter the dynamics over Kashmir and may trigger "water wars".[87]

Boundary disputes are also still an issue. To this day, the boundaries around the Siachen Glacier have still not been formally demarcated. And, the Sir Creek Maritime Boundary – between Pakistan's eastern province of Sindh, and Gujarat on India's west coast – has also remained unresolved. This dispute has meant that fishing agreements have also remained absent which has occasionally led to the arrest of fishermen on both sides. Pervez Musharraf has expressed frustration that these disputes remain needlessly unresolved. In conversation in 2018 he said, "the deal could have been signed yesterday. The Indian and Pakistani navies have demarcated the disputed areas both on the land and extending into the sea. The same counts for the demarcation of Siachen. Everything is in place. I told Manmohan Singh let us draw a line in between.[88]

CHAPTER 7

TRANSITIONAL JUSTICE: TWO CASE STUDIES

Independence for Timor-Leste

During Indonesia's occupation of Timor-Leste, the border between the then East Timor and Indonesia was a flashpoint of military incursions. From 1975 to 1999, Indonesian security forces killed tens of thousands of Timorese, while others died in the dense forests from starvation or illness. For almost a quarter of a century, twenty-five per cent of the population died which calculates to an estimated 250,000 Timorese, the vast majority of whom were civilians. Women and children who had fled to the forests were left to fend for themselves with no food, shelter and sometimes without basic clothing. When the Timorese wanted to travel outside the occupied territory, they needed a special permit, or *surat jalan*, issued by the Indonesian authorities.

In 1999, after years of international pressure, the international community brokered a referendum sponsored by the United Nations. The Timorese overwhelmingly, by a majority of 78.5 per cent, voted for independence. In retaliation, the Indonesia-friendly militia set the entire country systemically on fire in the days and weeks that followed. This violence and destruction, supported by the Indonesian Army, forced some 250,000 people to flee their homes.[1] In 1999 alone, an estimated 1400 political murders were committed.[2] Tens of thousands of East Timorese were forced to flee over the border into Indonesia and settle in refugee camps.

In an effort to bring back stability, United Nations peacekeeping forces arrived in Timor-Leste in 1999 and stayed there until 2006. In 2006, however, an internal crisis erupted which cost at least thirty-two deaths and led to approximately 150,000 people being driven from their homes.[3] On 11 February 2008, rebels attempted to assassinate both José Ramos-Horta and Xanana Gusmão, the founding fathers of today's independent Timor-Leste. Ramos-Horta was seriously injured when he was shot in front of his home – after which he was air lifted to Darwin in Australia where he received medical treatment. Gusmão narrowly escaped assassination and remained unharmed. Speaking about Ramos-Horta's assassination attempt, his brother Arsenio said, "My brother is a very forgiving person," and this attribute in Ramos-Horta undoubtedly made a huge contribution to the restoration of peace in Timor-Leste.

More than four decades after the conflict first erupted in 1975, the once volatile border is now safe, Timor-Leste is fragile but free, and bilateral relations between Timor-Leste and Indonesia have become an exemplar of peace resolution for conflict-ridden and post-conflict regions across the world. Very few could have foreseen that after such severe military oppression in Timor-Leste, that the leaders of these two nations would come to reconcile.

While visiting Timor-Leste in 2015, Arsenio and I met with two Indonesian soldiers after they had casually walked into Timor-Leste at *Batu Gede*, the border post with West Timor, Indonesia. When Arsenio told the soldiers about my project to showcase Timor-Leste's roadmap to peace and reconciliation as a case study in a book on Kashmir, they were keen that I should not forget to "write down in your book that today, the Timor-Leste and Indonesian border is one of the safest in post-conflict regions."[4] Today, anyone can freely cross the border between Indonesia and Timor-Leste without any hurdles, and families who live on both sides of the border can easily visit each other, even if they do not always have valid travel documents. When someone has passed away or gets married on one side of the border, friends and relatives are able to cross easily and are facilitated by the immigration authorities. It was with a real sense of pride that the soldiers we met said, "Indonesia and Timor-Leste are now at peace with each other, the two are friends, and we will remain friends."[5]

In conversation with the Nobel Peace Laureate and former president of Timor-Leste Dr. José Ramos-Horta, in 2015 (he is again president of Timor-Leste at time of publication), he shed light on how this reconciliation was achieved:

Right after the UN-sponsored referendum in August 1999 violence broke out in Timor-Leste. Xanana Gusmão and I travelled to Indonesia in October that year, one month after the eruption of violence. We met with the military leaders, and with President Gus Dur, and a sustained process of dialogue began that led to Indonesia's full cooperation with us and the United Nations in the transition period from 1999-2002. This culminated in President Megawati's attendance of the independence celebrations in May 2002. A strong commitment was made by leaders on both sides in starting the process of reconciliation; but this was made easier by twenty-four years of a firm and consistent policy of never demonizing the people of Indonesia and Islam. The word "enemy" does not exist in our vocabulary.[6]

It is widely acknowledged that another crucial factor in reconciliation was the respectful relationship that was cultivated between the commander of the guerrilla forces in Timor-Leste, Xanana Gusmão, and the Commander of the Indonesian Armed Forces, Try Sutrisno. In 2018, Try Sutrisno spoke of his respect for Gusmão, "I always treated Xanana Gusmão, the leader of the guerrillas, with the utmost respect. After my first meeting with him upon his arrest, it did not take long for me to conclude that Xanana was a brave man, a smart man, and a gentleman."[7] This respect between the two men was to have far-reaching positive implications for the people of Timor-Leste and the political relations between the two nations.

South Africa 1948-1990

Apartheid was not a new phenomenon in twentieth-century South Africa. Racial segregation in South Africa dates back to slavery and the forced labour that began with colonialism and the arrival in Table Bay of the Dutchman, Jan van Riebeeck, and three ships, on 6 April 1652.[8] In 1948, as the National Party led by the Afrikaners had come to power, apartheid became an official state mechanism and they introduced legislation to segregate the population on social, economic and political grounds. Hendrik Verwoerd, a South African professor in Sociology and Psychology, has been acknowledged as the architect of apartheid which he described as a policy of "good neighbourliness." Former South African Ambassador to the United States, Ebrahim Rasool, stated that the apartheid system effectively thought to legitimize itself scientifically and theologically through the hierarchy of creation and the assertion that the native population were indeed lesser human beings.[9]

In the 1950s, new apartheid legislation, or "Black Laws", formalized racial segregation. There were two types of legislation – security legislation and racial legislation – which were both enforced to oppress the black majority. In 1952, the African National Congress (ANC) led by Nelson Mandela, together with the South African Indian Congress, launched the Mahatma Gandhi-inspired Defiance Campaign. This was a campaign of non-violent resistance and demonstrations against the draconian laws that steadily spread throughout the country.

On 21 March 1960, the Pan Africanist Congress (PAC) organized a peaceful demonstration against the mandatory carrying of passes. Some five thousand people gathered around a police station in Sharpville (one of the black townships located just outside Johannesburg) without their passes – hence facing arrest. Without any warning, police officers opened fire, and according to official records, sixty-nine unarmed demonstrators were killed and 180 injured.

In the wake of this massacre, the days of peaceful protest came to an end, and the ANC founded its military wing, the *Umkhonto we Sizwe* or MK. In 1961, Arthur Goldreich and Harold Wolpe purchased Liliesleaf Farm located in Rivonia, Johannesburg, which became the headquarters of the underground activities of the South African Communist Party (SACP). Liliesleaf Farm also became the underground ANC and MK headquarters. On 10 July 1963, state security raided the farm, arrested its members, including Walter Sisulu, Govan Mbeki (father of Thabo Mbeki), Dennis Goldberg and others. The Rivonia trial in 1963 charged eleven members of SACP and ANC, including Nelson Mandela, with sabotage. They escaped the death penalty, but were sentenced to life imprisonment on Robben Island in Table Bay.

International efforts against apartheid in South Africa included the voluntary arms embargo imposed by the United Nations Security Council in 1963, and the banning, by the International Olympic Committee (IOC), of South Africa from participation in the Olympic Games in 1964. In 1966, the architect of apartheid, Hendrik Verwoerd, who had been elected prime minster in 1958, was assassinated in an act that shocked the regime. International pressure against apartheid intensified and in 1973, the OPEC nations imposed an oil embargo.[10]

In 1977, Steve Biko who had founded the anti-apartheid Black Conscious Movement (BCM) in the mid 1960s, died of injuries sustained in police custody. He had been stripped naked, held in chains, severely beaten and forced to stand in shackles; he died alone in a cell from a massive brain haemorrhage after a 1100 km drive from Port Elizabeth to the prison hospital in Pretoria. A year earlier, in 1976, Steve Biko and the BCM had played a major role in the Soweto Uprising that had called for the boycott of Afrikaans, the language of the oppressor, in black schools. In the aftermath of Biko's death, the United Nations Security Council passed UN Resolution 392 which condemned this barbaric act of violence perpetrated by the South African regime. In 1977, the United Nations Security Council adopted Resolution 418 to impose a mandatory arms embargo that would

Transitional Justice: Two Case Studies

be tightened by Resolution 591. In 1984, violent internal protests reached their momentum when township revolts began spreading rapidly throughout the country.

On 31 January 1985, P.W. Botha, the then president, offered Nelson Mandela a conditional release from prison on the proviso that he would denounce political violence and violent protests. But on 11 February 1985, during a political rally in Soweto, Mandela's daughter Zinzi rejected President Botha's offer, stating that her father said "your freedom and mine cannot be separated."[11] In July, Botha declared a state of emergency in thirty-six out of 260 districts and the next month, he stated that he would introduce further apartheid reforms.

In September of that year, in an effort to pressure the regime, the European Community imposed a set of very limited trade and financial sanctions on South Africa, and in October, the Commonwealth countries adopted similar measures. In the United States, the Reagan administration was opposed to South African sanctions but imposed a limited ban to head off stronger action in Congress.[12] In the fall of 1986, the second and more significant round of sanctions ensued.[13] As international sanctions against South Africa increased, the country fell further into economic and social crisis and the revolts against the oppression had no end in sight; it was becoming increasingly clear that the apartheid system was becoming unsustainable.

The promotion of a new system of government received much attention from President P.W. Botha and his colleagues during 1979-1983, but the constitutional ideas put forward by the government turned out to be so controversial that they led to a further breakdown of public order, followed by the re-imposition of a state of emergency between 1985 and 1990.[14] However, the fall of the Berlin Wall in 1989 and the disintegration of the Soviet Union played a vital contribution to the initiation of reform. It created a vacuum for the ANC which had received financial support, arms, and training, from the Soviet Union. On 2 February 1990, President F.W. de Klerk, who had been inaugurated in August 1989, delivered his famous speech in parliament in which he announced sweeping reforms that would mark the beginnings of the transition toward constitutional democracy. In May 1990, a series of talks began between the ANC, led by Nelson Mandela, and the leaders of all the South African political parties including President de Klerk and his delegates, and Joe Slovo of the South African Communist Party. The result of these talks in Cape Town was the historic document known as the "Groote Schuur Minute" which drafted a commitment towards the ending of violence on both sides and towards peace and a new beginning for South Africa.

Transitional Justice in Timor-Leste and South Africa

This chapter offers two examples of the process known as "transitional justice" – as it was practiced in Timor-Leste and in South Africa. These case studies both provide examples of successful transitions to democracy following decades of oppression. The human rights violations that occurred in both of these places, and the methods taken to address them, is a vital aspect of the transitional justice process. The reconciliation process that occurred between Indonesia and Timor-Leste is a concrete example of a mutual commitment being made by the uppermost leadership levels of two countries. In this example, instead of engaging in a journey of vengeance, these leaders were committed to looking toward the future and enabling effective dialogue – and this played a vital role in making peace possible.

South Africa provides a different example of transitional justice in which peace and stability was built after decades of apartheid (from 1948 to 1990) in a system whereby the government brutally suppressed its own people. The road to peace began between 1990 and 1994 when the country went through dramatic reforms in a process that included the drafting of a new constitution. It was during the Convention for a Democratic South Africa (CODESA) in 1991 that the vital new constitution was developed. The multi-party agreement – The National Peace Accord (NPA) – that laid out the commitment by both parties toward peace, also played a vital role in the curtailment of political violence that had been spreading. And lastly, the Truth and Reconciliation Committee (TRC), played another vital role in the peace process; it acted as a restorative justice body that provided witness to some of the most sensitive issues and human rights abuses that had affected the majority of the black and coloured population during apartheid.

It is important to emphasize that South Africa, in dealing with the perpetrators of political crimes, opted for a truth commission instead of an international tribunal. And Timor-Leste and Indonesia subsequently took inspiration from the South African model, as José Ramos-Horta explained in conversation in 2015:

> We had a national commission on truth and reconciliation based on the South Africa model. We had public hearings, undertook research, and compiled reports. Our message was consistent and we told the nation that as painful as our past was, we have to move forward and look to the future; we honour the victims, but we do not allow our past to freeze our thoughts against a better future. Political leaders, churches, and local communities have played a crucial role in rebuilding East Timorese

society and also in fostering good relations between Indonesia and Timor-Leste.[15]

Internationally however, many are of the opinion that international war tribunals are the most suitable way of bringing perpetrators of political crimes to justice. For example, in the case of Timor-Leste, the international community had been critical that the country had not been supportive of an international tribunal such as had occurred in Nuremburg or Tokyo after World War II. Notwithstanding the financial restraints in establishing such an international war tribunal, José Ramos-Horta explained the reasoning against it:

> Regardless of the crimes committed, and they were too many, Timor-Leste did not support the establishment of an ad hoc international tribunal. Such tribunals are set up to try those responsible for gross human rights violations, genocide and war crimes, typically in countries where there are no political rights and where the authorities are not willing to do so. Timor-Leste engaged in a patient and determined process of dialogue with Indonesian leaders that gradually removed the obstacles to a pro-active relationship. We have taken a pragmatic approach. We believe that one day the perpetrators will be brought to justice but Timor-Leste leaves this to Indonesia to decide. Indonesians have to decide what nation, society they want. They have to decide whether they want to uphold a society of justice or one that enjoys impunity. No one, not us, not the United Nations, or the United States, will force anything on Indonesia. We understand that Indonesia, like us, is a young and fragile democracy. If you force upon the judiciary the incarceration of powerful people, you undermine the fragile process of democratization that the country is going through. Pragmatism is not the avoidance of justice; pragmatism means understanding the difficulties that the other side (Indonesia) face, understanding their transition towards democracy, and being patient, and wise.[16]

In South Africa's case, Professor Tim Murithi, head of the Peacebuilding Interventions Programme at the Cape Town-based Institute for Justice and Reconciliation explained their reasoning as follows: "a criminal court is politicized and may not lead to reconciliation. A truth recovery process, however, is the process of a dialogue which is a vital starting point for reparation."[17] Moreover, the international criminal justice system is unable to prosecute the perpetrators of these crimes because they are protected by the political, diplomatic, and economic might of self-interested powerful countries that are not party to the Rome Statute that underpins the International Criminal Court.[18] Writing on this dilemma, the late Desmond Tutu wrote in his memoir:

> The human rights criminals are fellow citizens, living alongside everyone else, and they may be powerful and dangerous. If the army and police have been the agencies of terror, the soldiers and the cops are not going to turn overnight into paragons of respect for human rights. Their numbers and their expert management of deadly weapons remain significant facts of life.[19]

But criminal courts and trials are not only costly undertakings for respective governments, but they are also often ineffective in the search for truth, reconciliation and justice for victims of human rights abuses; the efforts of the perpetrators to escape incarceration may mean that they try to escape trial by twisting the truth or telling blatant lies which has the potential to lead to further division and violence. It also leads to the possible rejection of the acknowledgment that victims and family members are still in mourning – causing further distress to those victims.[20] It is for these reasons that South Africa opted for a Truth and Reconciliation Commission.

The examples of both Timor-Leste and South Africa can be taken as blueprints for peace building. In the same way that Timor-Leste took inspiration from the South Africa model, there are elements of these technical structures that can be used by India, Pakistan and by the Kashmiris as a roadmap to peace.

Timor-Leste: Leaving the Past Behind

In Timor-Leste, the prime message of its leadership was to leave the past behind. There were also many voices within Timor-Leste who were actively critical of the international community's preference for the establishment of an international tribunal vs. a Truth and Reconciliation Commission. When I met with the East Timorese investigative journalist, José Antonio Belo, in 2015, he said:

> The international community should remember that I can choose my friend, but I cannot choose my neighbour. Indonesia is located right next door and it is one of the largest countries in South-East Asia. We need good relations. Indonesia should establish its own justice system if they want to bring the perpetrators to justice, they can do that if they want …

Reconciliation is not about justice in a courtroom. Justice is sitting down with those who committed crimes against us. It is about knowing why friends of mine got killed. I want to hear from them why I was detained, tortured and treated so inhumanely. I want to find the remains of those Timorese heroes who were killed, I want to find the commanders who disappeared, and I want to bring back the stolen children of Timor-Leste [during Indonesia's occupation, it is said that thousands of East Timorese children were abducted by Indonesian armed forces. Until today, their whereabouts are unknown]. I found some in Jakarta. I talked to them. If those who harmed us will tell the truth, then there can be reconciliation which will benefit both sides.[21]

José Antonio Belo was actively involved in Timor's freedom struggle, and as part of this effort he connected foreign journalists to the guerrilla fighters who were hiding in the forest. One example of José Antonio's own reconciliation efforts after independence was when he sought out a member of the Indonesian Special Forces, or *Kopassus*, who had been one of his captors during the conflict. During the conflict in 1997, José Antonio was arrested and one night during his detention, a member of the *Kopassus*, named here "Arif" (his name has been changed), took him from the detention centre in the middle of the night. Arif was completely drunk. They drove out of the city for about an hour. The Indonesian soldiers had dug his grave and he was told to step inside. He stood there in his grave and was left there alone, waiting and ready to die. Some time later, Arif came back and, surprisingly, instead of pulling the trigger he pulled José Antonio out of the grave. They returned to the army vehicle and drove back to the detention centre where he was again held captive. The next day, Arif left the centre. This was the last time they met until, sometime after independence in 2003 or 2004, José Antonio sought Arif out and they met again. José Antonio asked him why he was not killed. All Arif said was, "I don't know, you're very lucky."[22] Today, José Antonio's belief in reconciliation and the search for answers remains, and he is one Timor-Leste's leading investigative journalists.

Another example of powerful reconciliation and forgiveness is that displayed by the then head of the Timor-Leste Defence Army, General Lere Anan Timur (he retired from his post in early 2022 and has since been promoted to Lt. General). He has a son who was abducted during the conflict – these children (or adults) are known as *anak dicuri*. While he was guerrilla commander during the occupation, he was living in the forest and his wife died in child birth. The Indonesian Armed Forces took the infant away and an Indonesian general adopted the child. The boy's name is Bobby. He was raised well, he grew up as a devout Muslim, and he graduated from university. His heritage was not kept secret from Bobby who returned to Timor-Leste and met his biological father, Anan Timur. Timur has made peace with the fact that his son has two fathers and tells Bobby that his actual father is the Indonesian general in Jakarta. This shows that reconciliation on the deepest personal and emotive levels is truly possible.

The younger brother of José Ramos-Horta, Arsenio Ramos-Horta, remained in Timor during, and since, the Indonesian invasion in 1975. When I visited him there, he generously gave his time to show me around. Having lived through the occupation, the memories of conflict are embedded in the landscape all around his home, "This is lake Tasi Tolu," he said, "those who were shot dead would be dumped into the lake at night. The following morning, we would recover some of the bodies. And the beach, on your right hand, was used for executions."

During occupation, Timorese guerrilla fighters were detained in the nearby Comarca Prison, in Dili. In another nearby building, which is today the Western Union building, prisoners were held and interrogated under the control of military intelligence. Arsenio was once detained there for a month. One day, as we drove past the building, I asked him what life was like in the detention centre. He seemed uninterested, "nothing special," he said, "sometimes we would stand behind the main gate and try to talk to people in the street but those who passed by would then walk faster and turn their face the other way." A few days later, however, when we drove past the building again, Arsenio sighed and remembered, "I was just waiting there, counting my days to be killed." Another landmark of torture lies in the city of Baucau; the Baucau Pousada is a pink, Mediterranean-style building built by the Portuguese and is the city's most important landmark. One of the buildings in the back of the Pousada was used as a torture centre. Anyone who was unlucky enough to be incarcerated there would be tortured there before being transferred to Dili and killed. There was no way of surviving. These are just a few examples of the bitter past that Timor-Leste is learning to leave behind.

Another East Timorese who was actively involved in Timor-Leste's peace-building process was Joel Pereira. When asked about his feelings on the conflict, on the sacrifices, and on the reconciliation, he said:

> Of course, it is hard to forget. Our personal feelings will always be there, we all remember the struggle for independence, and the sacrifices which were made by members of our families. Today, there is a young generation in Timor-Leste. We have to look forward. There is a Timor-

Leste of the past, and a Timor-Leste of the future. We all had to sacrifice to get what we want. It paid off, and we are now independent. It is not a time to complain, and instead we have to focus on economic development, on the people, and on the future of the nation.[23]

When I met with another active participant of the reconciliation process, Augusto Junior Trindade, in Dili in 2015, he made a short but powerful statement: *"Merdeka lebih besar dari pada hal-hal yang lain,"* which can be translated as "Freedom is bigger – more important – than anything else." He said that the resolution of conflict in Timor-Leste not only gave the citizens of Timor-Leste independence, but it also benefitted Indonesia: "Timor-Leste's independence helped Indonesia in the roadmap towards democracy. For more than three decades, Indonesia was ruled with an iron fist of an oppressive regime. Freedom in Timor-Leste opened doors for reforms and contributed to the development of a variety of sectors, including the military in Indonesia.[24]

Two decades after the independence vote in 1999, bilateral relations between Indonesia and Timor-Leste have continued to improve; Indonesia has boosted investment in Timor-Leste, and the former Timor-Leste prime minister, Rui Maria de Araujo, stated that the relationship is not only positive at the government-to-government and business-to-business levels, but that the people-to-people interaction is also strong.[25] And at its deepest levels, the roots that enabled the turning point toward solid bilateral relations can be seen to lie in Xanana Gusmão's relations with Indonesia following his capture by the Indonesian Armed Forces in 1992.

More recently, moreover, when José Ramos-Horta was re-elected President of Timor-Leste (in April 2022), and then made his first foreign state visit to Indonesia in July 2022, President Joko Widodo and other senior government officials warmly welcomed him. The following month, José Ramos-Horta awarded the Medal of Merit or "Ordem de Timor Leste" to both the then Commander of the Indonesian Armed Forces General Andika Perkasa and the former chief of Indonesia's State Intelligence Agency which is more commonly known by its acronym BIN, A.M. Hendropriyono. The "Ordem de Timor Leste" is the highest medal that is awarded to both civilians and military in contribution to Timor-Leste's peace and stability. Hendropriyono was the head of the BIN from 2001-2004 and his tremendous efforts contributed to peaceful relations between Indonesia and Timor-Leste in the aftermath of the independence vote in 1999.

Turning point in Timor-Leste-Indonesia Relations

When Gusmão was a rebel leader in Timor-Leste, he was arrested by the Indonesian Armed Forces while Try Sutrisno was their Commander. Remarkably, the relationship between the two commanders turned to friendship after East Timor became an independent nation in 1999 – and this is considered the turning point that enabled reconciliation. While Indonesia had been defeated by the loss of East Timor which it had considered an integral part of the Republic, the newly-created Timor-Leste, on the other hand, had to come to terms with the oppression and human rights violations that had taken place for more than two decades.

The "Hearts and Minds" Strategy

When I met with the former Indonesian Vice President and Commander of the Armed Forces, Try Sutrisno, in 2018, he disputed the idea that Indonesia had occupied or annexed East Timor in its efforts to expand territory on 7 December 1975. After Portugal started with its decolonization process following the Carnation Revolution in Lisbon in 1974, clashes broke out in East Timor between the right- and left-wing political parties. On 28 November 1975, the left-wing Revolutionary Front for an Independent East Timor (FRETILIN) unilaterally declared Portuguese Timor independent. This move was not recognized by Portugal, Indonesia, or Australia, and the next day, the four other East Timorese political parties – the Timorese Democratic Union (UDT), the Timorese Popular Democratic Association (APODETI), the Association of Timorese Heroes (KOTA), and Trabalhista – issued their *Proclamation of Integration.* The proclamation accused FRETILIN of obstructing a peaceful solution, and asked the Indonesian government and people to integrate East Timor into Indonesia. This proclamation subsequently became known as the *Balibo Declaration* and Try Sutrisno emphasised that there is a lot of controversy around it.[26] At the time, the UDT claimed to be the most popular party in East Timor.[27]

After Timor's integration into Indonesia in 1975, which occurred with the support of Europe, the United States and Australia, one of Indonesia's foremost strategies was the so-called "hearts and minds" strategy. This sought to win over the approval and acceptance of the Timorese through development such as investments in infrastructure and education. In this way, the Indonesian government sought to bring peace and security back to the region at a time when FRETILIN did not see a reason to lay down its arms and submit to Indonesia's governance. In the efforts of Indonesia to fully integrate the province and its people into the Republic, the armed forces developed a four-point strategy. When I met with him, Try Sutrisno laid out the strategy as follows:

- *Intelligence*: gain a better understanding of the region by spending time with the people and getting to know their character, culture, traditions, language, food and habits – in order to better be able to win hearts and minds.
- *Socio-political*: win over the hearts of the people through dialogue and through development; build infrastructures such as good roads in order to provide better access to towns and villages, and build seaports, airports, schools, churches, clinics and hospitals, and sport facilities, etc.
- *Territorial*: facilitate people-to-people contact through the support of culture, religion, education, sports and entertainment. In short, bring progress and uplift the living conditions of the people.
- *Use of arms*: use arms only if talks and negotiations fail.[28]

Sutrisno then further elaborated on the socio-political aspect of the strategy:

Indonesia's strategy in East Timor was to win over the hearts and minds of the people just like in other parts of Indonesia and in this, the Indonesian Armed Forces and the government took an objective approach. Firstly, a dialogue had to start with the people, who ethnically were not very different from other regions of the Indonesian eastern islands. In this way, Indonesia attempted to build people-to-people contact. East Timor had been left largely underdeveloped during Portuguese colonization and therefore the Indonesian government put a priority on development; they built schools, markets, churches and infrastructure such as a road that circled the whole island.[29]

In fact, under Try Sutrisno, the Indonesian Armed Forces (despite the limited budget) constructed the largest church, the *Dili Cathedral* in the capital. Education was important to the government of Indonesia and they relocated many Indonesian teachers to the region. Bahasa Indonesia became the official language. The Indonesian government provided education until senior high school, after which Timorese students were granted the opportunity to enrol in Indonesian universities throughout the country. They attended all the leading universities in Bandung, Jakarta, and Yogyakarta. However, there was some discrimination against the Timorese students who complained that they were bullied while some were even expelled from the universities based on their political convictions.

Timorese coffee remains one of the world's most prized, and it was the Portuguese who originally introduced it to the region. With decolonization in 1975, a lot of destruction occurred because many planters were forced to flee when the clashes broke out – but Indonesia helped the Timorese to rebuild and expand these coffee plantations. Try Sutrisno was proud of the Indonesian army's efforts in the area of agriculture, "the Indonesian Armed Forces were not only about keeping the peace and security in East Timor," he said, "the soldiers were also ordered to teach the people how to irrigate the land, how to make [rice] paddy fields, and how to grow vegetables."

East Timor is, after all, by and large agrarian. Especially in the mid-1970s, Indonesia as a whole was still very poor, and the eastern islands of the country were, and still are today, largely underdeveloped. Nevertheless, the Indonesian government felt a strong commitment to building and developing East Timor and it was subsequently transformed into one of the more prosperous provinces. It has been widely asserted that the Indonesian government invested more in East Timor than in any of its other provinces outside the main island of Java. The rapid development of Indonesia's urban areas only began in the early 1990s, but before this, during the worst years of the conflict in the late 1970s and early 1980s, many in East Timor died in the violence and from starvation. Some western scholars have asserted that although the Indonesian authorities were aware of the likelihood of upcoming famine, they made no efforts to provide food to the people. An estimated thirty per cent of East Timor's population died during the war. Most of the deaths occurred between 1977 and 1979.[30] During Try Sutrisno's tenure as commander of Indonesia's armed forces from 1988-1993, this changed, and he ordered his soldiers to share their rice and help the people to improve their overall livelihoods. When I met with him in 2018, it was clear that apart from his role as commander of the army, he had taken his responsibility to fulfil the requirements of the "hearts and minds" strategy very seriously.

Santa Cruz Massacre

However, the conduct of Indonesia's armed forces in East Timor attracted international condemnation when, on 12 November 1991, the Santa Cruz massacre occurred in the capital, Dili. It is just one example of the bloodshed that took place under Indonesia's rule since 1975, but it was by far the bloodiest massacre in the history of the conflict and is to this day commemorated in Timor-Leste. When I asked Try Sutrisno what happened, he said that the protestors had become violent in order to exploit the demonstrations to garner international support; whether this had been a deliberate ploy by the protestors or not, the violence of the Indonesian soldiers ensured that international attention was indeed achieved. The reason for the protest on that day in Dili was the cancellation of a visit to East Timor of a delegation of Portuguese Members of Parliament and a group of foreign journalists. The visit was cancelled by the Portuguese government because Indonesia had objected to the inclusion in the delegation of Jill Jolliffe – an Australian journalist and supporter of the left wing FRETILIN independence movement. Throughout the years, many similar visits and foreign inspections by government and non-government institutions, and organizations such as the United Nations, took place in East Timor. Try Sutrisno outlined his approach to keeping peace within the country as follows:

> It was my duty to keep the peace, and although I did not stop people from demonstrating to express their grievances against the Indonesian state, I also always insisted that those demonstrations should be conducted in an orderly manner. To keep the peace in East Timor or elsewhere in the country, there are some basic codes of conduct to which demonstrators should adhere. If these are being violated, then violence can easily break out resulting in the injury and killing of both civilians and military, as happened in Santa Cruz.[31]

An Indonesian gentleman I spoke with (who wished to remain anonymous), who had regularly visited East Timor during this time, had left Dili the day prior to the Santa Cruz massacre. He said in one of our many informal discussions on the conflict that, "the military commander who was assigned to ensure that the demonstration was conducted in a peaceful and orderly manner was provoked and stabbed on that day, sparking an outburst of anger among his fellow officers and subordinates." He insisted that until then, the fighting had mostly been limited to the forests and remote areas of the island, and that it was very unusual for a soldier to be attacked in the city. When the attack occurred, it provoked a spontaneous response from the soldiers out of solidarity for their commander which did not take long to spiral out of control.

"I gave no order to shoot at the demonstrators," Try Sutrisno said firmly during our interview. But he also pointed out that the Indonesian military had set out a clear set of rules, and that on the day, the protestors were reminded a number of times to abide by these rules and to protest in an orderly manner. He said, "my subordinates gave a number of warnings to the protestors to keep the demonstration in order, but they [the protestors] refused to listen." He made a distinction between what he sees as human rights violations, versus, procedures of the armed forces, and it is in this light that he said, "please do not compare Santa Cruz to the systematic killings that were instigated by Serbia, for instance."[32] The definition of violation of human rights within the military doctrine is based on the following three criteria: 1) Did the human rights violations take place by superior order? 2) Were the human rights abuses systematic killings? 3) Did the military specifically target the victims?[33]

The Gusmão-Sutrisno Nexus

Whether the horrific events in Santa Cruz are termed human rights violations or not, the killing of so many civilians is a shocking and sad reminder of the dangers of military rule, and is undoubtedly a controversial episode in General Try Sutrisno's military leadership. However, his subsequent reconciliation with the Timorese guerrilla leader Xanana Gusmão made an undeniably positive contribution towards future peace in the region. The treatment of prisoners in armed conflict is a vital factor in the subsequent peace-building process, and the Gusmão-Sutrisno nexus played a vital role in the shaping of the future of Timor-Leste and Indonesia relations.

During the conflict, it was common for guerrilla fighters to come down to the cities, and Gusmão was arrested during one of his visits to Dili, in 1992. At the time, Try Sutrisno was in Jakarta and when he was informed of the arrest, he flew to Dili where he and Xanana met for the first time. When remembering this time, he said, "I thought, being the chief of the guerrilla forces, that he was a dangerous man." But Try Sutrisno believed in talking with his adversary on the level of equality and respect – and it is this approach that was to be of great significance to the future relationship between the two sides. For Xanana Gusmão, this first encounter with the Chief of the Indonesian Armed Forces would become an important turning point in his life about which he still speaks publicly today.[34] When talking about this encounter, Xanana praises Try Sutrisno, often giving the example of Try's unchaining of him as a moment of great significance. "When I met Pak Try," Xanana has said, "he unchained me. Human rights were something important to him."

In turn, Try Sutrisno remembers Xanana as a gentleman and describes the encounter, and its aftermath, as follows:

I decided to treat Xanana with the utmost respect. Firstly, I called the army doctor. Conditions as a guerrilla fighter in the forest were poor, there were many diseases, and food was also scarce. Xanana as well, was in a rather poor physical condition as we met, so I ordered the doctor to have a thorough medical check and give him the appropriate treatment so he would fully recuperate. I then called my logistics officer, and ordered him to buy a shirt, trousers, jacket, hat, and shoes. My troops were protesting and complaining that he was Indonesia's most wanted enemy who had been hiding in the forest, and they did not understand why he should be given proper clothes. They said we are your soldiers but you never buy any clothes for us ... I then ordered him food, and told Xanana to eat something, as he was hungry, and then have a rest. The following day we would fly together to Jakarta where he would be brought to justice according to the Indonesian law. In Jakarta, I did not put him in jail and instead ordered him to be put under house arrest and be treated well. My troops would have a daily food allowance of 25,000 Rupiah per day, but I ordered to give Xanana food four times that amount. Only after the trial in 1993 – he received life imprisonment which was later commuted to twenty years – was he transferred to jail where he remained until 1999. After East Timor became independent and he became the country's first President in 2002, Xanana would proudly state to diplomats "the past is the past, and the future is our friendship with Indonesia." This would be the start of the reconciliation between Indonesia and Timor-Leste which was based on the sincere desire on the part of both nations to building peaceful relations – not only with their nearest neighbour but also with the entire South-East Asian region. Xanana continued to hold warm feelings towards Indonesia.[35]

Lasting Regional Peace

Ultimately, peace and reconciliation are universally desired, as are justice and development. This is outlined in the preamble to the constitution of the Republic of Indonesia that commits to, for example, improving public welfare, education, and freedom.[36] After Timor-Leste's independence, Indonesia has not only been committed to building peace with its neighbour, but it has also been committed to contributing to peace in the world at large by sending United Nations peacekeeping missions to conflict areas such as Cambodia, Vietnam, Lebanon – for which it has received several awards. Indonesia is also a member of the Association of Southeast

Asian Nations (ASEAN). ASEAN, to which Timor-Leste became a member "in principle" in 2022, promotes regional peace, stability and development through economic, political and military cooperation. When ASEAN was established in Bangkok in 1967, Indonesia, under President Suharto, was one its founding fathers. Indonesia, Malaysia, the Philippines, Singapore, and Thailand signed the ASEAN declaration which included the commitment to promoting "… regional peace and stability through abiding respect for justice and the rule of law in the relationship among countries of the region and adherence to the principles of the United Nations Charter …"[37]

And so, boosting ties with its nearest easterly neighbour has formed part of the Indonesian Government's wider commitments to economic development and peace in Southeast Asia as a whole. In recent years, bilateral relations have continued to strengthen and the two nations are committed to living peacefully side by side. The bitter past of oppression and human rights abuses may not be forgotten, but the message remains clear, the past is the past, and the future is friendship. Friendship and mutual respect are essential components in the reconstruction of the broken pieces after conflict, and in the building of strong and stable nations. The economic development of the country, and the revival of culture and education, cannot occur in the absence of a peaceful environment. In this regard, Indonesia (and now in the future, Timor-Leste) has benefitted from its membership of the ASEAN; and this type of cooperation between nations is another point on which Kashmir can draw inspiration.

Parallels with Kashmir

The Kashmiris have been the victims of what seems like a never-ending conflict during the past seven decades. Similar issues such as those in South Africa and Timor-Leste have been experienced by its people; human rights abuses such as state oppression, torture, incarceration and disappearances have been commonplace, and the basic survival of individuals has been put to the test. But if the people of Kashmir, or any other conflict zone, are to heal from the past – however horrific that past has been – they will need to take a forward-looking approach as the people of Timor-Leste have succeeded in doing. José Ramos-Horta emphasised this point when I spoke with him in 2015:

Be it India, Pakistan, Korea, China or Japan, they can all draw lessons from the Timor-Leste-Indonesia reconciliation. It is important to understand that there can be normalization of relations but only when there is strong mutual political will power. It is entirely in the hands of top leaders to get over issues of mutual dislike and to have normal friendly relations like cousins and friendly neighbours. Both India and Pakistan have weak leaders. India did not have any strong leadership after Mahatma Gandhi and Nehru. Likewise, ongoing instability, coups and counter coups, and internal problems in Pakistan have hampered peace efforts. In some respects, Pakistani leaders are keeping the Kashmir conflict alive as this serves Pakistan well domestically. India is a country of more than one billion people; it is an imperfect democracy but it is in a far stronger position than Pakistan. Unfortunately, its leadership has failed to address Kashmir. In this process, Kashmiris have suffered from the lack of visionary leadership of both India and Pakistan.[38]

Today in Timor-Leste, a new generation has grown up that has not been affected by the conflict. Although Timor-Leste's youth are being educated about the past and the conflict, this has not prevented or destroyed a positive outlook towards their neighbours in Indonesia. When I travelled to Timor-Leste in November 2017, I met a young Indonesian boy of about ten years old who was proud to be able to communicate with me in Bahasa Indonesia. When I asked him where he learned the language (as Bahasa Indonesia is no longer an official language in Timor-Leste and is no longer taught in the classrooms), he proudly answered *"belajar dari nonton TV"* (I learned it from watching television). It is this kind of encouragement of the local Timorese languages, alongside an openness to the cultures and languages of their neighbours, that Ramos-Horta has sought to encourage. He places great emphasis on the importance of a forward-looking and positive attitude as the primary requirement in building peace. He gives the following suggestions and recommendations for the Indian and Pakistani leadership:

If Indonesia and Timor-Leste had a similar attitude toward each other as India and Pakistan have had in the last decades, we would be at war with each other – we would have a violent border and the country would be rocked with internal instability. Wisdom, patience, and strong leadership are required to move towards a peaceful resolution. Kashmir could have had peace and stability now if there had been strong leadership. Kashmir could by now be either independent or jointly managed by the two neighbours – either way, both countries could have come together to guarantee the security of Kashmir.[39]

However, Ramos-Horta also emphasised the devastating role that the internal violence within Kashmir has played in the worsening and prolonging of Kashmir's problems:

> A failure of both India and Pakistan has been a tragedy for the Kashmiris. Having said this, there is no united Kashmiri voice that effectively advocates for the rights of the Kashmiris. The people of Kashmir should be smart and engage themselves. They should unite the Kashmiris on both sides of the Line of Control, and include different faiths as well. This way, they can create their own peaceful communities. If people choose to engage in violence, however, there will be repercussions. Kashmiris are the ones who should come up with a roadmap shared by Kashmiris on both sides of the Line of Control. They should make peaceful arrangements with the Hindus, the Muslims, the Buddhists. They are all Kashmiris. Kashmiris should attempt to reach out to each other to create peaceful and tolerant communities. If they work together, one day their actions will be successful because the Kashmiris have already done so much. India and Pakistan will then listen to the people of Kashmir. Unfortunately, these efforts are hampered by religious extremism, violence, and conflict. If individuals are weak and grudge-bearing, and have access to weapons, this can be of no advantage in any peace process. In other words, I would like to say, Kashmiris lay down your weapons, unite, and engage in a roadmap towards peace. Learn from Mahatma Gandhi's belief in change through peaceful means; implementing Gandhi's philosophy of non-violence will be a first step towards a peaceful resolution of the conflict.[40]

The example of Timor-Leste and the reconciliation not only of the political leaderships but also of military leaders – as seen in the peace-making that occurred between Try Sutrisno and Xanana Gusmão – shows that resolution is possible despite complicated histories of military oppression, injustice and gross human rights abuses. The achievement of peace in Timor-Leste provides an example of the success of using a humane approach towards adversaries and of a forgiving and forward-looking focus on positive outcomes for the people. It provides a potentially game-changing blueprint for India and Pakistan in their approach to Kashmir – provided that both nations actually want peace and reconciliation. In the "hearts and minds" strategy, the use of arms occurs only as a last resort in the event that democratic means, talks and negotiations completely fail. As seen in the deployment of the military in the Kashmir Valley – especially after the abrogation of Articles 370 and 35A – Kashmiris endured military rule without being given the chance to engage in any dialogue. Instead, the Indian government sent thousands of additional troops to the Valley in the anticipation that their upcoming ruling would be opposed. Such unilateral decisions can only add fuel to any already burning fire and serve to increase anger in the vast majority of the people who quite possibly had never wanted to be part of the Indian state.

However, demonstrations that spiral into violence – such as those that have occurred in Kashmir – are futile and only prolong the road to peace. The military, police and other security forces have to operate under a certain set of principles and have to take care of the wellbeing of their colleagues, superiors and subordinates. The dilemma faced in these circumstances is illustrated in the example of Indian Major Leetul Gogoi who went to extreme lengths during violent protests around a polling station in Jammu and Kashmir in 2017; in an effort to rescue staff who were inside the station that was being attacked by stone-pelters and petrol bombs, it occurred to Gogoi that if he tied one of the protestors to the front of his vehicle, the man would act as a human shield protecting his subordinates who were inside the vehicle. The Kashmiri shawl maker, Farooq Ahmad Dar, had been standing in the crowd when he was singled out by Gogoi for the task. This example shows the dilemma facing military leaders in these situations – between the successful fulfilment of their mission and the protection of the lives of their subordinates. Gogoi's act was widely criticized on the international stage as an inhumane abuse of human rights, but he insisted that it had saved multiple lives, and the Indian Army awarded him the Chief of Army Staff's Commendation Card for his bravery.[41]

In 1991, the protests in Santa Cruz spiralled out of control after the commander, Major Andi Gerhan Lantara, was stabbed by a Timorese protestor. His assistant, Private Domingos, was also injured.[42] The tragic events around Santa Cruz echo similar events that have occurred in Jammu and Kashmir where stone pelters have marched into the streets, venting their anger against Indian security forces. On multiple occasions, these protests have resulted in the deaths of scores of innocent civilians. One retired Indian police officer I spoke with (who wishes to remain anonymous) says that he had no choice but to use force in Kashmir against increasing political unrest – including against the militancy. He said that this came at the highest price and he considers himself lucky to still be alive.

Yet, the military cannot be allowed to act with impunity and regrettably, the Indian Armed Forces Special Powers Act facilitates this, and enables the continuation of human rights abuses in Kashmir to occur; even today, political detainees are often tortured. This inevitably leads to a continued and increasing antagonism towards the Indian state. With this in mind, the peace-making between Try Sutrisno and Xanana Gusmão provides another unique example that might be of benefit in Kashmir; if security forces treat their political detainees with respect and dignity, to which every prisoner has a right, this has the potential to bear fruit in later talks and negotiations.

Lastly, the South-East Asia organisation, the ASEAN, and its advocacy of regional peace, provides an example of a way in which long-lasting peace might be facilitated in the Kashmir region. Although the ASEAN adheres to a policy of non-interference in the internal affairs of its member nations, it also advocates settling any differences or disputes in a peaceful manner. It renounces the threat of the use of force and promotes mutual cooperation.[43] In the Asian region, South-East Asia sets an example, which is generally peaceful with only limited conflicts in some of its member states.

Breaking the Deadlock in South Africa

When President F. W. de Klerk announced the end of apartheid at the opening of parliament on 2 February 1990, it was a remarkable turning point for South Africa. During this famous proclamation, he said: "…our country and all its people have been embroiled in conflict, tension, and violent struggle for decades. It is time for us to break out of the cycle of violence and break through with peace and reconciliation. The silent majority is yearning for this. The youth deserve it…"[44] But this decision to initiate constitutional transformation was not the result of a road to Damascus moment.[45] During an interview in 2018, de Klerk said that it was instead the culmination of a long process of introspection and reform that started in 1978 when his predecessor, P.W. Botha, became Prime Minister. For de Klerk, the key point was simply the realization that the policies that the country had adopted, and that he had supported as a young man, had no chance of solving the critical problems that the nation faced and had only led to a situation of manifest injustice.[46]

A former South African military intelligence officer with whom I spoke in 2016, also expressed the view that by the mid-1980s the apartheid system no longer seemed sustainable:

Based on strategic political security issues, and an assessment made in the mid-1980s, we concluded that no political settlement was possible as long as the African National Congress was excluded. We also assessed that control of the security situation through black laws, state of emergencies, and reprisal methods against the people was not sustainable. Thirdly, we were also dealing with an economic implosion, sanctions, and a general dislike of apartheid that badly affected the country. President P.W. Botha, however, thought he could win and uphold the regime through military means. But then he fell ill in January 1989, he was forced to resign, and F.W. de Klerk became the country's new president.[47]

In the process of dismantling apartheid and ending the decades-long oppression, the "transition era" as it came to be known, between 1990 and 1994, saw many deaths as political violence erupted on all sides – until the first one-person-one-vote elections were held in 1994. However, during this time, the South African leadership remained steadily focused on a forward-thinking mindset; they introduced instruments for redress and reparation, and changed the language that they had, up until then, used when addressing their political opponents. This type of genuine commitment and conscientious focus on fairness and integrity – even in the midst of political turmoil – is vital at the highest levels when attempting to bring about such far-reaching socio-political change.

It has been widely acknowledged that the relationship between Nelson Mandela and President F.W. de Klerk did not always run smoothly. Despite these obstacles, both succeeded in overcoming their differences and working together during the transitional process. In 2018 de Klerk reminisced on this time:

> When we first met on 13 December 1989, both Nelson Mandela and I reached the conclusion that we would be able to do business with one another. Our relationship was, however, often extremely strained as a result of the continuation of faceless violence and the failure of the ANC to honour all of our agreements. This led to several angry exchanges between us. We were, after all, leaders of opposing parties locked in make-or-break negotiations on the future of South Africa. However, whenever the negotiations reached a deadlock, Nelson Mandela and I were always able to reach a reasonable agreement to end the impasse. Later, when both of us retired from active politics, we became friends. We had dinner with one another and he attended my seventieth birthday celebrations.[48]

The South African peace process brought resolution in the aftermath of one of the world's most oppressive regimes through a negotiated settlement that included a new constitution which is considered one of the world's most liberal and democratic. Although the international community played a contributary role in pressuring South Africa to end the apartheid regime – for instance by imposing sanctions – the conflict was ultimately resolved internally with the cooperation between South Africa's political parties. It was through the determined political will power of both Mandela and de Klerk that change occurred. Each unique peace process inevitably meets obstacles and setbacks, but the South Africa model remains a prime example of the achievement of relative peace and stability in a society that had been badly damaged by decades of oppression and militaristic rule.

De Klerk was awarded the Nobel Peace Prize along with Nelson Mandela in 1993, and when I conducted a written interview with de Klerk in 2018, he provided some key points that he considered essential for the success of any peace process. I asked de Klerk the following question, "with all the experience and expertise you acquired over the years in building peace, would you have any suggestions for the Pakistani and Indian leaderships on how to move ahead in the peace process?" He replied as follows:

> I learned the following lessons from my involvement in our – and other – peace processes which may – or may not – be relevant to the relationship between India and Pakistan:
> - Peace negotiations only succeed when all those involved genuinely accept that they will not be able to achieve victory through force.
> - Deep understanding of histories and peoples of the countries involved in the conflict is essential. Do not invade countries with ten thousand years of history and with complex societies that you do not understand.
> - Beware of asymmetric power relations. Leaders who believe they are overwhelmingly powerful will not make the concessions to weaker negotiating partners that successful negotiations always require.
> - Beware of the past. Negotiating parties often find it quite easy to agree about the future since most people want the same things – peace, prosperity, and progress. However, differences about the past often create insurmountable barriers.
> - Do not allow extremists on any side to sabotage peace processes.
> - All parties that can influence the outcome of conflicts must be included in the negotiations, even those that you like the least.
> - Sanctions will not influence the behaviour of parties that are convinced that they are confronted by existential threats. Economic growth and extensive engagement are often much more effective than ostracism.

- Accept the reasonable concerns of all parties – include those that you like the least. Why should parties enter into negotiations if they believe that the outcome will result in their destruction?
- Once agreements have been reached, the international community should help to ensure that they are faithfully implemented by all parties.
- The benefits that peace brings outweigh all the time, effort, painful compromises and frustration that are always involved.[49]

CODESA 1991-1994

In 1991, the Convention for a Democratic South Africa (CODESA) was established to negotiate the end of apartheid and a new democratic constitution. The meeting at the Groote Schuur in Cape Town on 4 May 1990 saw the political parties sign agreements, and it marked the beginning of the negotiations that would pave the way forward. "While we started talking, the violence was an underlying element," said Essop Pahad, who represented the African National Congress in the negotiations.[50] When I spoke with the South African mediator and author, Andries Odendaal, he also pointed out that "both the ANC and the Afrikaner right wing were heavily armed," at this time.[51] Essop Pahad continued:

The National Party also had military might at its disposal. During the negotiation process, things gradually changed. Although there was a bottom line from which the ANC negotiated, the main parties in the negotiation must also have the flexibility to make changes and compromises. During the transitional period, all difficult elements had come together. We had to integrate blacks into a sophisticated military regime. We had to find ways and means to cope with the difficulties that were ahead of us. The ANC had to make many concessions to stabilize the political situation. When Joe Slovo took the initiative and issued a declaration for the suspension of the armed struggle, many of the ANC supporters were not pleased with this development. They asked themselves the question, could they trust the people? Many ANC supporters were angry.[52]

Odendaal said, "it is important to understand that if the top leadership was talking and taking decisions, that did not mean that the local communities agreed."[53] When I spoke with the South African military intelligence officer, Nel Marais, he noted that it "took the ANC two years to lay down their weapons." Remembering these years, Marais said: "These were tough and emotional years. Sometimes talks were halted for weeks. Then individuals of the African National Congress and the National Party would come together and talk, not to negotiate. Roelf Meyer, the National Parties' chief negotiator played a major role in these talks."[54] Although countries like Britain did play a facilitating role in bringing opposing parties together, the negotiations toward a new South Africa were primarily internal. Even if foreign involvement had been desired by any of the parties, it would have caused problems because each political party – the National Party, the African National Congress and other parties – would have had their own preferences, be it Britain, a third country, or the African Union (which the ANC would have preferred).[55]

While talks and negotiations were underway, South Africa had to set an election date for the first free and fair elections – these were to be a hugely significant and critical breakthrough for the country. Meanwhile, Judge Albie Sachs was one of the leading negotiators in the creation of the new South African constitution; this constitution would give fundamental rights to people who had not witnessed any social, political or economic freedom for over four decades. It took South Africa six years to finalize the constitution. In Sachs' own words: "In due course, we also changed our language. We first talked about the 'enemy', then about the 'regime', the 'government', and finally the 'other side'."[56] In this way, all the parties eventually succeeded in overcoming their differences in an amicable way.

National Peace Accord

Containing the violence that erupted during the transitional period proved one of the biggest obstacles to achieving a peaceful resolution. Despite attempts by the church to contain the violence and encourage peaceful dialogue (following President F.W. de Klerk's initiative of reforms), the political violence did not dwindle and the private sector had to step in. On 22 June 1991, all political parties (except for three right-wing white parties) – the ANC, Inkatha Freedom Party, and the government – came together to discuss the ongoing violence. This was the first "Peace Meeting" where leaders of all the opposing parties, F.W. de Klerk, Buthezeli and Nelson Mandela, sat down together in one room. By this time, South Africans were anxious for peace to return. The late Archbishop Desmond Tutu played a crucial role. Five working groups were appointed to address the following issues: a code of conduct for political parties, a code of conduct for security forces, socio-economic development, implementation and monitoring of processes for the secretariat and for the media.[57]

This Peace Meeting resulted in the National Peace Convention on 14 September 1991, where the political leaders signed the National Peace Accord. All 26 political parties, with the exception of the extreme left and extreme right parties, signed the agreement. One other party did not sign the accord, the conservative party PAC, but they did not block it either.[58] Andries Odendaal, who was actively involved in the negotiations around the National Peace Accord, pointed out that:

> This was not a political agreement but merely a code of conduct to bring about peace. In this way, the country set clear rules regarding demonstrations, political rallies, and it provided guidelines for peace dialogue in local communities that were struck by clashes among different people and factions. For the first time, blacks and whites would actively work together. The regional coordinators and other staff played a facilitating role. Where and when hostilities were defused, it was as a result of talks between members of the peace committees – facilitated by the peace committee itself or staff of the National Peace Secretariat. The local peace committees worked as an 'early warning system' to prevent violence from occurring or to contain any clashes among different people and groups.[59]

Retief Oliver, who was the regional director of the Western Cape at the time, stated:

> Different structures were established to limit the violence. South Africa was divided and the National Peace Accord created a mechanism to build trust and enable dialogue among all parties. Through this dialogue, we came to realize that South Africans do have common grounds, and that we were able to work together. The National Peace Accord did not resolve major issues, but it created a mechanism to start talking about problems.[60]

Truth and Reconciliation Commission

The Truth and Reconciliation Commission (TRC) was established in South Africa in 1995 as one of the key elements of nation-building. As one of the elements of the transitional justice system, it is believed that a truth commission would lead to a more peaceful transitional period. The work of the commission was structured into three committees. Firstly, the Human Rights Violations Committee created a platform for the victims to express their grievances. Secondly, an Amnesty Committee was created whereby perpetrators of violence could apply for amnesty based on three conditions: the person had to tell the exact truth, the violence must have been politically motivated (e.g., not crime-based), and the condition of proportionality. Moreover, the act of violence must have occurred between 1960 and 1994.

Lastly, the Reparation and Rehabilitation committee was set up to make recommendations and assist victims. These recommendations included the award of a one-time financial payment to the amount of 30,000 South African Rand which was given to the victim or to their families. In the reconciliation process, the commission recommended reforms of the judiciary, of the security forces and the military, of the health sector, the media, the education system, and the religious sector. It recommended the rehabilitation of victims and the prosecution of those who were denied amnesty. It also included the establishment of the missing persons task force to exhume and bury the people who had disappeared and provide families with assistance in this.

In 2006, the TRC became actively involved in finding the locations of secret graves, exhuming the remains, and subsequently handing them over to the families for reburial.[61] And more recently in March 2016, the Gallows Exhumation Project was launched. This was set up to ensure that eighty-three political prisoners who were executed on death row were exhumed from the secret graves where they were buried by the apartheid government, and returned to their families for funerals and reburials.[62]

South African Parallels with Kashmir

There are a number of parallels between South Africa and Kashmir that are worth analysing here. Firstly, Kashmir had the equivalent of South Africa's so-called "black laws" – for example the Public Safety Act which allows detention of a person without any trial.[63] The other similarity, common to all areas that have endured long-term conflict, is that the Kashmiris, like the South Africans, have been raised to believe that oppression is a normal way of life. For example, a driver named Philip who I met in Pretoria, said that he grew up in a system of apartheid, which he thought was a "normal" way of living until his brother joined the Soweto uprising in 1976. Similarly, in Kashmir, children have been brought up to believe that the soldiers on the streets are there to protect you – only when those children grow up do they come to realize that those soldiers are there to control rather than protect.[64]

But the foundational parallels between both countries lies in their similar histories of colonialism and the resultant oppression, armed struggles and heart-breaking personal narratives of the political victims of the conflict. In South Africa, the native populations were oppressed as far back in history as the arrival of the Dutch VOC *Verenigde Oostindische Compagnie* (the Dutch East India Company) when they were considered lesser human beings. In Kashmir as well, the oppression of the Muslims started following the purchase of the Princely State of Jammu and Kashmir by a Hindu ruler through the Treaty of Amritsar in 1846. The decades long oppression in South Africa resulted in mass protests that started spreading throughout the country, and footage such as Johnny Clegg's song *Asimbonanga* and the video on YouTube depicting the mass demonstrations in South Africa resemble the struggles of Kashmir today. In both South Africa and in Kashmir, protests and protest movements that had started out as peaceful, turned violent when voices remained unheard and when there was continuously no political resolution in sight. Political activists like Nelson Mandela, Steve Biko, and other South African anti-apartheid leaders were arrested, imprisoned, tortured, and either killed or never returned home. The same has continued to happen in Kashmir.

Yet there comes a point in such long-standing conflicts when all parties realise that the use of arms can solve nothing. Nelson Mandela ultimately decided to follow Mahatma Gandhi's footsteps and pursue a peaceful struggle for justice – as did Yasin Malik, the leader of the Jammu and Kashmir Liberation Front. Yasin permanently denounced violence and aggression after his release from jail in 1994. Nelson Mandela's aim was to overcome hatred and antagonism towards the enemy, and to seek not to blame individuals, but the hatred-causing systems instead.[65] The Convention of a Democratic South Africa (CODESA), the National Peace Accord, and the Truth and Reconciliation Commission, all played important roles in overcoming that antagonism and opening the doors to a free and democratic South Africa. CODESA was established during the early stages of negotiations and it formulated an agreement about how negotiations were to proceed. It formulated a "Declaration of Intent", signed by all parties, that agreed to seek to include all parties in negotiations during the political transformation, to lay down all weapons, to keep the process internal without international interference, to work toward elections, and to write a new constitution. Elections and the new constitution are outside the scope of this book but the first three points need some elaboration here.

Firstly, despite the many obstacles that South Africa faced, the two opposing parties succeeded in bringing all parties, except for the extreme right and left wing, together around the negotiating table. In comparison to Kashmir, to date, there have been no talks in Kashmir, let alone negotiations or a peace dialogue. Moreover, in the past, any talks and negotiations at the official level have only taken place between India and Pakistan. As outlined in the first chapter, the Niagara Declaration, which favours inclusion of Kashmiris in any peace talks, is an example that could be used to move toward an all-inclusive dialogue that would include the Indian and Pakistani leaderships, as well as Kashmiri representatives from both sides of the Line of Control. An all-round inclusion of all stakeholders in the conflict, including those who carry guns, must become a guiding principle of any peace process. As long as stakeholders remain excluded, then successful talks cannot begin.

Secondly, another obstacle toward peace talks in Kashmir has been the ongoing violence. Both indigenous Kashmiris, and outsiders who have picked up arms, have often received support from outside Kashmir's borders. And, as long as Kashmiris in the Valley continue to harass the Indian security forces with stone-pelting, the deadlock against fruitful talks cannot be broken and the Indian government will continue to argue the need for draconian laws such as the Public Safety Act. All three stakeholders in the conflict – that is, India, Pakistan and the people of Kashmir – need to agree to lay down arms and denounce any violence or aggression.

Thirdly, India and Pakistan have continued to disagree on the issue of the relevance of the Simla Agreement on the one hand, and on the need, or not, for the involvement of the international community in finding resolution, on the other. While pressure from the international community might, of course, help to push India towards the negotiating table, the success of the South African peace process ultimately occurred as a result of internal efforts and because the political parties were willing to put fundamental differences aside in order to achieve resolution. Furthermore, as stated in CODESA, if international involvement had gone ahead, it would have been difficult to find agreement among the different political parties about which other nations should be involved. The same would be true for India, Pakistan and the people of Kashmir; for example, would India agree to Pakistan requesting the involvement of China? Or would Pakistan have faith in any peace process in which India requested Russia's involvement? And which country might the people of Kashmir want to be involved? The different parties and affiliations even within Kashmir would likely have different preferences which could potentially lead to obstacles and deadlock before any peace process could even begin.

Lastly, as seen in the South African peace process, a new awareness around the language used proved to be very important in bringing about trust and openness between the parties. As it stands today in Kashmir, each party still uses quite aggressive language when talking about its opponents, and in blaming them as the cause of Kashmir's ongoing problems. If each stakeholder in Kashmir is genuinely committed to building peace, then the language also needs to be changed; verbal aggression needs to be eliminated so that the antagonism has a chance to diminish and provide an opening for real dialogue to take place.

During the transition period in South Africa between 1990 and 1994, violence occurred as a result of disagreements arising between some of the opposing parties – especially between the parties on the extreme right and left ends of the political spectrum. As a result, South Africa created the National Peace Accord – from which Kashmir can take a great deal. To find a way out of the ongoing violence, the South African government included the church, the business community and charismatic leaders such as the late Desmond Tutu in the dialogue. Something similar would be of huge benefit in Kashmir where opposing parties will need to find ways of working together to denounce violence. This could occur with the help of religious leaders, mosques, community centres, civil society and it could also include involvement of the private and business sectors.

For example, if the Hizbul-Mujahideen declared a unilateral ceasefire and laid down their arms, then other armed groups may eventually follow. In taking lessons from Timor-Leste and South Africa, if a clear set of rules of conduct for demonstrations was created, then the people of Kashmir could express disagreements with the government in a safe manner that would prevent those protests from spiraling out of control. This should start at the community level in the areas of Kashmir that have been most prone to unrest. If a code of conduct was agreed among all parties, then violence in Kashmir could be reduced and incidents such as when the shawl-maker was tied to an army vehicle could be avoided.

The Truth and Reconciliation Commission is another area in which parallels with South Africa can be drawn. In 2015 in Kashmir, the former Jammu and Kashmir Chief Minister, Omar Abdullah, also demanded the establishment of a Truth and Reconciliation Commission in order to address the issues related to both the Pandit (Hindu) and Muslim communities who were affected by the over-two-decade-long violence.[66] Earlier, in 2011, he had suggested setting up a Truth and Reconciliation Commission in order to probe the death and destruction of militancy-related violence in Jammu and Kashmir – but unfortunately his suggestion was never taken up.[67] So far, India has refused any cooperation on the estimated eight thousand

Kashmiri men who have gone missing and the six thousand unmarked graves that have been discovered in the Kashmir Valley. And Kashmiri Hindus who have been victims of the militancy have also never received justice. A Truth and Reconciliation Commission, or any framework based on such a commission, would help victims and relatives find closure.

On the community level, small discussion groups might be created in order to address the suffering endured by those who were victims of human rights abuses when they were detained. But such commissions and groups need not necessarily be open to the general public as they were in South Africa (where anyone, including the media, could attend the sessions) – this would need to be decided at community and regional levels. Moreover, the victims in any conflict and their families, need an awareness, in advance, of the fact that Truth and Reconciliation Commissions may not always bring full closure.

However, the Truth and Reconciliation process is not without its critics. For example, although the aim of the TRC in South Africa was to avoid blanket amnesty of the perpetrators, Piers Pigou (who was actively engaged in the truth commissions in both South Africa and Timor-Leste) is somewhat critical of its limits. He considers the Truth and Reconciliation process "indifferent" and argues that although it may have brought "closure to some families and victims" it did not go far enough in prosecuting the military and security police. He therefore describes the TRC as a "truth recovery process with an emphasis on non-repetition."[68] A different criticism of the process has been made by Verne Harris, of the Nelson Mandela Foundation, who has argued that the "transitional justice discourse is dominated by experts from western countries who have an agenda to redeem the society for democracy, and to prevent all-out revolt."[69] In other words, he argues that the process could be seen as a form of appeasement that lacks the genuine desire to bring about real, long-lasting stability and peace. Nevertheless, although the truth and reconciliation process may fall short in many areas, the examples of Timor-Leste and South Africa show that it can serve to form a vital starting point for dialogue and for the healing of divisions that, although may ultimately take decades to heal, need to start somewhere. As Professor Tim Murithi has said, "peace and justice are moral imperatives and truth commissions are part of the process of initiating reforms."[70]

CHAPTER 8

PATHS TO RECONCILIATION

India and Pakistan

The main question is whether the parties involved in the conflict – India and Pakistan – can reconcile, and whether they can co-habit peacefully side-by-side in the longer term. These two nations have one of the world's most fractious relationships and began waging war with each other soon after the creation of their states in 1947. The conflict over Kashmir was brought to the United Nations Security Council soon after this, and around the same time as the Israel-Palestine conflict in 1948, and the beginning of war on the Korean Peninsula in 1950. To this day, none of these conflicts have been resolved. In 1998, India and Pakistan both announced their status as nuclear powers, and since then, they have both continued to grow their nuclear capacity – endangering not only the South Asian region but the world at large. While few are of the opinion that the two nuclear-armed nations currently face imminent war, there is no denying that since the Pulwama terrorist attack in Kashmir on 14 February 2019, security conditions have significantly declined.

Over the decades, the ideological attachments placed upon the Kashmir conflict by both individuals and states, have made peaceful resolution all the more difficult to achieve. As in all such ideological battles, each stakeholder believes that they are right, and as long as none of them are willing to make compromises, their attachment to their ideologies (whatever they may be, religious or non-religious, joining India, Pakistan or becoming an independent nation) will hamper all efforts to bring normalcy back to the region. For the past seven decades, the inability of the two nuclear-armed nations to let go of antagonism, has meant that all attempts to foster lasting peace have failed. India has continued to accuse Pakistan of state-sponsored terrorism, while Pakistan has directed criticism back at India for its ongoing oppression and human rights abuses in

Kashmir. In turn, India has accused Pakistan of violating human rights in Balochistan, and Pakistan has responded with credible evidence that India has orchestrated terrorist attacks in Pakistan to destabilize the nation. And so, the vicious cycle of blame and counter-blame continues.

As a result of this seeming never-ending deadlock, the people of Kashmir have increasingly shared the aspiration to create an independent nation. There is a danger however, that in this scenario, the people may simply find that the oppression that they experienced under the Indian security forces for seven decades, may then also continue with the subjugation by the Pakistani military. Moreover, even if most of Kashmir were to gain independence, the area of *Aksai Chin* would still likely remain under China's control – and a trade-off between peace and independence would still need to be made. Would further loss of innocent civilian life be worth the sacrifice? The famous Chinese war strategist *Sun Tze* said, "Do not start a war if you cannot win the battle for it only leads to destruction."[1] There is no doubt that the nations of India, Pakistan, and China are all too militarily powerful for a small region such as Kashmir to engage in military struggle with.

And politically, both India and Pakistan are against the creation of an independent Kashmir. During an interview with K.M. Bondevik, he pointed out that this shared standpoint against Kashmiri independence could actually form a useful starting point for dialogue between the two nations. He asserts that any such move towards lifting the deadlock should be supported by the international community:

> The non-independence factor is an important starting point for talks between India and Pakistan, and the international community can play a role in this regard. In fact, the international community should strengthen the non-independence factor by fully supporting this stance. This way, both countries can create a political platform to discuss and agree, for instance, on the status of the Line of Control, and the families that have been divided.[2]

In recent years, Bondevik has sought to bring about a working support group to kickstart dialogue, and he contacted the former president of Pakistan, Pervez Musharaf with this idea in mind. Musharaf supported the idea, and when I met with him, he remembered Bondevik's proposal:

> Mr. Bondevik came to London and wanted to meet me and he surprised me by saying that he would like to start an initiative on Kashmir. Our idea was to involve a small group of important personalities in Pakistan,

India, and Kashmiri leaders on both sides of the Line of Control. Perhaps we should also include an American; without their support, it appears that there can be no way forward. The initiative should start around a basic understanding of all stakeholders that we want to find ways and means to move forward. The United Nations and other world bodies would need to support Mr. Bondevik's initiative.[3]

The Inclusion of Kashmiris

It has been widely acknowledged that peace in Kashmir can never be achieved unless the different peoples and stakeholders within Kashmir are fully involved in talks – along with India, Pakistan, and with China playing a consensual role. For talks to be effective, they need to include Kashmiris from all walks of life, from both sides of the Line of Control, and from all the different religions, that is, Sikh, Buddhist, Hindu, Shia and Sunni, and also the small number of Christians living in Jammu and the Kashmir Valley. The barriers to such a process exist in the higher echelons of power in India and Pakistan – who first both need to agree on the importance of such inclusive talks before they can be established. The second potential problem is that up to and including the present day, both countries have corrupted talks by trying to get various sectors (such as local leadership, civil society, and other activists) on their side – often using financial incentives to do so. This has made it all the more difficult to establish a neutral commission that accurately reflects the needs of the people and that effectively addresses their grievances. So, to ensure that this does not happen again, a credible and fully inclusive representative mechanism will need to be established by the Kashmiris themselves. A credible document such as that created by Farooq Papa in 2012 – the *Niagara Declaration* – could lay the foundations or act as a starting-point, for such a process.

Violence and Terrorism in Kashmir

Farooq Papa, one of the founders of the Jammu and Kashmir Liberation Front (JKLF) whose insights are recorded in Chapter 2, is just one Kashmiri who asserts that the armed uprising of the 1990s occurred because the peaceful demonstrations that led up to it failed to bring about concrete peace talks. Consequently, the people of Kashmir were driven to the use of physical violence and were subsequently abetted in this endeavour with militaristic support from Pakistan. But after so many years of militant violence, it has become clear that any violence or aggression – whether carried out by native Kashmiris or those who enter the conflict from outside the borders of Kashmir – is not a course of action that can bring about positive societal change. Not least because the violence within Kashmir has provided an ongoing excuse for the Indian security forces to subject anyone suspected of using arms (even in the relatively minor case of stone-throwing), including innocent civilians, to ongoing human rights abuses.

Moreover, in recent decades, violence – especially terrorism and religious extremism – has contributed to increasing instability in the wider Middle Eastern region including in the predominantly Muslim regions of Afghanistan and Pakistan. This has resulted in a widening gap between the West and the Muslim World – especially post the 9/11 terrorist attacks and the subsequent invasion of Afghanistan. As outlined in the previous chapters, this global terrorism has played a detrimental role in Kashmir (via the incoming insurgents), so tackling terrorism on a global scale, as well as the specifically Kashmir-related anti-India terrorism, needs to form a part of any wider plan for peace in Kashmir as well as internationally.

Some of the armed militants who crossed the border into Kashmir in the last two or three decades, are still operating in the Kashmir Valley. Although it is believed that there are at present only a few hundred active armed militants in Kashmir, they make a significant contribution to Kashmir's instability. When the Indian government made the undemocratic and unprecedented decision to change the Indian Constitution in 2019, it created another vacuum for angry and dissatisfied Kashmiri youth to pick up arms – and some of these youths were radicalized whilst being wrongfully incarcerated.

The extent of the belief that violence is a justifiable expression of anger is not just illustrated by the number of youths who are actively drawn to it, but also by the population who make heroes out of those who have fought against Indian occupation. When the Indian security forces killed Burhan Wani in 2016, tens of thousands of Kashmiris went into the streets to declare his martyrdom. In their eyes, he died a *shaheed* (a martyr). Against this backdrop, for peace to prevail in the disputed region of Jammu and Kashmir, Pakistan would have to halt all its state-sponsored activities in the Valley, the Kashmiris would have to be determined to lay down their weapons, and India would have to commit to respecting the basic human rights of each individual. These would constitute the first steps towards the restoration of a peaceful society.

Gilgit-Baltistan and Azad Jammu and Kashmir

There is no guarantee that Pakistan will not incorporate Gilgit-Baltistan as an official province in a similar same way that India incorporated Jammu and Kashmir and Ladakh into the Indian Union when it undemocratically changed the constitution in 2019. Nevertheless, it is still widely assumed that despite some grievances against the Pakistani state, the vast majority of people in Gilgit-Baltistan still favour full integration with Pakistan. This differs to the situation in the Kashmir Valley (which lies on the Indian side of the Line of Control, in Jammu and Kashmir) where the vast majority of Muslims have never had aspirations to accede to India. For Pakistan, the strategic value of Gilgit-Baltistan, as outlined in chapter 3, is clear; the region's water assets and the proposed China-Pakistan Economic Corridor make it a region that Pakistan is very unlikely to want to cede.

In Azad Jammu and Kashmir, despite the claim that the people are "free" or "liberated", the dissatisfaction with their governance is clearer to see than it is in Gilgit-Baltistan. There are many individuals and movements from within this region who have become disillusioned with the policies of the Azad Jammu and Kashmir government. For example, there is frustration that in order to participate in Azad and Jammu Kashmir elections, people have to pledge allegiance to the Pakistani state. Moreover, Kashmiris from the region who have favoured independence, have faced imprisonment. The government has also refused to act upon the idea of facilitating greater people-to-people contact with the people of Gilgit-Baltistan. On the ground, new roads in this region would facilitate trade and boost people-to-people contact; and the people of Gilgit-Baltistan have expressed their desire to re-open ancient trade roads that connect Baltistan with Jammu and Kashmir. This plan formed part of the confidence-building measures during the Vajpayee-Musharraf years (*c*.2001-2004). It has not yet been realized – but is an initiative that could be rejuvenated as a valuable part of a larger peace-building plan in Kashmir. This people-to-people contact has the potential to play a crucial part in the establishment of conflict resolution institutions, and in the achievement of peace in Kashmir as a whole.

Another problem with governance in Azad Jammu and Kashmir, is that thousands of Kashmiris who crossed the Line of Control into the region in the 1990s, are still scattered in refugee camps there. This has left many families divided by the Line of Control, stuck in limbo, and having been unable to reunite for decades. K.M. Bondevik has visited the camps in Muzaffarabad and has sought to bring to light the humanitarian cost of the situation. He emphasises that peace is the only lasting solution, but action in the meantime – by arranging meetings between the divided families on both sides of the Line of Control – would act as an "important confidence-building measure." He questions why, when India insists on resolving the dispute through bilateral dialogue as per the Simla Agreement, does it not "take concrete action to start a peace dialogue with their archrival?"[4] This act of reuniting divided families could act as a neutral starting point for negotiation and dialogue between India and Pakistan.

Today, new generations are born in the refugee camps and the future of these Kashmiris remains uncertain. The camps have received some financial support from both the Pakistan government in Islamabad, and the Azad Jammu and Kashmir government in Muzaffarabad. Nevertheless, organizers on the ground have found it necessary to establish schools, medical clinics, and special cultural centres in the camps. Here, for example, the girls and young women have the opportunity to learn the arts of shawl-weaving and dressmaking, among other skills, in order to prepare them for life outside the camp. But more could be done.

Even if India and Pakistan were to agree to begin resolving the conflict bilaterally, without third-party mediation, the international community could still play a supportive role in the camps and among the underprivileged communities within Kashmir as a whole. International organizations or NGOs could, for example, provide financial assistance or technical know-how to the people in order to improve their daily living conditions – especially in the realm of education. These should only be interim measures, but any contribution to the improvement of the prospects of the Kashmiri youth in particular, may help to prevent them from aspiring to pick up arms and to fight in the name of *azaadi* against what they claim to be the occupying force.

The China Factor

As outlined in Chapter 4, the Kashmir conflict also plays a role in the context of China's geostrategic and geopolitical concerns. Aksai Chin and the Shaksgam Valley are areas that are currently controlled by China, but they have also been claimed by India. These areas are only very sparsely populated, and it is perhaps for this reason that the issue has not become heated between the two nations. But China has also adhered to a foreign policy principle of non-interference and had been increasingly distancing itself from the Kashmir dispute over the decades. India's abrogation of Articles 370 and 35A and its accompanying actions, clearly alarmed China who subsequently requested three closed-doors meetings with the United Nations Security Council to discuss the increasing tensions. But overall, the relationship between China and India has been a relatively peaceful one.

After China's opening up and modernization under Deng Xiaoping in 1978, they focused on resolving their border disputes and achieving peaceful relations with India as well as in the wider region. Today, China's focus on the Belt and Road Initiative (of which CPEC is an important part) means that peace in Pakistan and hence also in Kashmir has become even more crucial.

Another reason why China needs to foster peace in Kashmir, is that Gilgit-Baltistan borders the Xinjiang Province in western China which is home to a majority Muslim population that has historically never felt affiliation with Beijing's central leadership. China sees the East Turkestan Independence Movement (which many of the Muslim population in Xinjiang support) and its "three evils" of terrorism, extremism and separatism, as one of the foremost threats to its national sovereignty. The fact that the movement's influence spills out of China's borders, and that its fighters have received training in Pakistan, is another reason for fostering cooperation and trust with Pakistan.

However, despite China's many reasons for desiring peace in Kashmir, it is unlikely that it will play a prominent role in peace talks. It is more likely that it will remain a silent observer, only stepping-in to urge restraint and dialogue whenever tensions flare up between India and Pakistan. After all, China's bilateral trading relations with India are very important, and this is an area where cooperation between the two nations has increased in recent years and where further growth is no doubt desired.

Human Rights Abuses in Kashmir

Khurram Parvez, Shujaat Bukhari and Farooq Siddiqi (alias Farooq Papa) are just three examples of Kashmiris who have faced some of the worst consequences of conflict. Khurram lost a limb as a result of a landmine injury, and Shujaat paid the ultimate price when he was assassinated in 2018. In Farooq Papa's case, he endured torture at the hand of the Indian security forces when he was arrested, as a civil engineering student, at a peaceful demonstration in Srinagar. Shujaat once told me that he had been a fierce supporter of Farooq when the latter had addressed the crowds in Kashmir, criticizing the methods of Indian occupation in the region. Farooq recalled that after one of his arrests in the 1970s, his father had been determined to locate him; he had wanted to deliver Farooq some food that his stepmother had prepared for him. His father left home with the food, going from one detention centre to another, looking and asking for his son, but he was nowhere to be found. After a long search, Farooq's father had to return home with the container of food; the Indian security forces had detained him in a centre located far outside the city.

If we are to learn from the case studies of Timor-Leste and South Africa, international criminal tribunals are not the best method of addressing human rights abuses. Such a tribunal would very likely only aggravate the already dire security conditions in the Valley and increase the likelihood of officers on both sides of the Line of Control seeking revenge. Powerful people, in both India and Pakistan, who have been responsible for human rights abuses as well as for supporting the militancy, may still hold power. Any decision-making that does not include all parties, and any punitive justice that a tribunal might trigger, has the potential to lead to retaliatory violence and the disruption of the entire peace process.

Tim Murithi, head of the justice and peace-building program at the Institute of Justice and Reconciliation in Cape Town, South Africa, also discourages the idea of an international tribunal. Instead, he recommends the establishment of a *joint* India-Pakistan Truth and Reconciliation Commission to address the human rights abuses in Kashmir.[5] When I met with Murithi, he highlighted that such a Truth and Reconciliation Commission would need to be established by both India and Pakistan, as *both* nations have violated human rights in the Kashmir region. Any success of such a commission in Kashmir would depend on the joint cooperation of India and Pakistan and their joint ambition to achieve peace in the region.

However, governments may not always be open to establishing such a commission. When I spoke with Piers Pigou, a South African expert on Truth and Reconciliation Commissions, he pointed out that human rights violations are a delicate subject of discussion for governments and that they may well do all they can to relegate such commissions to an indefinite back-burner rather than face public humiliation. Some of the victims may also prefer a tribunal, being disappointed that although a Truth and Reconciliation Commission will bring the abuse to light, it may not always result in trial or punitive consequences for the perpetrators. In all likelihood, the architects of the oppression and the on-the-ground perpetrators of human rights abuses, will not be brought to trial and will continue to enjoy (albeit not necessarily formally) immunity from being prosecuted. So Pigou, recommends that (whichever formal route is eventually taken) truth and reconciliation be started on the ground, in small groups, where individuals' and families' grievances and hardships can be heard and addressed at the local community level.[6]

India-Pakistan Relations and Kashmir

In the post-Cold War era, India has become a strong player on the international political stage. In contrast, Pakistan has played a comparatively weak role (at least in part due to its ongoing state-sponsored terrorism and the consequential reluctance of the international community to engage). As a result of this imbalance between the two nations, it is India's voice – and its refusal to take any multilateral approach to resolution in Kashmir – that has, thus far, won the day. India's refusal to accept any involvement of the United Nations Security Council, has meant that the international community has, generally, remained silent on Kashmir – only wanting to play a mediatory role provided that both India and Pakistan agree.

It seems contradictory that, despite India's insistence on exclusively bilateral negotiations with Pakistan, it sought third-party intervention (from the International Court of Justice in The Hague, the Netherlands) to prevent the execution of their naval spy Kulbhushan Jadhav. India has rejected Jadhav's video confession – as, perhaps, it would. But if the confession holds any truth, then it reveals a sustained, Indian-state-run operation to destabilize Pakistan through the funding of terrorist groups in Balochistan. It seems likely, therefore, that both India and Pakistan have funded terrorist activity over the years.

But it is Pakistan that seems to have displayed a more genuine desire to achieve resolution in Kashmir – and the continued failure of bilateral talks to get off the ground is the reason why Pakistan has continued to advocate for the implementation of the United Nations Resolutions. If India has a real desire to find a peaceful resolution in Kashmir, then it needs to take action to stabilise its relationship with Pakistan. As K.M. Bondevik has said, although Pakistan is willing to discuss the terrorism-related factor with India, India continues to refuse unless certain conditions are met.[7]

The terrorism factor should not continue to be the hurdle in lifting the deadlock; it could, in fact, become a starting-point for talks provided that both nations genuinely want a peaceful resolution. Any effort on behalf of the Indian authorities to draw one step closer to Pakistan would be a game-changer in the efforts towards normalization in Kashmir. Moreover, any peace plan between the two nations would be a vital boost to India's reputation on the international political stage – especially in its efforts to acquire a permanent seat on the United Nations Security Council. If India wants success on the international political stage, addressing the Kashmir dispute with Pakistan would be a wise place to start.

The Case Studies of Transitional Justice in South Africa and Timor-Leste

The aim of this study has not been to find a solution to the *territorial* dispute between India, Pakistan, and China. It has not sought to suggest ways to redraw or rename the borders that divide the region. As Farzana Yaqoob (the former minister for Social Welfare and Women Development in Azad Jammu and Kashmir) pointed out, nothing has been achieved for the people of Kashmir in the past by the resolutions that have affected the territorial integrity of India and Pakistan. She further pointed out that in fact, these changes have only ensured that the status quo (of everyday conflict in the lives of the people) has been maintained.[8] The territorial dispute therefore, needs, on the one hand, to remain in the hands of the top leaderships of India, Pakistan, and eventually China, but on the other hand, it also needs to take a back seat to the more important issue of creating peace and improving the quality of life for everyday Kashmiris in the whole region.

The case studies of the practice of transitional justice in South Africa, and between Indonesia and Timor-Leste, provide two concrete examples of antagonistic parties overcoming their differences, and of top leaderships finding ways to peacefully cohabit side by side despite the oppression and hardships that their peoples had endured. The main lesson learned from the South African peace and reconciliation process is that no matter how difficult the roadmap to peace may seem, a positive outcome is possible if the leadership at all tiers is committed to building peace; be it the politicians, the business community, the religious institutions, or other community leaders. It is within local communities that the onset of violence can so easily occur, and so it is as important to foster change at this level as it is at the state level; it is evident from these case studies, that commitment in all areas of society is essential in bringing aggrieved parties together and in encouraging dialogue.

Furthermore, all parties need to be willing to make the necessary concessions. CODESA (Convention for a Democratic South Africa) and the National Peace Accord (the multi-party agreement that formalized the commitment to a negotiated settlement at the end of apartheid) are two examples of detailed strategic plans that paved the way for a democratic South Africa. The new constitution that was drawn up in the post-apartheid era is another example of a document that provided a framework for long-lasting peace. Both the Indian and Pakistani leaderships, as well as the people of Kashmir, can draw valuable inspiration from the South African model of peace building.

The Nobel peace prize-winning president of East Timor, José Ramos-Horta, emphasized the strong mutual will power that will be needed by both India and Pakistan to enable them to move ahead in peace negotiation – specifically will power defined by wisdom, patience, and strong leadership. He pointed out that issues within the leadership of both Pakistan and India have proved to be significant hurdles in the process – which makes it even more important that Kashmiris on both sides of the Line and Control should unite in their desire for peace. If the people of Kashmir are strong, then the leaderships in India and Pakistan will have no choice but to listen to them. In turn, violence and the use of weapons should be completely renounced by the people of Kashmir because the continuing on-the-ground violence is rapidly becoming one of the biggest hurdles to achieving peace.

One example of a leader who was able to make concessions and adapt to the needs of the time, is the former Indonesian Vice President Try Sutrisno who was actively involved in armed conflict in East Timor when he was Commander of the Armed Forces. Yet, he was also involved in the peace process that followed in the aftermath of the 1999 referendum. He is not the only individual who was involved at the leadership level both during the years of conflict (between 1975 and 1999) and also after the independence referendum. Leaders who have been through such processes in their own countries might just be the best people to act as mediators in conflict negotiations such as on Kashmir. Figures such as diplomats, foreign ministry officials, and retired military officers, could potentially play the significant role of silent mediator whether it be behind closed or around the negotiating table. Many Indonesian officials, whether civilian or military, active or retired, have a wealth of knowledge on the art of negotiation and mediation. Many active Indonesian military officers also work in conflict regions around the world under the banner of the United Nations peacekeeping forces, and are well-known for their negotiating skills and ability to bring antagonistic parties to agreement. Traditionally, Indonesia has been a close friend of India; after all, Indonesia was a Hindu nation before the arrival of Islam but it is also a close friend of Pakistan which is a Muslim nation. As such, Indonesia has the potential to be uniquely impartial and ideally placed to act as mediator between the two nations on Kashmir. Moreover, its foreign policies are based on its non-alignment ideology as outlined by the founding father of the Republic of Indonesia, former President Sukarno. This ideology was formulated during the first Asia-Africa Conference that took place in Bandung in 1955 and is a fundamental aspect of Indonesia's overall handling of its foreign affairs.

When I spoke with Try Sutrisno, he summed up his lifelong experience as military commander and politician with the following wisdom:

If nations want to develop and thrive, it is impossible for two nations that are neighbours to be in conflict with one another. We need to live peacefully side-by-side. Whenever there is conflict, we need to find ways and means to reach out to each other and reconcile; after that we start with the reconstruction, and we make our nations strong. Investment in arms is no solution but investing in education makes our people brighter. Peace is a serious asset required for all of humanity around the globe, and which is the basic human right each individual on this planet deserves.[9]

He emphasised the importance of the role that ASEAN (The Association of Southeast Asian Nations) has played in maintaining peace and security in Southeast Asia, and recommended that such a collaboration also has the potential to play a vital role in promoting peace in Kashmir.

One association that currently incorporates both India and Pakistan is SAARC (the Asian Association for Regional Cooperation). But SAARC only focuses on regional cooperation and does not get involved in bilateral issues such as the Kashmir dispute. However, another organization, the Shanghai Cooperation Organization does have the potential to serve as a platform where both Indian and Pakistan might hold bilateral talks on the side-lines of their regular meetings.[10] This organization, formed in 2003, is an association of nations that includes China and Russia as full members, and India and Pakistan as observer members; its wider membership covers a huge portion of Eurasia. Essentially, it focuses mainly on the most predominant regional security issues which are jointly addressed as "extremism, terrorism, and separatism." Within this association of nations, China (as mentioned previously) has fostered what it calls its "all weather friendship" with Pakistan, and Russia and India have developed their friendship that started during the Cold War. In addition, Russia and China have formed closer ties than ever before. So, perhaps this quartet of India, Pakistan, China, and Russia, could engage in talks and create a neutral space within which talks between Pakistan and India could be held. After all, it was the erstwhile Soviet Union that mediated the ceasefire at the end of the 1965 Indo-Pakistan War over Kashmir.

The Independence *(azaadi)* Factor

As part of the conclusion to this study, a brief analysis of the idea of Kashmiri independence is necessary. As things currently stand, the move towards an independent Kashmir would likely result in the creation of yet more complexity and deadlock in the relationship between India and Pakistan. The consequences of a vote for independence – both in Kashmir as a whole and/or in its regions – would have to be considered in advance. Plans would need to be drawn up detailing the processes before and after the referendum (or referendums). Contingency plans in case of conflict and violence would need to be made. Each post-plebiscite scenario – taking into account factors such as the election of officials, the allocation of basic resources, and the movement of people – would need to be planned-for. In the long term, India and Pakistan need to stabilize their relationship with each other, but the relationship between Kashmir and both India and Pakistan also needs to be stabilized. And at the inter-regional level within Kashmir, more communication needs to occur. These factors, and a multitude of potential scenarios, would all need to be considered to avoid history repeating itself in this region that has seen so much violence.

One Kashmiri I met who shared the opinion that an independent Kashmir is unattainable, questioned how bureaucrats and politicians would manage an independent Kashmir with so many different religions and ethnic groups. He wondered how a region that had seen so much corruption could pull through that history and develop a functioning democracy. He was concerned, for example, about what might happen if ethnic or religious fanaticism took hold; how could the minorities in Kashmir's regions – for example the Hindus in Jammu or the Buddhists in Ladakh – be kept safe? How, and where, would the Pandits from the Valley be resettled? Would the minority Sikhs and Christians in Kashmir have a voice? Would China allow a Muslim majority state to be created right next-door to where radical elements could potentially find root? My Kashmiri friend, who wished to remain anonymous, pointed out that it had been Sheikh Abdullah (the long-standing Jammu and Kashmir politician who held office until he died in 1982) who had created the idea of a utopian independent Kashmir. He continued, saying, "Alas, the Indians are obsessed in their rivalry with Pakistan (and vice versa) and they have ignored the plight of the people of Kashmir." But he also said that now, in order to break free of the deadlock, the Kashmiri people themselves need to accept that times have changed since the days of Sheikh Abdullah, and that they now "have to accept the ground realities" and "learn to live with the world as it is today."[11]

In particular, stone-pelting and violent protests need to stop in order to provide the chance of stability returning to the Valley. The killings of civilians, whether it be by extremists or by the authorities, can no longer be tolerated. The Indian government should look to abrogate the draconian laws that it introduced in recent decades. Kashmir may have to find new administrators who work with the government in India and who are held accountable for keeping peace and fostering freedom. India could also, for example, make improvements and provide re-training to the local police force. But it is perhaps in the minds of the Kashmiris that the most important change needs to occur; the compulsion toward martyrdom and religious extremism needs to be left behind and a renewed self-image, based upon the region's rich cultures and its peace and stability, needs to be fostered in their place.

In conclusion to this study of Kashmir and its conflict, there is evidently no easy solution. But as José Ramos-Horta has said, the conflict can be resolved provided that there is a strong political will at all levels. Therefore, let us all join hands and initiate ways that will ultimately lead to peace in this disputed region. Let us put our differences aside and let go of the past so that someday the children of Kashmir can go out into the streets with their friends, ride bikes, and play hide and seek without the fear of bloodshed. Let us work together to make this a world in which Kashmiris can live lives free of the oppression of the gun. Let us strive for change and unite for the ultimate goal of freedom and peace for the people of Kashmir – for the goal of *azaadi*!

APPENDIX

THE NIAGARA DECLARATION

Historical Background

During British rule in India, Jammu and Kashmir was the largest of the princely states on the Indian subcontinent. The ruler of Jammu and Kashmir was a Hindu Maharaja. The majority of the population, however, was, and is, Muslim. With the partition of the British Raj in 1947, Jammu and Kashmir had the choice of either joining India or Pakistan. Based on the majority religion, geographic contiguity, and the wishes of the people, it was generally assumed that Kashmir would join with Pakistan. However, the Maharaja then signed the Instrument of Accession with India.

India and Pakistan have subsequently fought three wars over Kashmir. The initial conflict in 1947 was prompted by the signing of the Instrument of Accession and was followed by another war in 1965. The countries fought a limited war in 1999 (Kargil) and again in 2003 (Siachen). The 1971 Indo-Pakistan War that led to East Pakistan's (today's Bangladesh) secession, started over Kashmir. The issue has been referred to the United Nations Security Council which has passed a series of United Nations Security Council Resolutions specifying the need for a plebiscite. More than six decades later, the situation in Kashmir is deadlocked with no resolution to the conflict in sight.

Against this backdrop, the Canadian-based World Kashmir Diaspora Alliance has initiated a proposal to hold an All-Parties Peoples Convention.

The All-Parties Peoples Convention

The World Kashmir Diaspora Alliance (WKDA) which is headed by Farooq Siddiqi, alias Farooq Papa, intends to hold an All-Parties Peoples Convention in the City of Niagara Falls, a border city between the United States and Canada. The significance of the venue is seen as symbolic of the peace between two neighbouring countries that have been at war in the history of North America, but who have progressed to the status of two friendly countries. The idea, originated by Farooq Papa, is to bring the various leaders of Kashmir – from different religious, sectarian, ethnic, linguistic and political groups – together for formal discourse and to arrive at a consensus that can eventually lead to a working roadmap to peace in South Asia.

It is noted that India and Pakistan have not been able, to date, to maintain steady progress towards peace; both countries have intermittently engaged in bilateral talks, but these talks have repeatedly failed, and no outcome that could have benefited either the Kashmiri people, or the people of South Asia as a whole, has been achieved. The rigid stand that both countries have taken with respect to the resolution of Kashmir is manifest in deadlock and will continue to be so without the political will to change the situation. In such a state of antagonism, the Kashmiri people – irrespective of their religious group, linguistic background, political ideology and social class – have suffered the most in the absence of any hope for peace.

Niagara Declaration

The "Niagara Declaration" is the final declaration that will be agreed upon after thorough discourse, via working meetings, has taken place. This discourse will involve about four hundred delegates comprising of political and religious leaders, civil society activists, academics, journalists and representatives of all minority sections from both sides of the "Line of Control" (LoC). The All-Parties Peoples Convention in Niagara Falls will be attended by Indian and Pakistani parliamentarians, representatives of the United States Congress, Canadian Parliamentarians, European Union Parliamentarians, and Chinese Communist Party (CCP) representatives as observers, moderators, and monitors.

Farooq Papa emphasizes that the convention is not intended to challenge the stated stands of India and Pakistan, but to find a way for the people of Kashmir to participate in the progress that South Asia will witness in the 21st century given the condition of peaceful co-existence. It will be left for India and Pakistan to resolve the Kashmir conflict when they become prepared to put the needs of the people of Kashmir first – in the interests humanity and of peace in the region as a whole. India and Pakistan, together with the international community, must help to remove the impediments that confront the Kashmiri people.

Farooq Papa is of the opinion that Kashmiris themselves have to find the way out of continued sufferings. This can only be done through dialogue, and through peaceful means, so that the people of Kashmir can progress alongside other nations in the sub-continent.

The goal of the declaration is to provide an indigenous road map for peace, reconciliation, and governance. This road map shall be accountable to the people of Kashmir, economic growth, and environmental conservation of Kashmiri forests, water bodies and wildlife. It shall provide recommendations for the settlement of the issue of Kashmir for the countries that are a party to the dispute. The declaration will also aim at preserving the cultural heritage and creating opportunities for employment by direct foreign investment and development of infrastructure, which at present is lacking.

To be successful, Farooq Papa appeals to India, Pakistan, Canada, the United States, the European Union, China and other countries to support this event by allowing the delegates from both sides of the Line of Control to travel abroad and to support this initiative of the people of Kashmir. Lastly, the World Kashmir Diaspora Alliance appeals to the Kashmiri Diaspora, and the Indian and Pakistani people living outside the South Asian subcontinent, to provide their support through volunteering and sponsorships.

NOTES

Chapter 1: Introduction to Kashmir

[1] Shujaat Bukhari, *The Dirty War in Kashmir*. New Delhi: LeftWord Press, 2018, 9.
[2] Farooq Siddiqi, in phone conversation with the author, June 2018
[3] Shujaat Bukhari, in discussion with the author, Jakarta, November 2016
[4] Statement by India at the 38th Session of the Human Rights Council, 18 June to 06 July 2018, on Agenda Item 2. Oral update by United Nations High Commissioner for Human Rights, delivered by Ambassador Sh. Rajiv K. Chander, Permanent Representative of India 19 June 2018, Geneva, *DD News*, 20 June 2018. http://ddnews.gov.in/international/india-condemns-un-report-human-rights-jammu-and-kashmir
[5] India had planned missile attack in Pakistan, *The News International*, 4 March 2019, https://www.thenews.com.pk/latest/439698-india-planned-to-hit-karachi-bahawalpur-sources
[6] 450 People on temporary no fly list in Jammu & Kashmir after August 5, *Economic Times*, 2 November 2019, https://economictimes.indiatimes.com/news/politics-and-nation/450-people-on-temporary-no-fly-list-in-jammu-kashmir-after-august-5/articleshow/71865497.cms
[7] Kashmiri Journalist Gowhar Geelani stopped at Delhi Airport, not allowed to fly out of country, *India Today*, 1 September 2019, https://www.indiatoday.in/india/story/kashmiri-journalist-gowhar-geelani-stopped-at-delhi-airport-not-allowed-to-fly-out-of-country-1594230-2019-09-01
[8] Cross-border shelling marks escalation in Kashmir dispute, *The Guardian*, 20 October 2019, https://www.theguardian.com/world/2019/oct/20/cross-border-shelling-marks-escalation-in-kashmir-dispute
[9] EU Calls for India-Pakistan dialogue with involvement of Kashmiris, *The Nation*, 24 September 2019, https://nation.com.pk/24-Sep-2019/eu-calls-for-india-pakistan-dialogue-with-involvement-of-kashmiris
[10] Two days before Royal visit, Sweden sends tough statement on Kashmir, *The Hindu*, 28 November 2019, https://www.thehindu.com/news/national/2-days-before-royal-visit-sweden-sends-tough-statement-on-kashmir/article30107906.ece
[11] Interview with the author in Muzaffarabad, 8 February 2015
[12] *Ibid.*
[13] Former Pakistan President Pervez Musharraf, in conversation with the author, Dubai, 27 April 2018
[14] Kwasi Karteng, *Ghosts of Empire*. (New York: Public Affairs), 2011, 140

[15] Former Norwegian Prime Minister K.M. Bondevik, in telephone conversation with the author, 21 March 2019
[16] Parvez Imroz, email to the author, September 2018
[17] Sameer Ahmad Bhat, Yasir Nazir, Ausif Ali Mir, *Diverse Meanings of Freedom Struggle in South Asia Movements against Dogra Rule in Kashmir*, (International Journal of Science and Humanities Research: 2014)
[18] ISIS is a live treat: GoC, *Rising Kashmir*, 29 November 2015
[19] Khurram Parvez, in conversation with the author, Jakarta, 21 September 2015
[20] Former Norwegian Prime Minister K.M. Bondevik, in telephone conversation with the author, 21 March 2019
[21] Sumantra Bose, *Contested Lands* (Cambridge: Harvard University Press, 2010), 193
[22] Bose, *Contested Lands*, 193
[23] Former Pakistan President Pervez Musharraf, in conversation with the author, Dubai, 27 April 2018
[24] World Kashmir Diaspora Alliance, *The Niagara Declaration*
[25] *Ibid.*
[26] Statement issued and endorsed by Yasin Malik on 24 December 2015 by text message from Srinagar, Indian Kashmir with acknowledgement of Farooq Siddiqi
[27] Kwasi Karteng, *Ghosts of Empire* (New York: Public Affairs, 2011), 136
[28] Pakistan has lost out in Kashmir: Dulat, *Rising Kashmir*, 14 May 2015
[29] Bose, *Contested Lands*, 190
[30] Pakistan has lost out in Kashmir: Dulat, *Rising Kashmir*, 14 May 2015
[31] *Ibid.*
[32] Former Pakistan President Pervez Musharraf, in conversation with the author, Dubai, 27 April 2018
[33] *Ibid.*
[34] Former Norwegian Prime Minister K.M. Bondevik, in telephone conversation with the author, 21 March 2019
[35] Josef Korbel, *Danger in Kashmir* (Karachi: Oxford University Press, 2002), 56
[36] Alastair Lamb, *Kashmir a Disputed Legacy 1846-1990* (Karachi: Oxford University Press, 1991), 135-137
[37] Victoria Schofield, *Kashmir in Conflict* (London: I.B. Tauris, 2003), 58
[38] https://www.pakun.org/kashmir/history.php
[39] The future of Kashmir, *BBC News*, http://news.bbc.co.uk/2/shared/spl/hi/south_asia/03/kashmir_future/html/
[40] Gilgit Baltistan: The home of 5 Highest Mountains, *Skardu.Pk*, https://www.skardu.pk/gilgit-baltistanthe-home-of-5-eight-thousanders-mountains/
[41] https://www.dawn.com/news/484648/education-in-hunza
[42] Karakoram International University
[43] Pak PM Imran Khan gives provisional provincial status to Gilgit-Baltistan, *Hindustan Times*, 1 November 2020, https://www.hindustantimes.com/world-

news/pak-pm-imran-khan-gives-provisional-provincial-status-to-gilgit-baltistan/story-O5mtkrQDQLh1VtSgF2yoaJ.html

[44] Provincial Status for Gilgit Baltistan, *The Daily Times*, 11 April 2021, https://dailytimes.com.pk/744069/provincial-status-for-gilgit-baltistan/

[45] Yousuf Hussain Abadi, in conversation with the author, Skardu, 3 May 2018

[46] *Ibid.*

[47] The Azad Jammu and Kashmir Interim Constitution Act, 1974

[48] Kashmir: Paths to Peace, *Chatham house*, May 2010, https://www.chathamhouse.org/sites/default/files/field/field_document/Kashmir%20Paths%20to%20Peace.pdf

[49] Interview with a Kashmiri who wishes to remain anonymous

[50] International Boundary Study, *US State Department*, 15 November 1968

[51] Lamb, *Kashmir a Disputed Legacy 1846-1990*, 40

[52] The Black Hand: ETIM & Terrorism in Xinjiang, *CGTN*, 14 December 2019, https://news.cgtn.com/news/2019-12-07/The-black-hand-ETIM-and-terrorism-in-Xinjiang-MepKpOPAKA/index.html

[53] Kwasi Karteng, *Ghosts of Empire* (New York: Public Affairs, 2011), 137

[54] Khurram Parvez, in conversation with the author, Jakarta, 21 September 2015

[55] *Half Widow, Half Wife? Responding to Gendered Violence in Kashmir* (Srinagar: Association of Parents of Disappeared Persons, 2011)

[56] *Ibid.*

[57] Ernesto Gallo, Laura Schuurmans, *Kashmir: A Denied Reality* (Brussels: Kashmir Council E.U, 2014), 7

[58] Interview with a retired senior Indian police officer, Bangkok, 24 May 2018

[59] Khurram Parvez, in conversation with the author, Jakarta, 21 September 2015

[60] *Ibid.*

[61] A.S. Dulat with Aditya Sinha, *The Vajpayee Years* (Noida: Harper Collins Publishers India), 98

[62] Dulat, *The Vajpayee Years*, 98

[63] Jean-Luc Racine, *Cashemire: au péril de la guerre* (France: Autrement, 2002), 6

[64] Racine, *Cashemire: au péril de la guerre*, 7

[65] Racine, 5

[66] Racine, 6

Chapter 2: India and Kashmir: The Armed Struggle

[1] Raja Muzaffar, in telephone conversation with the author, August 2018

[2] Khurram Parvez, in conversation with the author, Manila, April 2017

[3] Farooq Siddiqi, in conversation with the author, Kunming, 1 November 2015

[4] *Ibid.*

[5] Kallol Bhattacherjee, *The Great Game in Afghanistan. Rajiv Gandhi, General Zia and the unending war* (Noida: Harper Collins Publishers India, 2017), 20

[6] Panel discussion, visit of Ms. Laura Schuurmans researcher/writer on Kashmir from Indonesia, *Islamabad Policy Research Institute*, 27 March 2015, http://www.ipripak.org/kashmir-issue/#sthash.FUBlmyC6.dpbs

[7] Bhattacherjee, *The Great Game in Afghanistan. Rajiv Gandhi, General Zia and the unending war*, 20

[8] Bhattacherjee, 20

[9] Farooq Siddiqi, in conversation with the author, Kunming, 1 November 2015

[10] *Ibid.*

[11] *Ibid.*

[12] J&K police conspired with Hizb to kill Dr. Guru: CIC chief, *Outlook India*, 31 July 2008, https://www.outlookindia.com/newswire/story/jk-police-conspired-with-hizb-to-kill-dr-guru-cic-chief/594159

[13] Farooq Siddiqi, in conversation with the author, Kunming, 1 November 2015

[14] Sumantra Bose, *Contested Lands*, 180

[15] Behara Navrita Chadha Behera, *Demystifying Kashmir* (Washington, DC: Brookings Institution Press, 2006)

[16] Farooq Siddiqi, in conversation with the author, Kunming, 1 November 2015

[17] *Ibid.*

[18] *Ibid.*

[19] *Ibid.*

[20] *Ibid.*

[21] State department terrorist designation of Hizbul Mujahideen, *US Department of State*, Press Release, 16 August 2017

[22] *Ibid.*

[23] US designates Hizbul Mujahideen as terrorist group, slaps sanctions, *Hindustan Times*, 17 August 2017, https://www.hindustantimes.com/india-news/us-designates-kashmiri-militant-group-hizbul-mujahideen-as-terrorists-places-sanctions-on-it/story-mHtgvyciIAaem10e4rdxCI.html

[24] Most wanted Hizbul terrorist killed in encounter in JK, *Rediff*, 15 December 2021, https://www.rediff.com/news/report/most-wanted-hizbul-terrorist-killed-in-encounter-in-jk/20211215.htm

[25] US decision to label Hizbul Mujahideen a terrorist group is saddening: Foreign Office, *Dawn*, 17 August 2017, https://www.dawn.com/news/1352124

[26] Farooq Siddiqi, in conversation with the author, Kunming, 1 November 2015

[27] India's Secret Army in Kashmir New matters of abuse emerge in the conflict, *Human Rights Watch*, May 1996, Volume 8, No.4

[28] Farooq Siddiqi, in conversation with the author, Kunming, 1 November 2015

[29] Kashmir rebels kill Israeli tourist, marking new phase in conflict, *The New York Times*, 28 June 1991

[30] Farooq Siddiqi, in conversation with the author, Kunming, 1 November 2015

[31] Kashmir rebels kill Israeli tourist, marking new phase in conflict, *The New York Times*, 28 June 1991

[32] Farooq Siddiqi, in conversation with the author, Kunming, 1 November 20155

³³ Operation Balakot was a militant group against Pakistan launched by Azam Inqilabi who now lives in reclusive life in Srinagar. There was no significant activity and within a couple of years it fizzled out.
³⁴ Farooq Siddiqi, in conversation with the author, Kunming, 1 November 2015
³⁵ *Ibid.*
³⁶ Ghulam Nabi Khayal, Abducted Israeli tourist freed by Muslim militants, *United Press International Archives*, 4 July 1991, https://www.upi.com/Archives/1991/07/04/Abducted-Israeli-tourist-freed-by-Muslim-militants/9445678600000/
³⁷ How custodial killings were covered up in Kashmir, *Al Jazeera*, 6 March 2018, https://www.aljazeera.com/indepth/features/custodial-killings-covered-kashmir-180227140255001.html
³⁸ Farooq Siddiqi, in conversation with the author, Kunming, 1 November 2015
³⁹ *Ibid.*
⁴⁰ Khurram Parvez, in conversation with the author, Manila, April 2017
⁴¹ Bose, *Contested Lands*, 182
⁴² *Ibid.*
⁴³ Interview with a retired senior Indian police officer, Bangkok, 24 May 20188
⁴⁴ Bose, *Contested Lands*, 182
⁴⁵ Violence down, infiltration attempts up in Valley after 370 move, says govt, *Hindustan Times*, 4 December 2019, https://www.hindustantimes.com/india-news/violence-down-infiltration-attempts-up-in-valley-after-370-move-says-govt/story-QsbLEb9PmgVT0UPW412iwI.html
⁴⁶ Anonymous interview
⁴⁷ *Ibid.*
⁴⁸ Kashmir militant leader announced as head of new Al-Qaida linked cell, *The Guardian*, 17 July 2017, https://www.theguardian.com/world/2017/jul/27/kashmir-militant-leader-announced-as-head-of-new-al-qaida-linked-cell-zakir-musa
⁴⁹ Anonymous interview

Chapter 3: Pakistan and Kashmir

¹ Lamb, *Kashmir a Disputed Legacy 1846-1990*, 53
² *Ibid.*
³ K. Warikoo (Ed), *The other Kashmir: Society, Culture and Politics in the Karakoram Himalayas* (New Delhi: Pentagon Press, 2014), 172
⁴ Gilgit Baltistan: The home of 5 Highest Mountains, *Skardu.Pk*, https://www.skardu.pk/gilgit-baltistanthe-home-of-5-eight-thousanders-mountains/
⁵ John Keay, *India A History: From the Earliest Civilisations to the Boom of the Twenty-First Century* (New York: Grove Press, 2010), 423
⁶ Lamb, 18-19

[7] *Ibid.*
[8] Warikoo (Ed), *The other Kashmir: Society, Culture and Politics in the Karakoram Himalayas*, 136
[9] CPEC involves China in risks of Indo-Pak relations: US-China expert, *Rising Kashmir*, 11 March 2017
[10] China's first domestically-built aircraft carrier officially enters service, *CNN*, 18 December 2019, https://edition.cnn.com/2019/12/17/asia/china-aircraft-carrier-shandong-intl-hnk/index.html
[11] Why developing the Chabahar port in Iran is important for India; 10 points, *Times of India*, February 16, 2018, https://timesofindia.indiatimes.com/india/why-developing-the-chabahar-port-in-iran-is-important-for-india-10-points/articleshow/62944859.cms
[12] Coordinates NJ9842 is referred to the part of disputed region of Jammu and Kashmir where the Line of Control ends and the land has not been demarcated by India and Pakistan.
[13] Eric S. Margolis, *War at the Top of the World: The Struggle for Afghanistan, Kashmir, and Tibet* (New York: Routledge, 2002), 189
[14] Quote from anonymous Kashmiri
[15] Warikoo (Ed), 136
[16] Gilgit-Baltistan empowerment and self-governance order 2009, opportunities and challenges, *Gilgit-Baltistan Policy Institute (GBPI)*, July 2010. http://gbpolicyinstitute.org/wp-content/uploads/Report%20GBPI%20Seminar%202010.pdf
[17] Gilgit-Baltistan to become a new province of Pakistan announces Khan government, *The Diplomat*, 2 November 2020, https://thediplomat.com/2020/11/gilgit-baltistan-to-become-a-new-province-of-pakistan-announces-khan-government/
[18] Christopher Snedden, *Understanding Kashmir and Kashmiris* (London: Hurst & Company, 2015), 219
[19] Martin Sökefeld, *Anthropology of Gilgit-Baltistan: Introduction* Ethnoscripts Vol 16 no 1, 2014, 11
[20] , *Ibid.* 16
[21] Martin Sökefeld, interview by email, 25 January 2018
[22] Unheard voices: Engaging youth of Gilgit-Baltistan, *Conciliation Resources*, January 2015, 3
[23] Inspector General (Rtd) from Skardu in conversation with the author, Islamabad, 29 April 2018
[24] Yousuf Hussain Abadi in conversation with the author, Skardu, 3 May 2018
[25] Martin Sökefeld, interview by email, 25 January 2018
[26] Future of Gilgit-Baltistan: Hanging in the balance, *Rising Kashmir*, 24 January 2017
[27] Gilgit-Baltistan: A province or not, *The News*, 24 January 2016 https://www.thenews.com.pk/tns/detail/560233-gilgit-baltistan-province
[28] Martin Sökefeld, interview by email, 25 January 2018

[29] Kashmir: Paths to Peace, *Chatham House*, May 2010, https://www.chathamhouse.org/sites/default/files/field/field_document/Kashmir%20Paths%20to%20Peace.pdf
[30] Snedden, *Understanding Kashmir and Kashmiris*, 209
[31] John Keay, *India A History: From the Earliest Civilisations to the Boom of the Twenty-First Century* (New York: Grove Press, 2010), 423
[32] Keay, *India A History: From the Earliest Civilisations to the Boom of the Twenty-First Century*, 423
[33] John Keay, 423
[34] Warikoo (Ed), 102
[35] Ali Changezi, in telephone conversation with the author, March 2017
[36] Warikoo (Ed), 159
[37] Gilgit-Baltistan empowerment and self-governance order 2009, opportunities and challenges, *Gilgit-Baltistan Policy Institute (GBPI)*, July 2010. http://gbpolicyinstitute.org/wp-content/uploads/Report%20GBPI%20Seminar%202010.pdf
[38] Aiman Shah, in conversation with the author, Gilgit, 28 March 2018
[39] Museum for rock art, *Dawn*, 05 July 2010, https://www.dawn.com/news/842938/museum-for-rock-art
[40] Warikoo (Ed), 62
[41] Ali Changezi, in telephone conversation with the author, March 2017
[42] *Ibid.*
[43] Seema Sehkhawat, Sectarianism in Gilgit-Baltistan, *South Asian Terrorism Portal*, 18 January 2011
[44] Snedden, 219
[45] Seema Sehkhawat, Sectarianism in Gilgit-Baltistan, *South Asian Terrorism Portal*, 18 January 2011
[46] Aiman Shah, in conversation with the author, Gilgit, 28 March 20188
[47] Martin Sökefeld, interview by email, 25 January 2018
[48] Muhammad Najib, interview by email, 10 April 2017
[49] Muhammad Najib, interview by email, 10 April 2017
[50] *Ibid.*
[51] Profile of Farzana Yaqoob
[52] Farzana Yaqoob, interview by email, April 2017
[53] *Ibid.*
[54] *Ibid.*
[55] Muhammad Najib, interview by email, 10 April 2017
[56] Ershad Mahmud, interview by email, April 2017
[57] *Ibid.*
[58] *Ibid.*
[59] *Ibid.*
[60] Devolution of Power in AJK, *The News*, June 10, 2018
[61] *Ibid.*
[62] Azad Government of the State of Jammu and Kashmir Commission of Rehabilitation

⁶³ Visit to Kashmir Model School, Muzaffarabad, February 2015

Chapter 4: China's Geostrategic Context

¹ First since 1965, UN Security Council to hold rare closed-door meeting on Kashmir today on China, Pak request, *News 18 India*, 16 August 2019, https://www.news18.com/news/india/first-since-1965-un-security-council-to-hold-rare-closed-door-meeting-on-kashmir-today-on-china-pak-request-2271795.html

² UN Security Council to meet on Kashmir at China's request, *Reuters*,17 December 2018

³ Will Line of Actual Control with China become like Line of Control with Pakistan, *India Today*, 18 August 2017, https://www.indiatoday.in/india/story/line-of-actual-control-line-of-control-india-china-pakistan-1030323-2017-08-18

⁴ India-China Border Dispute: A conflict explained, *The New York Times*, 17 June 2020, https://www.nytimes.com/2020/06/17/world/asia/india-china-border-clashes.html

⁵ New India-China border clash shows simmering tensions, *The New York Times*, 25 January 2021, https://www.nytimes.com/2021/01/25/world/asia/india-china-border.html

⁶ Xhuxian Luo, *China's land border law: A preliminary assessment*, Brookings, 4 November 2021

⁷ India Slams New Chinese Border Law, *VOA News*, 2 October 2021

⁸ India-China relations at 'most difficult phase in 30-40 years', *Al Jazeera*, 10 December 2020, https://www.aljazeera.com/news/2020/12/10/most-difficult-phase-india-china-relations-continue-to-sour

⁹ Han Suyin, *Eldest Son: Zhou Enlai and the making of modern China 1898-1976* (London, Pimlico, 1994), 239

¹⁰ Suyin, *Eldest Son: Zhou Enlai and the making of modern China 1898-1976*, 239

¹¹ Suyin, 239

¹² Susan Shirk, *China Fragile Superpower* (New York: Oxford University Press, 2008), 117

¹³ John Byron, Robert Pack, *The Claws of the Dragon* (New York: Simon & Schuster, 1992), 432

¹⁴ *Ibid.*

¹⁵ Shirk, *China Fragile Superpower*, 113

¹⁶ China is now the world's largest oil & gas importer, *Forbes*, 20 October 2019, https://www.forbes.com/sites/judeclemente/2019/10/17/china-is-the-worlds-largest-oil--gas-importer/?sh=caab50354413

¹⁷ Scott Kenney, David A. Parker, *Building China's One Belt, One Road*, Center for Strategic and International Studies, 25 November 2015

[18] Jonathan Holslag, *China + India Prospects of Peace* (New York: Colombia University Press, 2010)

[19] Stapled visas not issued to Kashmiris in recent times: China, *The Indian Express,* 23 March 2012

[20] Indian Media –Hurriyat Chief Mirwaiz Umar Farooq invited to China, *Pakistan Defence*, 22 November 2009, https://defence.pk/pdf/threads/indian-media-hurriyat-chief-mirwaiz-umar-farooq-invited-to-china.39725/

[21] India to get Romeo, Apache choppers after signing USD 3 billion defence deals with US, *The New Indian Express*, 25 February 2020, https://www.newindianexpress.com/nation/2020/feb/25/india-to-get-romeo-apache-choppers-after-signing-usd-3-billion-defence-deals-with-us-2108277.html

[22] India is the second largest importer of weapons in the world after topping the list for 8 consecutive years, *India Times*, 11 March 2019, https://www.indiatimes.com/news/india/india-is-the-second-largest-importer-of-weapons-in-the-world-after-topping-the-list-for-8-consecutive-years-363512.html

[23] US, India take steps to increase cooperation ties between 2 largest democracies. *US Department of Defense*, 11 April, 2022, https://www.defense.gov/News/News-Stories/Article/Article/2996395/us-india-take-steps-to-increase-cooperation-ties-between-2-largest-democracies/

[24] India is the world's largest arms importer. It aims to be a big weapons dealer, too, *Washington Post*, 16 November 2014, https://www.washingtonpost.com/world/asia_pacific/india-is-the-worlds-largest-arms-importer-it-aims-to-be-a-big-weapons-dealer-too/2014/11/15/10839bc9-2627-4a41-a4d6-b376e0f860ea_story.html

[25] China has built the world's largest navy, now what's Beijing going to do with it? *CNN*, 6 March, 2021, https://edition.cnn.com/2021/03/05/china/china-world-biggest-navy-intl-hnk-ml-dst/index.html

[26] Sweet as can be? *The Economist*, 12 May 2011, http://www.economist.com/node/18682839

[27] China's arms trade; which countries does it buy from and sell to? *South China Morning Post*, 4 July 2021, https://www.scmp.com/news/china/military/article/3139603/how-china-grew-buyer-major-arms-trade-player

[28] Majer, Ondrejcsak, Tarasovic, Valasek (Ed), 441

[29] The Black Hand. ETIM & Terorrism in Xinjiang, *CGTN*, 7 December 2019, https://news.cgtn.com/news/2019-12-07/The-black-hand-ETIM-and-terrorism-in-Xinjiang-MepKpOPAKA/index.html

[30] The East Turkestan Islamic Movement (ETIM), *Council on Foreign Relations*, 4 September, 2014

[31] *Ibid.*

[32] The Black Hand. ETIM & Terorrism in Xinjiang, *CGTN*, 7 December 2019, https://news.cgtn.com/news/2019-12-07/The-black-hand-ETIM-and-terrorism-in-Xinjiang-MepKpOPAKA/index.html

[33] The Guardian view on Xinjiang's detention camps: not just China's shame, *The Guardian*, 18 March 2019,

https://www.theguardian.com/commentisfree/2019/mar/17/the-guardian-view-on-xinjiangs-detention-camps-not-just-chinas-shame

[34] Building the New Silk Road, *Council on Foreign Relations*, 25 May 2015, https://www.cfr.org/backgrounder/building-new-silk-road

[35] Chronology of China's Belt and Road Initiative, *Xinhua*, 28 March 2015

[36] The Silk Road Economic Belt, *SIPRI*, 2017, https://sipri.org/sites/default/files/The-Silk-Road-Economic-Belt.pdf

[37] Scott Kenney, David A. Parker, *Building China's One Belt, One Road*, Center for Strategic and International Studies, 25 November 2015

[38] *Ibid.*

[39] Ali Changezi, in conversation with the author, September 2017

[40] Islamabad a pivot for China's involvement in Islamic world, *China Daily*, 22 April 2015, http://www.chinadaily.com.cn/opinion/2015-04/22/content_20507080.htm

[41] The China-Pakistan Economic Corridor: India's dual dilemma, *China and US Focus*, 25 June 2015, http://www.chinausfocus.com/finance-economy/the-china-pakistan-economic-corridor-indias-dual-dilemma/

[42] India not worried over Pakistan-China Economic Corridor: High Commissioner T.C.A. Raghaven, *The Economic Times of India*, 22 April 2015, https://economictimes.indiatimes.com/news/politics-and-nation/india-not-worried-over-pakistan-china-economic-corridor-high-commissioner-tca-raghavan/articleshow/47018523.cms

[43] India raises CPEC after China, Pakistan voice concern about action in Kashmir, *The Wire*, 10 September 2019, https://thewire.in/diplomacy/india-pakistan-china-cpec-kashmir

[44] *Ibid.*

[45] John W. Garver, *Protracted Contest. Sino-Indian Rivalry in the Twentieth Century* (Seattle: University of Washington Press, 2001), 227

[46] Garver, *Protracted Contest. Sino-Indian Rivalry in the Twentieth Century*, 228

[47] Garver, 216

[48] *Ibid.*, 228

[49] *Ibid.*, 231

[50] India Slams China, Pakistan over joint statement on Kashmir, The Week, 10 September 2019, https://www.theweek.in/news/world/2019/09/10/india-slams-china-pakistan-over-joint-statement-on-kashmir.html

[51] *Ibid.*

[52] China's Taiwan Strait provocations need a US response, *Foreign Policy*, 8 August 2018, https://foreignpolicy.com/2018/08/08/chinas-taiwan-strait-provocations-need-a-us-response

Chapter 5: Silence is a Crime in Times of Conflict

[1] The origins of impunity: Failure of accountability in Jammu & Kashmir since the start of the conflict, *Human Rights Watch*, 2006 https://www.hrw.org/reports/2006/india0906/5.htm

[2] Khurram Parvez, in conversation with the author, Jakarta, 21 September 2015

[3] *Ibid*

[4] Why the death of militant Burhan Wani has Kashmir up in arms, *BBC*, 11 July 2016, https://www.bbc.com/news/world-asia-india-36762043

[5] Hizbul poster boy, killed in encounter, *The Hindu*, 8 July 2016, https://www.thehindu.com/news/national/other-states/Burhan-Wani-Hizbul-poster-boy-killed-in-encounter/article14479731.ece

[6] Gowhar Geelani, *Kashmir Rage and Reason* (New Delhi: Rupa Publications India, 2019), 8

[7] Twitter/Facebook post of Syed Shujaat Bukhari, 19 July 2016

[8] Facebook post of Syed Shujaat Bukhari, 18 July 2016

[9] Valley of Fire, *Frontline*, 21 July 2016, https://frontline.thehindu.com/the-nation/valley-of-fire/article8870797.ece

[10] *Ibid.*

[11] Interview with a Kashmiri who wishes to remain anonymous, July 2016

[12] *Ibid.*

[13] China 'concerned' over Kashmir clashes, *Times of India*, 19 July 2016, https://timesofindia.indiatimes.com/world/china/China-concerned-over-Kashmir-clashes/articleshow/53271118.cms

[14] Kashmir in crisis, *The New York Times*, 21 July 2016 http://www.nytimes.com/2016/07/21/opinion/kashmir-in-crisis.html?_r=0

[15] *Ibid.*

[16] Letter of Dr. Sajjad Karim MEP to Commissioner Mogherini, 19 July 2016

[17] Kashmir clashes due to terrorist 'Burhan Wani's Death', *The Newshour Debate*, 11 July 2016, https://youtu.be/e5MPn8q2v04

[18] First-ever UN human rights report on Kashmir calls for international enquiry into multiple violations, *United Nations Human Rights Office of the High Commissioner*, 14 June 2018, https://www.ohchr.org/EN/NewsEvents/Pages/DisplayNews.aspx?NewsID=23198&LangID=E

[19] Khurram Parvez, in conversation with the author, Jakarta, 21 September 2015

[20] *Ibid.*

[21] *Ibid.*

[22] *Ibid.*

[23] *Ibid.*

[24] *Ibid.*

[25] *Ibid.*

[26] *Ibid.*

[27] *Ibid.*

[28] Press release, *Ludovic-Trarieux Human Rights Prize*, 2006, http://ludovictrarieux.org/pdf/pressrelease2006.pdf
[29] Kashmir's Torture Trail, UK's Channel 4 Documentary on Kashmir
[30] *Ibid.*
[31] Dulat, A.S. *Kashmir, The Vajpayee Years*, Harper Collins, 2015, 83
[32] PSA only alternative to control stone pelting: IGP, *Rising Kashmir*, 7 February 2016
[33] India: Impunity Fuels Conflict in Jammu and Kashmir, *Human Rights Watch*, 12 September 2006
[34] *Ibid.*
[35] "DENIED" Failures in accountability for human rights violations by security personnel in Jammu and Kashmir, *Amnesty International*, June 2015
[36] Amnesty International slams India 'for clampdown on civil liberties' in Kashmir, *The Kashmir Walla*, 7 April 2021, https://thekashmirwalla.com/amnesty-international-slams-india-for-clampdown-on-civil-liberties-in-kashmir/
[37] *Ibid.*
[38] *Ibid.*
[39] Farooq Siddiqi, in conversation with the author, Kunming, 1 November 2015
[40] *Ibid.*
[41] Wikileaks cables; India accused of systematic use of torture in Kashmir, *The Guardian*, 16 December 2010, https://www.theguardian.com/world/2010/dec/16/wikileaks-cables-indian-torture-kashmir
[42] Kashmir unmarked graves hold thousands of bodies, *The Guardian*, 21 August 2011, https://www.theguardian.com/world/2011/aug/21/kashmir-unmarked-graves-thousands-bodies
[43] Buried Evidence: Unknown, unmarked, and mass graves in Indian-administered Kashmir, a preliminary report, *International People's Tribunal on Human Rights and Justice in Indian-administered Kashmir*, November 2009
[44] *Ibid.*
[45] *Ibid.*
[46] *Ibid.*
[47] *Ibid.*
[48] *Ibid.*
[49] *Ibid.*
[50] *Ibid.*
[51] European Parliament resolution of 10 July 2008 on allegations of mass graves in Indian-administered Kashmir http://www.europarl.europa.eu/sides/getDoc.do?type=TA&reference=P6-TA-2008-0366&language=EN
[52] *Half Widow, Half Wife? Responding to Gendered Violence in Kashmir* (Srinagar: Association of Parents of Disappeared Persons, 2011)
[53] *Ibid.*

54 *Ibid.*
55 Parvez Imroz, email to the author, September 20188
56 Allegations of abuse in Indian-administered Kashmir, *Al Jazeera*, 01 July 2015, http://www.aljazeera.com/programmes/insidestory/2015/07/kashmir-human-rights-abuse-150701222455840.html
57 That horrific night in Kunan Poshpora, *Rising Kashmir*, 23 February 2016
58 *Ibid.*
59 Rape in Kashmir: A Crime of War, *Asia Watch, A division of Human Rights Watch*, https://www.hrw.org/sites/default/files/reports/INDIA935.PDF
60 *Ibid.*
61 *Ibid.*
62 Militarization with impunity: A brief on rape and murder in Shopian, *International People's Tribunal on Human Rights and Justice in Indian-administered Kashmir (IPTK)*, 19 July 2009
63 Asiya & Neelofar: Where is Justice, *Rising Kashmir*, 30 May 2018
64 Militarization with impunity: A brief on rape and murder in Shopian, *International People's Tribunal on Human Rights and Justice in Indian-administered Kashmir (IPTK)*, 19 July 2009
65 Parvez Imroz, email to the author, September 2018
66 The Origins of Impunity: Failure of Accountability in Jammu and Kashmir Since the Start of the Conflict, *Human Rights Watch*, 2006
67 *Ibid.*
68 The Anatomy of a Massacre: The Mass Killings at Sailan, August 3-4, 1998, *Jammu and Kashmir Coalition of Civil Society*, August 2014
69 Centre Bans JKLF under anti-terror law, *The Hindu*, 23 March 2019, https://www.thehindu.com/todays-paper/yasin-maliks-jklf-banned/article26615178.ece
70 United States Congress House of Representatives Committee on Government Reform, Subcommittee on Human Rights and Wellness. Decades of terror: exploring human rights abuses in Kashmir and the disputed territories. *US government*, 2004, 15
71 *Ibid.*
72 *Ibid.*
73 *Ibid.*
74 Khurram Parvez, in conversation with the author, Manila, April 2017
75 Sumantra Bose, *Kashmir: Roots of Conflict, Paths to Peace* (Cambridge: Harvard University Press, 2003), 120
76 Bose, *Kashmir: Roots of Conflict, Paths to Peace*, 120
77 ,121 *Ibid.*
78 1998 Wandhama Massacre: When 23 Kashmiri pandits were killed in the dead of night, *Greater Kashmir*, 26 January 2018, https://www.greaterkashmir.com/news/kashmir/1998-wandhama-massacre-when-23-kashmiri-pandits-were-killed-in-the-dead-of-night/

[79] Tributes paid to victims of Wandhama massacre, *Greater Kashmir*, 25 January 2018, https://www.greaterkashmir.com/news/kashmir/tributes-paid-to-victims-of-wandhama-massacre/
[80] Heavy firing at Kashmir temple, *CNN*, 24 November 2002, https://edition.cnn.com/2002/WORLD/asiapcf/south/11/24/kashmir.temple/index.html
[81] 19 villagers massacred in Kashmir Valley, act suspected to polarize two communities, *India Today*, 15 May 2006, https://www.indiatoday.in/magazine/states/story/20060515-19-villagers-massacred-in-kashmir-valley-act-suspected-to-polarise-two-communities-783119-2006-05-15
[82] India: Impunity Fuels Conflict in Jammu and Kashmir, *Human Rights Watch*, 12 September 2006
[83] *Ibid.*
[84] Valley of the Brawl: Tensions Rise in Kashmir, *Foreign Affairs*, 11 February 2016
[85] *Ibid.*
[86] Interview with a Kashmiri who wishes to remain anonymous, 2016

Chapter 6: The India-Pakistan Discord

[1] Narendra Modi & US-India relations, *Carnegie Endowment for International Peace*, 1 November 2018, https://carnegieendowment.org/2018/11/01/narendra-modi-and-US-india-relations-pub-77861
[2] US backs India's bid for permanent UN Security Council seat, *The Economic Times,* July 2018, https://economictimes.indiatimes.com/news/defence/us-backs-indias-bid-for-permanent-un-security-council-seat/articleshow/49070474.cms
[3] *Ibid.*
[4] Ambivalent Nativism; Trump supporters' attitude towards Islam & Muslim immigration, *The Brookings Institution*, 24 July 2019, https://www.brookings.edu/research/ambivalent-nativism-trump-supporters-attitudes-toward-islam-and-muslim-immigration/
[5] Christophe Jaffrelot (Ed), *Hindu Nationalism* (Princeton: Princeton University Press, 2007), 117
[6] Jaffrelot (Ed), *Hindu Nationalism*, 194, 196
[7] Narendra Modi defends contentious citizenship law and protests, *The Guardian*, 22 December 2019, https://www.theguardian.com/world/2019/dec/22/narendra-modi-defends-contentious-citizenship-law-as-clashes-continue-india
[8] India's policies of hate have erupted for all the world to witness, *The Washington Post*, 26 February, 2020, https://www.washingtonpost.com/opinions/2020/02/25/indias-politics-hate-have-erupted-all-world-

witness/?fbclid=IwAR3S0OiD0AUpkfurs9hWj5x5Jy9TbBHIFqF8_WXimxwA7A_sdIYMF4Xz-Yk

[99] Peer Bashrarat, *Curfewed Night*, 83

[10] Trump's Flawed Pakistan Policy, *Foreign Affairs*, 10 January 2018, https://www.foreignaffairs.com/articles/pakistan/2018-01-10/trumps-flawed-pakistan-policy

[11] Pakistan, Terrorism and meeting Trump, *Council on Foreign Relations*, 18 July 2019, https://www.cfr.org/blog/pakistan-terrorism-and-meeting-trump

[12] Trump, Modi discuss Indian Occupied Kashmir at G7, *Geo News*, 26 August 2019, https://www.geo.tv/latest/245854-trump-modi-discuss-indian-occupied-kashmir-at-g7

[13] No change in US policy on Kashmir, says State Dept, *Dawn*, 11 February 2021, https://www.dawn.com/news/1606744

[14] Madiha Afzal, *Post Afghanistan, US-Pakistan relations stand on the edge of a precipice,* Brookings, 13 October 2021

[15] *Ibid.*

[16] Former Pakistan President Pervez Musharraf, in conversation with the author, Dubai, 27 April 2018

[17] *Ibid.*

[18] Lashkar killed Shujaat Bukhari: J&K police, *The Hindu*, 28 June 2018, https://www.thehindu.com/news/national/let-behind-shujaat-bukhari-killing-jk-police/article24279550.ece

[19] Hizbul, Lashkar blame India for journalist Shujaat Bukhari's murder, *Hindustan Times*, 15 June 2018, https://www.hindustantimes.com/india-news/hizbul-lashkar-blame-india-for-journalist-shujaat-bukhari-s-murder/story-Yy7VkI8pwfhsAuowePN1fL.html

[20] Jurisdictions under Increased Monitoring, *The Financial Task Force*, June 2021 https://www.fatf-gafi.org/publications/high-risk-and-other-monitored-jurisdictions/documents/increased-monitoring-june-2021.html

[21] Implications of Article 370, *The Nation*, 17 August 2019, https://nation.com.pk/17-Aug-2019/implications-of-abrogation-of-article-370

[22] Washington and the 'Most Dangerous Place in the World', *Foreign Policy*, 24 February 2019, https://foreignpolicy.com/2019/02/24/washington-and-the-most-dangerous-place-in-the-world/

[23] War with India not an option says Qureshi, *Dawn*, 29 September 2018, https://www.dawn.com/news/1435702

[24] Dulat, 22

[25] Former Pakistan President Pervez Musharraf, in conversation with the author, Dubai, 27 April 2018

[26] Simla Agreement July 2, 1972, Ministry of External Affairs Government of India, http://mea.gov.in/in-focus-article.htm?19005/Simla+Agreement+July+2+1972

[27] *Ibid.*

[28] *Ibid.*

²⁹ Robert G. Wirsing, *India, Pakistan, and the Kashmir Dispute* (New York: St Martin's Press, 1994), 69

³⁰ Muhammad Khan, in conversation with the author, Islamabad, 30 April 2018

³¹ Simla Agreement July 2, 1972, Ministry of External Affairs Government of India, http://mea.gov.in/in-focus-article.htm?19005/Simla+Agreement+July+2+1972

³² *Ibid*

³³ Office of the Spokesperson Press Release PR No. 391/2016, *Ministry of Foreign Affairs, Government of Pakistan*, Islamabad, 15 August 2016

³⁴ Let us talk PoK, terror: S Jaishankar to Pakistan foreign secretary, *Economic Times of India*, 12 July 2018, http://m.economictimes.com/news/defence/let-us-talk-pok-terror-s-jaishankar-to-pakistan-foreign-secretary/articleshow/53762173.cms

³⁵ *Ibid.*

³⁶ Pakistan ignores India's condition, sends invite for talks again, *Times of India*, 19 August 2016, https://timesofindia.indiatimes.com/Pakistan-ignores-Indias-condition-sends-invite-for-talks-again/articleshow/53776626.cms

³⁷ India is building a more prosperous Kashmir, *The New York Times*, 19 September 2019, https://www.nytimes.com/2019/09/19/opinion/india-pakistan-kashmir-jammu.html

³⁸ J.N. Dixit, *India-Pakistan in War & Peace* (New Delhi: Books Today, 2002), 118

³⁹ United Nations Security Council Resolutions: On 1 January 1948, Indian P.M. Jawaharlal Nehru was the one who brought the case of Kashmir to the United Nations Security Council, in which it was agreed that the accession of Kashmir would be addressed and resolved according to the aspirations of the Kashmiri people. Since 1948, the UN Security Council has adopted eighteen resolutions, directly or indirectly dealing with Kashmir. In its first of a series of resolutions, on 6 January 1948 the UNSC adopted Resolution 38 in which the President called on India and Pakistan to take part in direct talks under his guidance in an effort to find some common ground on which the structure of a settlement might be built. As the two countries went to a war for the second time, in 1965 alone, the UN Security Council adopted five resolutions in relation to the India-Pakistan question, and in which (Resolution 214) it demanded that the parties urgently honour their commitments to the Council to observe the ceasefire, and further called upon the parties to promptly withdraw all armed personnel as necessary steps in the full implementation of resolution 211.³⁹ In 1998, the UN adopted Resolution 1172, the last in the long string, in which it not only condemned India's and Pakistan's nuclear tests in May 1998, the Resolution also urged both to resume the dialogue amongst them on all outstanding issues, particularly on all matters pertaining to peace and security, in order to remove the tensions between them, and encouraged them to find mutually acceptable solutions that address the root cause of tensions, including Kashmir.

⁴⁰ United Nations Military Observers Group for India and Pakistan

[41] United Nations Military Observers Group for India and Pakistan
[42] *Ibid*
[43] Wirsing, 71
[44] Muhammad Khan, in conversation with the author, Islamabad, 30 April 2018
[45] Pak's Nawaz Sharif praises 'vibrant, charismatic' militant Burhan Wani again, *Hindustan Times*, 5 January 2017, https://www.hindustantimes.com/india-news/pak-s-nawaz-sharif-praises-slain-militant-burhan-wani-again/story-Qwwj2q3WY6N0G2ODbOOJAP.html
[46] Former Pakistan President Pervez Musharraf, in conversation with the author, Dubai, 27 April 2018
[47] Pakistan ignores India's condition, sends invite for talks again, *Times of India*, 10 August 2016, https://timesofindia.indiatimes.com/Pakistan-ignores-Indias-condition-sends-invite-for-talks-again/articleshow/53776626.cms
[48] LeT leader Zaki-ur-Rehman Lakhvi sentenced to 5 years in jail in terror financing case, *The Hindu*, 9 January 2021, https://www.thehindu.com/news/international/pak-court-sentences-lakhvi-to-5-years-in-terror-financing-case/article33529260.ece
[49] Pakistan home to most internationally proscribed terrorist entities, India tells UNHCR, *India Today*, 25 February 2021, https://www.indiatoday.in/india/story/pakistan-home-to-most-internationally-proscribed-terrorist-entities-india-tells-unhrc-1772848-2021-02-25
[50] Pakistan calls in US ambassador to explain Biden comments, *Deutsche Welle*, 15 October 2022, https://www.dw.com/en/pakistan-summons-us-ambassador-over-bidens-nuclear-remarks/a-63452501
[51] George Perkovich, *India's Nuclear Bomb: The Impact on Global Proliferation* (Berkeley: University of California Press, 1999), 59
[52] Naeem Salik, *The Genesis of South Asian Nuclear Deterrence, Pakistan's perspective* (Karachi: Oxford University Press, 2009), 56
[53] Avoiding another close call in South Asia, *Council on Foreign Relations*, July - August 2002
[54] Salik, *The Genesis of South Asian Nuclear Deterrence, Pakistan's perspective*, 7
[55] In 1974, under the pretext of a peaceful nuclear explosion code-named the Smiling Buddha, India test-fired its first nuclear device. It is widely believed that India's aspirations to develop nuclear weapons were aimed to achieve international status. After China tested its first nuclear bomb in the Taklamakan desert on 16 October 1964, India also realized its vulnerability against its giant neighbour with whom it had fought a short but brutal border war in 1962. In1964, India became determined developing nuclear weapons. India was not the only one worried about China's regional intentions, which, during the Cold War, fought wars with almost all of its neighbours.
[56] Perkovich, *India's Nuclear Bomb: The Impact on Global Proliferation*, 86
[57] Feroz Hassan Khan, *Eating Grass: The making of the Pakistani Bomb* (Stanford: Stanford University Press, 2012), 7
[58] Khan, *Eating Grass: The making of the Pakistani Bomb*, 6

59 Khan, 213
60 *Ibid*
61 The Nuclear Suppliers Group (NSG) is a group of nuclear supplier countries that seeks to contribute to the non-proliferation of nuclear weapons through the implementation of two sets of Guidelines for nuclear exports and nuclear-related exports.
62 Zahir Kazmi, *Normalizing Pakistan*, International Institute for Strategic Studies, 21 May 2014
63 Press release, Seminar on Pakistan's non-proliferation efforts and strategic export control system, *Institute of Strategic Studies Islamabad*, 3 May 2016
64 If Pakistan wants a "normal" nuclear status, it must give up terrorism, *The Diplomat*, 5 September 2015, https://thediplomat.com/2015/09/if-pakistan-wants-a-normal-nuclear-status-it-must-give-up-terrorism/
65 Pakistan calls in US ambassador to explain Biden comments, *Deutsche Welle*, 15 October 2022, https://www.dw.com/en/pakistan-summons-us-ambassador-over-bidens-nuclear-remarks/a-63452501
66 Lahore Declaration
67 Pervez Musharraf, *In the Line of Fire* (London: Simon & Schuster, 2006), 300, 302.
68 *Ibid.*
69 *Ibid.*, 303
70 *Ibid.*
71 *Ibid.*
72 *Ibid.*
73 Former Pakistan President Pervez Musharraf, in conversation with the author, Dubai, 27 April 2018
74 *Ibid.*
75 *Ibid.*
76 *Ibid.*
77 *Ibid.*
78 *Ibid.*
79 *Ibid.*
80 *Ibid.*
81 *Ibid.*
82 Pakistan brings up Kulbhushan Jadhav in UN Security Council debate, *Hindustan Times*, 20 January 2018, https://www.hindustantimes.com/india-news/pakistan-brings-up-kulbhushan-jadhav-in-un-security-council-debate/story-pwB67FuQSvCfwLWkRjKXKK.html
83 Former Pakistan President Pervez Musharraf, in conversation with the author, Dubai, 27 April 2018
84 Press Release, *International Court of Justice*, 18 May 2017
85 Fact Sheet: The Indus Water Treaty 1960 and the role of the World Bank, *The World Bank*, 11 June 2018, https://www.worldbank.org/en/region/sar/brief/fact-sheet-the-indus-waters-treaty-1960-and-the-world-bank

[86] *Ibid.*
[87] Indus Water Treaty: 10 things experts say about the agreement and why PM Narendra Modi should not withdraw it, *Financial Express*, 26 September 2016, https://www.financialexpress.com/india-news/indus-waters-treaty-10-things-experts-say-why-pm-narendra-modi-should-not-withdraw-indus-river-all-you-need-to-know/391373/
[88] Former Pakistan President Pervez Musharraf, in conversation with the author, Dubai, 27 April 2018

Chapter 7: Transitional Justice: Two Case Studies

[1] Reconciliation and Conflict Resolution in East Timor, lessons for future peace operations, *Institute for Ethics, Law, and Armed Conflict*, 2012
[2] East Timor, Country Summary, *Human Rights Watch*, 2005
[3] Reconciliation and Conflict Resolution in East Timor, lessons for future peace operations, *Institute for Ethics, Law, and Armed Conflict*, 2012
[4] Visit to Batu Gede, border post between Timor-Leste and Indonesia on 16 September 2015, meeting with "Sersan Dua" Roberth A. Fahiberek and "Sersan" José Matos de Araujo Nunes
[5] *Ibid.*
[6] Nobel Peace Laureate José Ramos-Horta, in conversation with the author, Dili, September 2015
[7] Former Indonesian Vice President Try Sutrisno, in conversation with the author, Jakarta 14 September 2018
[8] T.R.H. Davenport, *South Africa a Modern History* (London: The Macmillan Press, 1992), 19
[9] Lecture by H.E. Mr. Ebrahim Rasool, South Africa's Ambassador to the United States of America. 20th Annual Hesburgh Lecture in Ethics and Public Policy at Notre Dame University, *Kroc Institute for International Peace Studies*, 8 April 2014
[10] Sanctions on South Africa: what did they do? *Yale University*, February 1999 http://aida.wss.yale.edu/growth_pdf/cdp796.pdf
[11] Lecture by H.E. Mr. Ebrahim Rasool, South Africa's Ambassador to the United States of America. 20th Annual Hesburgh Lecture in Ethics and Public Policy at Notre Dame University, *Kroc Institute for International Peace Studies*, 8 April 2014
[12] Sanctions on South Africa: what did they do? *Yale University*, February 1999 http://aida.wss.yale.edu/growth_pdf/cdp796.pdf
[13] *Ibid.*
[14] Davenport, *South Africa a Modern History*, 433
[15] Nobel Peace Laureate José Ramos-Horta, in conversation with the author, Dili, September 2015
[16] *Ibid.*
[17] Tim Murithi, in conversation with the author, Cape Town, 18 February 2016

[18] Tim Murithi, *The Ethics of Peacebuilding* (Edinburgh: Edinburgh University Press, 2009)
[19] Desmund Tutu, *No Future Without Forgiveness* (New York: Doubleday, 1999), 23
[20] *Ibid.*
[21] José Antonio Belo, in conversation with the author, Dili, 12 September 2015
[22] *Ibid.*
[23] Joel Pereira, in conversation with the author, Dili, September 2015
[24] Augusto Junior Trindade, in conversation with the author, Dili, September 2015
[25] Discourse: Indonesia, Timor Leste have developed a mature relationship: PM, *The Jakarta Post*, 31 August 2015, http://www.thejakartapost.com/news/2015/08/31/discourse-indonesiatimor-leste-have-developed-a-mature-relationship-pm.html
[26] Companion to East Timor - Indonesian covert military operation in East Timor, *University of South Wales*
[27] Ali Alatas, *The Pebble in the Shoe: The diplomatic struggle for East Timor* (Jakarta: Aksara Karurnia, 2006), 64
[28] Former Indonesian Vice President Try Sutrisno, in conversation with the author, Jakarta 14 September 2018
[29] *Ibid.*
[30] Companion to East Timor – the politics of starvation, *University of South Wales*,
[31] Former Indonesian Vice President Try Sutrisno, in conversation with the author, Jakarta 14 September 2018
[32] *Ibid.*
[33] *Ibid.*
[34] *Ibid.*
[35] *Ibid.*
[36] Excerpt from the preamble "Subsequent thereto, to form a government of the state of Indonesia which shall protect all the people of Indonesia and all the independence and the land that has been struggled for, and to improve public welfare, to educate the life of the people and to participate towards the establishment of a world order based on freedom, perpetual peace and social justice, therefore the independence of Indonesia shall be formulated into a constitution of the Republic of Indonesia which shall be built into a sovereign state based on a belief in the One and Only God, just and civilized humanity, the unity of Indonesia, and democratic life led by wisdom of thoughts in deliberation amongst representatives of the people, and achieving social justice for all the people of Indonesia."
[37] About ASEAN, *ASEAN*, https://asean.org/asean/about-asean/
[38] Nobel Peace Laureate José Ramos-Horta, in conversation with the author, Dili, September 2015
[39] *Ibid.*

[40] *Ibid.*
[41] Major who tied JK civilian to jeep as 'human shield' awarded, *The New Indian Express*, 22 May 2017, https://www.newindianexpress.com/nation/2017/may/22/major-who-tied-jk-civilian-to-jeep-as-human-shield-awarded-1607789.html
[42] Companion to East Timor- Santa Cruz and the aftermath, *University of New South Wales-Canberra*,
[43] ASEAN overview, *ASEAN*, https://asean.org/asean/about-asean/overview/
[44] Quote from President F.W. de Klerk's speech at the opening of Parliament on 2 February 1990
[45] Definition of Damascus Road Experience: Road to Damascus refers to a sudden turning point in one's life. It's in reference to the conversion to Christianity of the apostle Paul while literally on the road to Damascus from Jerusalem. Prior to that moment, he had been called Saul, and was a Pharisee who persecuted followers of Jesus.
[46] Former South African President F.W. de Klerk, interview by email, August 2018
[47] Nel Marais, in conversation with the author, Pretoria, 8 February 2016
[48] Former South African President F.W. de Klerk, interview by email, August 2018
[49] *Ibid.*
[50] Essop Pahad, in conversation with the author, Johannesburg, 15 February 2016
[51] Andries Odendaal, in conversation with the author, Cape Town, 16 February 2016
[52] Essop Pahad, in conversation with the author, Johannesburg, 15 February 2016
[53] Andries Odendaal, in conversation with the author, Cape Town, 16 February 2016
[54] Nel Marais, in conversation with the author, Pretoria, 8 February 2016
[55] *Ibid.*
[56] Albie Sachs, in conversation with the author, Cape Town, 16 February 2016
[57] Peter Gastrow, in conversation with the author, Cape Town, 17 February 2016
[58] Andries Odendaal, in conversation with the author, Cape Town, 16 February 2016
[59] Andries Odendaal, in conversation with the author, Cape Town, 16 February 2016
[60] Retief Oliver, in conversation with the author, Cape Town, 18 February 2016
[61] Taphelo Mokushane, interview by email, April 2016
[62] *Ibid.*
[63] In the 1950s new apartheid legislation, or "black laws", formalized racial segregation. This legislation was enforced to oppress the black majority and to protect the white minority. There were two types of legislation: security legislation, and racial legislation. Based on racial grounds, blacks, coloured and Indians were separated from the whites. The coloured people from the Cape enjoyed more rights than the blacks. People of different race, however, would go to separate schools, separate offices, and separate beaches during the summers.

The law also prohibited mixed marriages. This legislation badly affected the general population.[63] The apartheid regime, however, sustained its political power through the security legislation that was gradually put in place to suppress all political opponents. The *Suppression of Communism Act* was enacted to curb communism but was also used to suppress any political opponents of the regime. In 1952 the *Natives Act* had been implemented to compel all Africans to carry special passes as a mode of identification, and failure to produce one would face immediate arrest and severe punishment.

[64] Essar Batool, Ifrah Butt, Munaza Rashid, Natasha Rather, Samreena Mushtaq, *Do you Remember Kunan Poshpora* (New Delhi: Zubaan books, 2016)

[65] Lecture by H.E. Mr. Ebrahim Rasool, South Africa's Ambassador to the United States of America. 20th Annual Hesburgh Lecture in Ethics and Public Policy at Notre Dame University, *Kroc Institute for International Peace Studies*, 8 April 2014

[66] Omar Abdullah demands establishing truth & reconciliation commission, *Economic Times*, 2 January 2015

[67] *Ibid.*

[68] Piers Pigou, in conversation with the author, Johannesburg, 15 February 2016

[69] Verne Harris, in conversation with the author, Johannesburg, 11 January 2016

[70] Tim Murithi, in conversation with the author, Cape Town, 18 February 2016

Chapter 8: Paths to Reconciliation

[1] Sun Tze, *The Art of War* (East Bridgewater: Signature Press Editions, 2007)

[2] Former Norwegian Prime Minister K.M. Bondevik, in telephone conversation with the author, 21 March 2019

[3] Former Pakistan President Pervez Musharraf, in conversation with the author, Dubai, 27 April 2018

[4] Former Norwegian Prime Minister K.M. Bondevik, in telephone conversation with the author, 21 March 2019

[5] Tim Murithi, in conversation with the author, Cape Town, 18 February 2016

[6] Piers Pigou, in conversation with the author, Johannesburg, 15 February 2016

[7] Referring to former Norwegian Prime Minister Mr. K.M. Bondevik in chapter 1

[8] Farzana Yaqoob, interview by email, April 2017

[9] Former Indonesian Vice President Try Sutrisno, in conversation with the author, Jakarta 14 September 2018

[10] Shanghai Cooperation Organization or SCO is a relatively new initiative. Originally known as the *Shanghai Five* (China, Russia, Kazakhstan, Kyrgyzstan, and Tajikistan), it was established in 1996 to resolve the border issues with China in the Central Asian region as outlined in Chapter Four. In 2001 it was renamed the Shanghai Cooperation Organization and Uzbekistan joined membership. In 2007, India and Pakistan were accepted in the organization.

[11] Interview with a Kashmiri who wishes to remain anonymous.

AFTERWORD

As this book moves towards publication in January 2023, after months of tense relations between New Delhi and Islamabad, the International Crisis Group has marked (on its CrisisWatch webpage) the status of the conflict in Kashmir as "deteriorated". The new status (after remaining "unchanged" for some time) comes after Hindus were brutally attacked by anti-India militants in a village in Jammu early in the month. In the first incident in which minority Hindu civilians have been targeted in Jammu in over a decade, six people (including two children) were killed and seven injured. India's response has been to rearm thousands of Hindus with the incentive of 4,000 rupees ($48) per month under the guise of "Village Defence."

www.ingramcontent.com/pod-product-compliance
Lightning Source LLC
Chambersburg PA
CBHW060951230426
43665CB00015B/2151